Emil Ludwig is one of the foremost writers of biography today, already known in this country for his studies of Napoleon and Wilhelm Hohenzollern. In his new book, prefaced by an introduction on the writing of history, he deals with nineteen men of genius: Frederick the Great, Bismarck, Wilson, Lenin, Da Vinci, Voltaire, Shakespeare, Rembrandt, Byron, Goethe, Balzac, and eight others.

Ludwig writes with a mingling of the critical and the lyrical. He neither attempts that kind of "valet" biography (interpreting men in terms of their indiscretions) nor does he make portraits like statues. His work in its energy is reminiscent of Carlyle and it has something of the color of Philip Guedalla. And underlying all these studies the shrewd reader will find the portrait of a man, the interpretation of his character, and Ludwig's theory of the causes and effects of the appearance of a world genius in human society.

"A challenging and absorbing book."— *Forum.*

"Bound to be one of the most discussed books of the season."—*Chicago Tribune.*

DA VINCI

GENIUS AND CHARACTER

By
EMIL LUDWIG

Translated by
KENNETH BURKE

> With me, as you know, the great men come first, and the military heroes last. I call those men great who have distinguished themselves in useful or constructive pursuits; the others, who ravage and subdue provinces, are merely heroes.—VOLTAIRE.

NEW YORK
HARCOURT, BRACE AND COMPANY

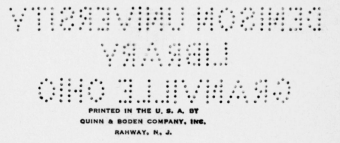

CONTENTS

LIST OF ILLUSTRATIONS

GENIUS AND CHARACTER

INTRODUCTION: ON THE
WRITING OF HISTORY

THE most modern of all portraitists has been dead now for no less than eighteen hundred years. I refer to Plutarch, who was—paradoxically enough—a Bœotian. But actually, he was an Athenian in culture, a Frenchman in psychological acumen, English in his Puritanism, and in thoroughness a German. At the time of Trajan he explicitly formulated, and exemplified in his own work, those principles of procedure which we, again today, are attempting to utilize.

"I record, not history, but human destiny. The evidences of vice or virtue are not confined to famous accomplishments; often some trivial event, a word, a joke, will serve better than great campaigns and battles as a revelation of character. The painter employs details of feature and expression to procure an external likeness of the inner man—and similarly, I should be allowed to focus my attention upon those subjects which bear directly upon the spirit, selecting such matter as this to give my portrait form and leaving it for others to write of wars and exploits."

In every age there have been great men who loved Plutarch: for here the student of mankind could find the replica of his own impulses, potentialities and failings. Napoleon carried Plutarch with him for twenty years, often reading in his tent, on the eve of a battle, the life of Cæsar. And even his mortal enemy, the Baron vom Stein, writes of how "great men have found in history an incentive to noble action in their youth, practical advice in riper years, and in old age—on looking back upon the drama of their own lives—a source of encouragement and solace for all that they have suffered."

After a period which attempted to define man in terms of descent and breeding, we enter upon an era totally alien to the Darwinian mentality; once again we turn our attention to the personality *per se*, the personality almost devoid of temporal coördinates, considering the volume, intensity, and resistance of its vital forces, the restless fluid of its emotional configurations, and the balance between its impulse towards action and its repression through precept. Whereas our fathers asked, "How did the individual harmonize with his world?" our first question is, "Does he harmonize with himself?" Questions of success and responsibility have been shifted from the environment back to the individual, so that the analysis which was formerly expended upon the milieu now seeks to penetrate within. Further, the renewed interest in memoirs is biological: and perhaps the portraitist of today, who is first of all a psychologist, is much nearer to the biologist than to the historian.

And he has correspondingly greater freedom in his method of treatment. He can exploit the dramatic form, or the short essay, the detailed, exhaustive life history, or the editorial. He should be at home in all these methods of approach, and should select them in accordance with the subject and purpose of his work—just as his colleague, the speechless portrait-painter, makes use of oil, crayon or charcoal, etching needle or water color.

His problem remains a constant: it is the discovery of a human soul. Of course, the portraitist reworks the material supplied by the purely scientific biographer and is always indebted to him. With a kind of naïve cynicism, he appropriates the scientist's laboriously collated facts for purposes of his own: an artist who ransacks the flower beds and leaves a pillaged garden behind for the grumbling caretaker, while he himself goes off with a superb bouquet gleaming in his arms.

For if the philologist begins with an investigation and gradually assembles the picture of a man, the portraitist begins with the concept of a character and searches in the archives for what is at bottom the corroboration of an intuition. But woe to him if he is tempted to improvise, to shift his dates ever so little, thereby encroaching upon the novelist!

For the historical novel is always the unhistorical novel—and for this reason it is the bugbear of the genuine portraitist. To take the liberty of fabrication under the ægis of history does not merely entail a transgression against one's subject; also, it is a deliberate choice of inferior materials, since God is expert, is more imaginative than the poet, and has always imbued the course of His creatures' lives with a deeper logic than even the most skilled constructor can invent. If a writer does not stand with *reverence* before the inevitable sequence of all the dates in a human life, he should never attempt the restoration of a character in history. Let him, rather, remain in the realm of undisciplined dreaming!

It is best that the portraitist should confine himself to characters who have died and who are therefore, as expressed in the vernacular, finished. For often the time, the nature and the circumstances of a death determine the interpretation of all preceding events. The portrait of a living figure can only be correct with reservations; and the last picture that is made of a man, the death mask, will always remain the truest, although not always by any means the most beautiful.

The nature of a man is summarized in his portrait—and the great portrait-painters with pen or brush have all been great physiognomists. So that pictures, these silent betrayals, provide the biographer with material as valuable as letters, memoirs, speeches, conversations—when the scientific investigator has found them authentic—or as handwriting. For this reason, the biographer cannot obtain adequate results unless he has a picture of his subject to work from.

The same applies to the accounts of a man's daily habits. These were formerly inserted like curiosities, little bonbons for the reader's palate. Anecdotes were recorded skeptically, shamefacedly, and as though by a lowering of professional dignity. Yet for us, the most trivial habit will often suggest the interpretation for some major trait of character, and the accredited anecdote becomes an epigram.

Scientific biographies occasionally close with a chapter designed to show us the hero "as a man"—which is put in as a kind of insert, like the diagram of a battle or the facsimile of a page from a note book. But how is the portraitist to represent his subject except as a man? And what else must he do but trace this man's every thought and act, every motive and impulse, back to the indivisible elements of his personality?

For this purpose, he must have more than the knowledge of a period: he must be versed in the study of man, must be a psychologist and an analyst. He must be skilled, through both intuition and training, in interpreting a character by the symptoms of its behavior. Surely, there are great biographers latent in great diplomats; and biographers could be profitably employed in diplomatic service.

Yet a knowledge of genius is demanded also—and herein lies the most formidable difficulty of all. To understand and interpret a poet, one must have the creative gift; to discuss the man of the world, a taste for worldly living is necessary; the biography of a statesman demands political insight; an understanding of women is called into play when an erotic character is analyzed— in a word, when writing of genius one must draw upon resources in himself which are akin to its dominant characteristics. "I take pleasure in the thought," wrote Vauvenargues, "that the man who understands such great deeds would not have been incapable of performing them—and fate seems unfair in confining him to the mere recording of them."

If we conceive of our task in so wide a sense and are determined to make our accounts of a human life serve also as an instance of the nature of genius, if we see in our hero merely a kind of pretext for tracing the outer limits of mankind, then we are immune to all dangers of partisanship: beyond chauvinism and other prejudices, we face our heroes with impartiality, avoiding—like the two creators of human beings, Shakespeare and Balzac—the strictures of any so-called philosophy of life.

But here a new problem arises. Must the biographer be cold, like a judge, or take an impassioned stand, like the attorney? The purely Platonic attitude seems insipid and dull to us; yet it is unreasonable to demand that the author be wholly devoted to his hero.

Here too Plutarch is prototype and master. By his practice of matching a Greek with a Roman, he can make evaluations totally devoid of prejudice. He invariably recognizes genius, and remains incorruptible in its presence. With the intuition of the poet he penetrates his heroes' motives, tracking down the sources of their passions and their acts. He senses the significance behind the most imperceptible of signs, and is not misled by any event which happens heretofore to have been given undue prominence. And whereas he studies character without regard for genius, when he is finished genius has automatically resulted.

The French are adept at this art. Among the Germans perhaps the only successful attempt has been Goethe's psychography of Winckelmann, which is very close to a dramatic sketch.

Such are the prototypes of the accompanying essays. The reader will find here men of action and contemplation, practical men and organizers, all of them geniuses, all of them raising matters of issue. The aim is to define that unchanging substance of which these qualities are but the varying aspects. Even when the men discussed are active in politics and have a close bearing upon the questions of our day, the attempt is made to view them from a distance. And though these twenty portraits, which span six centuries and nine nations, have only an internal connection with one another, this internal connection is a strong one.

From sketches of this sort human standards can arise. And precisely this is the meaning and purpose of this work. Our educational intent is to show all readers, and especially youth, that great men are not gods, that they have been gripped by the same all-too-human passions, repressions, and encumbrances as afflict every other mortal, and that they have fought through, regardless, to their goals. In this way one is incited to minimize all shortcomings and to exact of himself the fullest utilization of his powers.

There is another method of approach, now current in the universities, which discusses the genius in terms of his work, whereas we resolve the work in the personality. This method, though it affords the reader the advantages of a system which we lack entirely, compensates for this by its inadequacy to serve as a living model. While psychiatry, with all its arrogance and pretense, can never treat of a complete man, but must confine itself to its own restricted province.

Why write of characters at all, unless an example, or perhaps even a warning, can result from the process! This was always the purpose of the drama, and it should also constitute the aim of the portraitist when he turns to biographic forms.

Thus, to be equipped for this work, we must always perceive the rhapsody of our own life as though it were foreign to ourselves. We must feel in our experiences, however unvaried they may appear on the surface, a parallel or an equivalent to lives which have been marked by great vicissitudes. If we are to make copies of men, we must see ourselves mirrored in mankind. It is not until our own life appears to us as symbolic that we are prepared to discern the symbolism behind the lives of others.

For as we sense the logic of our own life, similarly we will observe with awe the logic of other destinies—and will interpret cautiously the past recorded on that complicated tapestry of human characters in which the hand of God is manifest.

FREDERICK THE GREAT

The bullet that strikes me
will come from on high.

MANY characters begin in perfect balance, are later
deranged by the trend of their experiences, and end in
complete disharmony. Many harbor within themselves
from the very start so deep a sense of conflict that even
the most fortunate subsequent developments can not
relieve them. But there are few who, after early years
of unrest, darkness, and inner dissent, gain clarity and
certainty in their advance from decade to decade until
at the close of their lives they have attained that harmony to which they had been foreordained by nature.

Frederick is to be counted among these few.

Two propensities endangered him: his interest in
philosophy and his predilection for the life of the "man
of the world."

Two factors matured him: the anger of his father
and the consequences of his hunger for fame.

At sixteen Frederick was simply a frail, pretty boy
with long hair meticulously curled and too great a liking
for the parlor arts. His father was right in berating him
for effeminacy, since no Van Dyck prince belonged on
the throne of Prussia. He came to the court in Dresden,
where he was caught in a swirl of brilliant festivities.
Prematurely sensual, languid and feminine as he was,
his first step showed preciosity: he fell desperately in
love with a bright racy girl older than he, the beautiful

Countess Orzelska, who could hardly be recognized when in men's clothing. Yet when, at a masked ball, another beauty in thin disguise was pointed out to him behind a curtain, he abandoned the Countess forthwith. And from then on he danced passionately.

Returning to Berlin, he became melancholy and wrote his first love poetry. This augured a kind of life totally unworthy of a Prussian prince. By nature he was anything but bold. His father berated him for acting so disgracefully—yet when Frederick was asked to renounce his right to the throne on condition that he might follow his own inclinations in peace, he firmly refused. Then came two attempts at flight, both of them failures. Could it be wished for him that they had been successful? What would have become of this unsteady young man in England? His harmony was reserved for maturer years: in the meantime he must grope blindly and restlessly, and take his punishment.

He swore that he would never yield. Two months later, in his cell at Cüstrin, he promised under oath to do everything his father asked of him, to obey the king like a vassal. Before his window his dear friend, Katte, was executed. He saw it, and trembled for his own life, distrusted the priest who handed him a glass of water to calm his nerves, distrusted his words of encouragement, taking them as a last consolation before death.

More of a man in every way, he returned to freedom and office. This was the beginning of Frederick's reserve, his rationalism. Despite his aversion to the woman selected for him, he readily accepted his betrothal and marriage as a means to greater freedom. Since the thought of progeny never troubled this intellectualistic man, whose nonconformity made him alien even to his own forefathers, he remained quite contented without children. He neither expressed a wish to have them by his wife, nor did he become a father irregularly. His unrest derives from other sources.

His credo at twenty: "I have been unhappy all my life. Perhaps I would have grown too haughty had a sudden happiness followed after so much discontent. There is still one escape open to me: a pistol shot can liberate me from the sufferings of this life. I feel that when any one hates restraint as much as I, his hot-bloodedness will always drive him to extremes."

The years at Rheinsberg are generally considered to have been Frederick's happiest period. But they were merely his quietest. At twenty-five he was anticipating the kind of life which he was to perfect twenty years later at Sanssouci. A young man, totally untested, very eager for exploits, and in no position to know when he would be called to action, he had Knobelsdorff carve above the entrance of his country-house: *"Frederico tranquillitatem colenti."* Pleasure boats on the lake; he himself as patron playing the part of Philoctetes and of Mithridates; the founding of make-believe orders of knighthood, reinstating old French styles of chivalry; the immature discussion of intellectual matters at table; de luxe editions of the "Henriade"; importation from Paris of the newest writings by Herr von Voltaire, whom Frederick called "my golden fleece"; the composition of bad verses in the style of the age—and that is all.

Yet there are traces of resignation: for it is resignation to brand oneself a Platonist when the yearning for happiness is denied a practical outlet. "I belong to the category of meditative men—a status more agreeable than any other." We can sense the masterly reserve. "More agreeable"? Then why does he call poetry and philosophy merely a "solace" for inclement times, mere "blissful drunkenness"? And can we class among the category of meditative men any one who, with the entire range of philosophy to choose from, confines himself to practical ethics, since it offers the most immediate returns in terms of living? He despised metaphysicians, whom he compared to Chinese mystagogues. And on one occasion, when a volume of Wolf's metaphysics was being handed to him, an ape, one of those exotic freaks which he kept about his rooms, reached forward, lifted the work from his hands, and hurled it unbidden into the blazing fireplace.

He completely misunderstood Machiavelli's "Book of the Prince." It was intended purely for the age in which it was written, being an Italian handbook for conditions around 1500, and it should not have turned up again, two hundred years later, in chilly Prussia. Yet as he afterwards confessed to Voltaire, it was not moral fervor, but the inactivity and boredom of a Crown Prince, which prompted him to write his "Anti-Macchiavel." Usually people lay too much stress upon his attachment to this pathetic, cynical genius, overestimating its importance as a revelation of his own state of mind. Frederick saw in Voltaire purely the concentration point of an attitude and a method which were shared by any person of intellectual bent who happened to be living around the year 1740.

The prince was shielded from the over-development of his literary interests by his temperament, lurking in ambush.

His credo at twenty-seven: "I finally begin to see the

dawn of a day which does not yet shine full upon me."
And elsewhere: "Yet it must be a pleasure to be king
all alone in Prussia!"

At seventeen demonic through restraint, at twenty-
seven Platonic through restraint. The synthesis of the
two was a king.

Now finally, freed of all obstructions, passion found
its channel of escape. It could not be converted into the
erotic: "I love women, but my love is very unstable, a
mere gratification of desire followed by disgust." It
turned into ambition, the hunger for fame. This man
was seized and carried away by the love of glory.

He had been king but a few months—and he took the
first opportunity, the death of Charles VI, to renew old
claims against Silesia. All Europe called him mad, and
he himself hardly realized what he was doing. "I plan
to strike on the eighth of December, thus beginning
the boldest, greatest, and most far-reaching enterprise
ever undertaken by a prince of my house." To his friend
Jordan: "Old man, the intensity of my passion, the
hunger for fame, even sheer curiosity (to conceal
nothing from you), some mysterious instinct in short,
have robbed me of my sweet repose. I have been lured by
the thought of seeing my name in the papers and in the
archives of history." This was the Frederick who said
of himself that he could never devote himself half-
heartedly to a cause: "I must go at it headlong."

On the battlefield he was horrified at his presumption.
Before his first encounter, at Mollwitz, he had fled, and
did not appear again until sixteen hours later, when all
was over and won. He was no general. Frederick was
never a military hero, never a man like Napoleon, who
loved the exhilaration of battle. He hated the hunt, but

loved the dance. At that time he was so wild that he was represented in an almanac as Orlando Furioso. Everything went at a gallop. He was determined to enjoy to its fullest all the power at his command.

On the very day and hour of his coronation he had shown himself to be an autocrat: Leopold of Dessau, "*der alte Dessauer*," rode with him. Frederick was tolerant, yet he despised the masses. *Canaille* was the word which this enlightened monarch preferred in speaking of them. In late years he gained popular favor by donning the mask of sociability, but he genuinely loved only his soldiers and his dogs.

Two precipitate wars were followed by a decade of peace. In Sanssouci Frederick became an Augustus. "If you come here," he wrote Voltaire, "you shall be among the first of my titles: Frederick, King of Prussia, Elector of Brandenburg, Proprietor of Voltaire." Proprietor? Even if this is figurative, it doesn't sound well. He gathered philosophers around him much the way his father had once gathered his "Potsdamned" giants: not as a philosopher, but as a fancier. That was not so unusual. Were there not, at that time, philosophers who served as ambassadors, and princes who wrote on free will? "A man who devotes all his time to science and lives without friends is an educated werewolf. In my opinion friendship is a necessary ingredient of our happiness." No one lived a more "clubby" life than he, yet as the "philosopher of Sanssouci" he should have lived in retirement.

This court was naturally much different from the earlier one at Rheinsberg. Now Frederick was king, with power and fame, freedom and money. A ruler, highly cultivated, endowed with genius, he was now in a position to set himself up as a prince in high style. Whatever did not immediately concern the state, he shared as an amateur with others, in the sociable style of the Rococo: letters, memoirs, essays, even flute-playing, which, he reports, sometimes gave rise to new thoughts as he practiced while walking.

This author followed in his own tracks: as early as 1746 he was writing the history of his second war, which had ended in '45. Yet his pen gradually fell behind, his ability as a commander outstripping his ability as a writer. Being a "man of the world," he wrote in French, though he spelled as poorly in French as in German, and it was not only his legal documents which had to be corrected by secretaries. His most famous sayings were nearly always couched in German. Unintentionally, his marginal notes in German contain a highly Prussian philosophy.

He began now to show remarkable signs of maturity. Among other things he built himself a tomb which supported a narrow plinth topped by marble flora. And each day he looked across from his window at this symbol of life and death.

Credo of the Brandenburger at thirty-five: "I love war because of the fame that goes with it; but were I not a prince I should devote myself entirely to philosophy. After all, every one in this world must have his trade."

The momentous consequences of his first injudicious venture exerted a sobering influence upon the king. It was not until now, in the Seven Years' War, that his gifts were developed to their fullest. He was purged by danger and profound despair. At the beginning of the war he wrote more verses in three months than ever before in a whole year—so great was his need of relief.

After Kunersdorf he gave himself up as lost: he thought that both crown and life were in peril, and began addressing his nephew as King. In the tumult of the battle he cried out, "Is there no damned shot for me!" And after Kolin, the only battle in which Frederick ever drew a sword, he said to the young Count von Anhalt: "Do you know that every man has certain blows of fate coming to him?"

Berlin, Potsdam and Sanssouci all fell into the hands of the enemy, and the king could not foretell how they would be treated. Despite his difficulties in youth, he was now facing for the first time the evil consequences which resulted from acts of his own choosing. As he beheld those very forces which he himself had unloosened gaining in magnitude like an avalanche and turning against him, Frederick became more resolute, more conscientious. He began now to manifest the same traits of character which he had once hated so strongly in his father. He gave definite orders that in case of capture no ransom was to be paid for his release. He feared pain, but not death: "Pain an eternity, death an instant." Now, of a sudden, he discovered that he did not belong among the "category of meditative men." "It seems," he wrote at fifty to D'Argens, "that we are much better fitted for action than for thought." It seems so.

He returned home, tired but victorious.

Credo at fifty-five: "Glory is vain. Did men ever merit praise? They were praised merely because they made such a clamor."

The great man sits in his little house. For twenty years now this marvelously chastened mind has brought blessings upon the realm. There is no longer any Voltaire, no Round Table. Frederick has driven off most of the Frenchmen. His sister, the only human being he ever loved, is dead, and he has built a temple to her memory. All his life he has sought friends. Hardly a one has remained loyal to him. He cared for his generals, but they were not his friends. Fouqué and Lord Keith are here, growing old beside him. He sends them wine a century old, devises mechanisms for their failing speech, gives them wheel-chairs when they cannot walk. Menzel has furnished us the details: Frederick, still hale and hearty, descending the terrace alongside his friend's wheel-chair. Then they die off. And those at a distance, with whom he corresponded, die off: Voltaire, D'Alembert. The king no longer plays on his flute.

Old Freddy works. On the morning after his return from the long war, literally on the very next morning, this king had begun rebuilding his territories, going about his work systematically, like a man doing penance. Much of the country had been laid waste, but he removed all signs of devastation. He drained swamps, planted new forests, built roads and innumerable houses. After a long life of passion and reflection, of truculence and coldness, of European plans and international achievement, his ripest wisdom is like that of the last Voltaire.

Credo at seventy: "To improve one's territories, to reclaim waste land and to drain swamps—this is a victorious advance against barbarism."

He is alone, retiring within himself. He even loses his nephew, whom he has cared for most. Only his animals remain with him. His greyhounds lie about in his chairs and on his bed. When they die, the king buries

them beneath marble tablets, near his busts of the
Roman emperors. Condé, the white horse, runs about at
will, goes up to his master and eats fruit from his hand.

The last visitor is by name Mirabeau. It is Fortinbras.

Frederick, whose life was totally different from
Goethe's, finally arrives at the same philosophy of resignation. His last words were:

"La montagne est passée, nous irons mieux."

BARON VOM STEIN

THE BARON VOM STEIN

I have but one fatherland, and that is Germany.

THE framework of a massive body supports a squared skull with delicately vaulted forehead and thin uncommunicative lips. Yet two clear blue eyes and a gigantic nose—evidences respectively of faith and energy—stand out upon this face with an aggressive and commanding prominence. For faith and energy are the fundamental traits of this powerful and simple man.

No other German statesman possesses in such marked purity the fusion of these two qualities. Crystallinely practical, Stein never questioned the value of his purposes; and the purity of his intuition showed no tendency to weaken his will power—yet the lifelong competition between faith and action was fatal to his work, since it denied him the possibility of an ultimate consistent solution. Despite his disillusionment with specific individuals, whom he condemned severely, he was not open to that misanthropy and cynicism in general which was indispensable to Bismarck, so that at the crucial point he attained nothing positive. He had too much faith for such sound practicality, and was too capable in practical matters for so profound a faith in mankind. As a consequence his ideal of a German empire was much purer than that of Bismarck, who, coming after him, carried to completion in one way the work which Stein had planned in another.

Thus, throughout the whole of his life, the hopes of the Baron vom Stein burned as a lonely torch in the

political gloom of Germany's kings and diplomats—
burned alone until they were extinguished by death, but
they did not pass until they had transmitted their flame
to a torch of the future.

In common with every idealist who attempts to put
his schemes into practice, Stein's unceasing battle against
human inertia gradually sharpened his temper. But since
he was aware that irascibility would ruin his chances of
success, he forced himself to remain calm and steady.
He was tireless by nature, and a genuine pride in his
social position drove him to adopt the most rigorous
standards of nobility. Hard pressed by the rapid tempo
of the age, strengthened by his hatred of the victorious
enemy, and encouraged by the endless possibilities which
the mounting chaos of politics seemed to offer, he fought
with greater and greater vehemence for his idea, for
that Fatherland whose union he believed in fervidly.

He fought against the Fatherland. Where he succeeded, as in the emancipation of the serfs, the work
was only partially his: in the last analysis it was the
result of alliances which it had not been his direct task
to organize and of military measures which he had not
dictated. But the union, which failed, was his own fundamental idea, his grand passion, the very core of his
energy. Of course, the first Napoleon was his enemy
in a much more drastic sense than the third Napoleon
could ever be to Bismarck. But for both of them, war
with the French was merely the means of procuring
internal union through war and victory abroad.

Stein, who was a true champion of the masses, wanted
to combine all people of German blood. Since he detested
the ruling houses and could endure at the most but six

princes out of a total of thirty-six, he exhausted himself
in open resistance to the courts, the intrigues and the
caprices of the remaining thirty—and at the end of his
journey he stood face to face with a state of disunion
which was even worse than at the start. Bismarck, whose
sympathies were with the dynasties and against the people, fulfilled the possibilities of German unity so thoroughly that the nation survived even after the ruling
houses had collapsed—which is all the more astounding
in that he would have chosen precisely the reverse
condition.

Given a problem in construction, and given two persons of equal energy to solve it, it seems as though an
unmoral mind will prove superior to an open heart.

For Stein had faith. Always relying on Providence,
always considering himself an instrument in nobler
hands, always conscious of a responsibility to both God
and man, he was a thoroughgoing Protestant. Complete
resignation to the will of heaven never made him for one
moment the passive fatalist: and he never grasped more
strikingly this inexplicable antinomy between resignation and activity than in the days when the fate of his
mortal enemy was being decided. Stein was in St. Petersburg, and had invited his friends to drink to Napoleon's
retreat from Moscow. Whereupon, in a kind of spiritual
drunkenness such as this sober man seldom experienced,
he raised his glass and called out to his guests the splendid
words: "Many times in life I have thrown my pack
behind me. Drink up! Since we must die, let us be
brave!"

He was. For seventy years he was, and more so than
many a general. Civil courage was the moral aspect un-

der which Stein's energy chose to manifest itself. He feared no one; and since, furthermore, he owed obedience to no one, he was among the freest of the free. He voluntarily subjected himself to one man, the King of Prussia, who had become his overlord purely by virtue of being Frederick's heir.

For Stein served under both the strongest and the weakest of German rulers. He was the first to speak of "Frederick the Only." On Frederick's account he had entered the service of Prussia, the old king with his eagle eye soon recognizing his talents and putting them to good use. And afterwards he had to bear up under the weak character of Frederick's grand-nephew, whom he learned to despise.

By nature fearless and quixotic, he was open in the expression of his opinions. A naïve vigor, which had behind it his sterling integrity and his powerful intellect, prompted him to talk with disconcerting frankness about people who were later to become prominent. And he did not stop at saying such things in private, but publicly aired them in his writings. He branded Queen Louise as weak and coquettish, Hardenberg as dishonest and superficial. Jahn, the founder of German gymnastics, he called unbearably chauvinistic, and refused consistently to receive him. Concerning the king alone he maintained public silence.

And yet instead of finding, like Bismarck, a Prussian king who would follow him and uphold his policies, he found a Hohenzollern who was narrow, obstinate, cowardly and domineering, who discharged him from office after two scant years, and then on discovering a year later that he was indispensable recalled him without even enough good grace to vouchsafe him one word of apology.

Although the imperial Barons vom Stein had dwelt for seven centuries in their castle in Nassau above the river Lahn, it was not until now—when their line was about to die out—that the name of "Stein," which means "stone," became a metaphor. For there was actually something rocklike in the strength and independence of this knight. And we can feel still more strongly the symbolism of his origin when we consider that his house owed fealty to the empire alone, having escaped until the present generation the fate of mediatization, a process then common in the German states whereby the territories of the lesser nobles were absorbed into some larger adjoining political unit. For this Baron stood literally in the immediate service of the empire. And being directly a part of the empire, he was subject to no subsidiary prince. He had planned that his own estates should be absorbed in the empire. Staunchly conservative by reason of both race and training, he recognized the emperor alone as a higher authority.

But he felt that the privileges of rank also entailed obligations; and through expecting so much of the nobles he became their most acrid critic. What other member of this class has ever dared, before or since, to address the German rulers in such language as he! In 1804, when the Duke of Nassau appropriated two of his villages under the pretext that the independent imperial knighthood had been dissolved by Napoleon, Stein retorted that if these territories should fall in turn to one of the two major German powers the Duke's action would have proved a benefit to the empire—and he hoped to see the day when this would happen. But where, he asked, had these petty rulers, who were now pilfering everything they could lay hands on, been during the recent wars? "They avoided all participation, and contrived to prolong their decrepit existence by emigration, by treaty, and by the bribing of French army officers." Then he becomes still more ominous, but suddenly interrupts himself in the middle of a sentence and closes: "—yet there is a Conscience to pass judgment and a Divinity to wreak vengeance. Humbly I remain your ——— ——— Stein." Literally so, with the dashes.

His memoirs, which were written for distribution among the kings and princes, contain fiery sentences such as no other European of the day, not even a revolutionary, dared to write. "Fifteen million Germans are being sacrificed to the caprice of thirty-six petty despots . . . sacrificed to the whims of tiny sultans and viziers. . . . But these autocrats should not forget that the common people are, by the grace of God, free!"

When in St. Petersburg after Napoleon's retreat the old dowager empress, *née* Württemberg, ended dinner with the mincing words, "But now if a single French soldier escapes through the German boundaries, I shall be ashamed to call myself a German," the Baron arose, flushed to the very back of his neck, bowed, and said, "Your Majesty is very unfair in saying such things about so great, loyal, and courageous a people to which you have the honor to belong! You should have said, 'I am not ashamed of the people, but of my brothers and cousins, the German princes.' For had they done their duty in the nineties, then no Frenchman would have reached the Elbe or the Oder, to say nothing of crossing the Dniester!"

This detestation of the princes, who outraged his keen sense of duty by placing honors before honor, was Stein's first and deepest emotion. It underlay his entire social scheme, and was a basic concept in his vision of the new empire. When he saw the princes bartering with the French, and taking provinces and titles in payment for treason against the common Fatherland, it seemed unthinkable to him that a unified state could be built of such questionable materials. And he felt that at least thirty of these princes should be set aside, since the empire and the constitution were not a matter of caste, but of race.

For the class next in rank to the princes, the knighthood of which Stein himself was a member, had also done what they could to show him the presumption of the nobility and make him the first democrat amon͡g titled Germans:

"If the aristocracy wish to retain the leading position in the state to which they lay claim, they must rely less upon their arid pretentiousness, their dogs, horses and pipes, and more upon culture and an active interest in matters of real dignity and importance. It cannot be done by exemption from taxation and the social ostracism of every one who lacks a pedigree. . . . In their best days our people knew nothing of lineage. Archbishop Willigis of Mainz was the son of a poor woman; Duke Billung of Saxony the son of a man who owned seven hides of land." And in a secret session prior to the campaign against Napoleon, Stein proposed to the generals in all seriousness that the king should abrogate all titles and afterwards recognize only those nobles who had distinguished themselves in the war!

Stein naturally opposed the Revolution. But like

Goethe, he did so for democratic reasons, and in almost the same words: "The surest way to halt the spread of the revolutionary spirit is to meet all reasonable demands of the people." This sympathy for the masses, which derived from a love of mankind in general and a keen sense of duty, conditioned the entire structure of his reforms.

He had much hard-won practical experience behind him. At twenty-four, an official in the mining department; from twenty-seven to forty, head of the administration of mines and manufactures on the Ruhr; then, until forty-seven, supreme president of the provincial chamber of Westphalia. Such work, by bringing him in close contact with the people, sharpened his sympathies. For a man as serious-minded as he, this was an opportunity to study human needs and learn the means of betterment. And the nest in which he spent many years of this period was called Wetter.

This was Stein's happiest period, his only happy period. He could curb his hot temper by meticulous attention to business. He could praise "quiet, solitude, regular work." After forty he seldom had fits of rage, as on the occasion when a messenger had sprinkled ink instead of sand on his signature and Stein wiped the wet sheet on his face. The next day, when the servant reappeared, Stein arose quickly and pressed a crumpled bit of paper in his palm: it contained two gold pieces. But he could not bear to lose time. One of his associates speaks of him as "clear and curt in stating his opinions, and so vigorous as to terrify persons of a timid or compliant nature."

But his work on public improvements and his ex-

tensive dealings with the people trained him in stability.
After a brief mission for old Freddy, Stein declined to
render his successors any service involving courts and
diplomats, whom he called a "breed of frivolous, pre-
tentious, good-for-nothing idlers." He was now content
to confine himself to the narrower sphere (itself broad
enough) of his mines, factories, canals, and highways.
At times he would advance the state as much as ten
thousand thalers out of his own pocket.

Throughout this period of strenuous moderation he
committed but one mistake.

After several years of careful observation, he decided
that he would marry a certain countess "because of her
purity of character and her soundness of judgment."
For "the spectacle of this soft benevolent creature and
the utterances of her calm mind will moderate all the
hardness, gruffness, and precipitancy of my nature."
But this twenty-one-year-old, who could almost have
been his daughter, turned out to be less interested in
composure than in sociability. Soon after their marriage
she went to live with her sister. Her husband, who was
unpracticed in intimacy with women, was left alone.
He wrote to an elderly friend to confess how much he
needed the sympathy of a companion. And furthermore, his wife failed to bear him the male child required
to carry on his name.

His activities as a statesman broke in upon this domestic bitterness. At the age of forty-eight, like Bismarck, he became minister, being summoned—again
like Bismarck—by a king who called upon him skeptically and almost unwillingly. Yet Stein had barely three
years in which to carry out the ideas that were seething

in his brain as the result of twenty years' experience. To resist the growing pressure from abroad—we are writing of 1804-1806—he tried to improve the national morale; and to this end he successfully combated all forms of political corruption—nepotism, inefficiency, and bureaucracy. In the last analysis, he was working towards the abolishment of class distinctions.

But there was one class which he had accepted as beyond question; and the arch representative of this class, the absolute king of Prussia (who was in reality a very limited one) remained unsurmountable. Stein's greatest efforts were shattered against this impregnable wall. He was courageous, but not superhuman: and the first time he pitted himself against the full onslaught of reality (in his narrower sphere he had been an autocrat, and thus a victor) his lance was shattered. "I cannot," he wrote in Protestant loyalty about the king, "complain against any one who has been made weak by nature, any more than you can find fault with me because I am not Newton. I see in this the will of Providence, and there is nothing else to do but to have faith and to resign oneself."

Yet almost immediately afterwards he made one last dogged attempt to gain his point. In a grotesque document which he sent to the queen, who was in turn to hand it on to the king, he stated as abruptly as a court fool that the councilors were enjoying the confidence which the king should place in his minister, and that these councilors were, in the last analysis, dictating the policies of the state.

After explaining at length why a government could no longer be conducted in this manner, he drew the king a picture of his three councilors and intimates.

The first was "a victim of his wife's arrogance"; and his relationship with the family of the second councilor was "undermining his morals." This second councilor was "physically and morally maimed and stunted"; his knowledge was "confined to the fopperies of the French," for "this frivolous man has never given a thought to the serious sciences." Now as to the third: "In a period which has no parallel in modern history, the guidance of the diplomatic affairs of this state is entrusted to the weak and unclean hands of a low-born French poetaster, a roué, who combines physical decrepitude with moral corruption, and fritters away what shallow brains he does have with his worthless cronies of the gambling table."

In closing he described the minister of foreign affairs: "branded as a sneaking traitor . . . a dullard and a lecher." With the result that "the people of this state are dissatisfied with their present government . . ." and "a change is imperative." And should your Royal Majesty decide not to accept the proposed reforms, we may expect either that the state of Prussia will be dissolved or that it will lose its autonomy, and that the love and respect of its subjects will completely vanish."

Written six months before the battle of Jena, by the minister of the interior to his king, courtesy of the queen. She had carefully spared the eyes of her husband the closing admonition.

Collapse, flight, treaty of Memel.

When the perplexed king offered the baron the ministry of foreign affairs, Stein—afflicted with gout as he was—accepted on condition that one of the councilors should be dismissed. Then the king broke into a rage: "Now I see . . . that you are to be considered an ob-

stinate, obstreperous, disobedient, and defiant public
servant who, boasting of his talents and his genius, has
little real concern for the best interests of the state, but
is activated solely by caprice and dominated by his passions and motives of personal hatred and embitterment.
. . . And if you are unwilling to modify your disre-
spectful and indecent conduct, the state can henceforth
dispense with your services. Königsberg, January 8,
1807."

Eight months later, when the king recalled him in
desperation, Stein was lying ill with a fever in his castle,
but he wrote like a Prussian: "As to Your Majesty's
distinguished orders concerning return to ministry. . .
I obey unconditionally, and leave to Y. M. the arrangement of all particulars." Only partially recovered, he
traveled from Nassau through Kopenhagen to Tilsit
(which is the way the map of Germany looked at that
time).

Yet it seems as though Stein had a premonition of the
brief period of office in store for him. It was to be
scarcely a year. He seized this half-demoralized state
with both hands, to shape it after his own ideas. On one
sheet of paper he canceled the serfdom of the Prussian
peasants; on a second he bestowed self-government upon
all cities; on a third he extended military duty to all
classes, including the nobility; on a fourth whipping
was abolished and the opportunity of becoming an officer was opened to every private soldier; a fifth did away
with the cabinet system of government; a sixth converted the peasants on the royal domains of East and
West Prussia into free proprietors; a seventh cut in half
all the higher salaries in the state, including the king's—

all this having been thought out in twenty-five years of solitude, executed in exile within a few months, and made possible by the national distress.

He had already begun plans for carrying out the project nearest to his heart, the establishment of a Prussian parliament with universal suffrage, when one morning in Berlin he picked up the latest "Moniteur" from Paris and found printed there, with angry comments, a frightfully frank letter of his which the French had intercepted while on its way to a trusted correspondent and which they were now displaying before the world as evidence of an insurrection. This was soon followed by a *lettre de cachet* condemning the "nommé Stein," and signed: Napoleon, Madrid.

Despite his thirty years of service, and a tradition of seigniorial privileges which had extended for seven centuries, Stein had to give up his office and leave the country immediately. For a time he lived off the sale of his silver, locating in Bohemia, where he agitated, advised, and wrote until the beginning of Napoleon's invasion into Russia, when Czar Alexander sent him a cordial letter inviting him to St. Petersburg.

The German baron despised the German rulers, even those of Berlin and Vienna; he hated Frenchmen and distrusted Hanoverians; but he found the czar of Russia a paragon of idealism, energy, uprightness, patience, tact, courage—all the princely virtues that he had been dreaming of for thirty years. Stein fought through these last and most exciting years of his public life in the pay of Russia, first as Alexander's adviser in camp and at the capital, and afterwards at Paris without definite office. He consistently praised the czar, and acclaimed him as a liberator. Now this stern and scrupulous man thought that he had found at last the ruler after his heart. For a time he literally considered the czar as an avenging angel who had come to destroy the demon Napoleon.

1813. Stein was in a fever of activity. Unremittingly, even in the pauses between battles (Stein, being a genuine statesman, looked upon war purely as the means to an end) he distributed prospectuses, letters, and memoranda among the allied kings and ministers. All these proposals were written with the one aim of promoting unity. In style they are succinct, clear, and simple. It was only in his letters to friends that the pathos of his devotion to the great cause betrayed itself in a subdued murmur of complaint.

Napoleon's reverses gave him new hope. After years of banishment, with their hours of depression, he awoke to a last brief period of youth. Suddenly a letter of five lines to Gneisenau: "What are you doing in England, when Russians and French are maneuvering in Germany? I beg you earnestly, come! Farewell and come! Stein." Such was the fighting mood he was in at present. When he met Madame de Staël, these two choleric natures were so overwhelmed by their common cordial hatred of Napoleon that Arndt, who was present, saw them "at tables and on divans, poking and ramming against each other in their excitement."

Frightful recoil! If all these plans, all this triumph, were to have no permanent value! If this one opportunity of a century were to be lost for Germany! If the coalition formed to combat and expel the conqueror were, immediately after the victory, to be dissolved again through jealousy and ill will, plot and intrigue,

and every last one of these rulers were to begin plot-
ting for the aggrandizement of his own house at the
expense of national unity! When he first went to Paris,
Stein still had faith in his czar.

Trembling at the promise of success, Stein mapped
out during the summer all that he intended laying before the congress in the fall. After thinking over the
matter for a lifetime, he still felt that the best possible
arrangement for Germany would be a division into two
sections with a balance of power which he tried painfully to equalize. As a means of binding Austria to the
empire and of counteracting the centrifugal tendency
of her alien population, he planned that her ruler should
have the rank of emperor with the right to veto all
acts of the proposed parliament. The emperor could
make war, however, solely in conjunction with a triple
council of princes, Prussia among them.

But now came Vienna! Salons and fêtes, castles and
antechambers, nepotism, a politics of private interests,
of secretaries, of lackeys, of the alcove. If all courts were
interrelated with one another, how could they injure
the good Bourbon, how deprive him of land? Should the
minor German states have a subordinate position?
Would not Metternich himself derive greater advantage
from a loose alliance as neighbors than from the arrangement which this remarkable baron had been advocating
now for decades? Stein was personally honored, to be
sure, but he had no official standing, and gradually came
to be looked upon as a positive nuisance. For these people were much less interested in a German empire than
in the maintenance of traditional and recently acquired
prerogatives.

And Alexander? Was he, too, one of those who were

thinking only of their own immediate interests? With
horror his adviser and admirer saw him siding with
England to prevent any increase in the strength of Germany and to oppose all cession of French territories,
while showing great enthusiasm, on the other hand, for
the subjection of Poland to Russia. No one, either German or non-German, seemed to have the least interest
in establishing the empire: the realities which had once
been dreams now vanished again before his very eyes
and became dreams once more. He wrote: "The shallow-
ness and diffidence of the one [Alexander], the senile
obtuseness and sluggishness of another [Hardenberg],
the commonness and intellectual feebleness of the third
[Nesselrode], and the combined triviality of them all
made it impossible for any great and noble idea to be
thoroughly and consistently carried out." This was the
second—and the greater—disillusionment of his life.

Stein took his hat and returned to his ancestral
fortress.

Yet in this same summer of 1815, when he was definitely and safely installed in his castle for the first time
in years, he learned one evening that the minister Von
Goethe was stopping over in Nassau. And although they
had never met, Stein went down to the "Lion" and
brought him as a reluctant guest to the castle. The next
day they traveled to Cologne together. Stein was fifty-
eight, Goethe eight years older. For a lifetime they had
seen each other in action. Stein, highly cultured, respected the poet who had admired his mortal enemy and
had never believed in German unity. Goethe, who had
been unsympathetic to all of Stein's specific activities
while respecting him as a personality, was now entering
a new, more German period, discovering Dürer and his

associates, and returning with a deeper attachment to the charming streams and valleys of his youth.

As they stood side by side in the Cologne cathedral, Stein said softly to Arndt: "Be quiet, don't disturb him. In matters of politics we can't, of course, praise him. But let him alone, he is too great."

Such deep humility as this the fiery-tempered old man felt in the presence of the genius whom he had sternly condemned as a "citizen of the world"; for Stein had always raged at this cosmopolitan attitude in philosophers and savants which he considered inimical to nationalistic progress. And now, despite this excellent opportunity to take Goethe to task for his views, his truculence vanished, and he grew tactful and reticent. "I have never," Arndt writes, "heard Stein converse in a quieter voice."

Sixteen years, most of them healthy ones, were still in store for the baron. But Germany had no further need of him. All that he had worked for, and especially the constitution, sank into the archives of history. Freedom paled, reforms grew moldy, plans withered away. Sixty years were to pass before Stein's projects to defeat bureaucracy were realized, ninety before the Prussian nobles granted the peasants self-government. And at the same time as old Stein, with shattered hopes, was shutting himself up in his Rhenish castle, a man was born in a castle of Brandenburg who was, though only partially and in his own way, to make Stein's dream a reality two generations later.

To be sure, the recluse was offered the presidency, or Prussian representation, in the alliance; but he did not relish being in any way dependent upon his old rival,

Hardenberg, who was still in power and who "would victimize me on the slightest provocation." The next and most natural move, to put Stein at the head of Prussia, never occurred to the king. Even when endowments were being lavished upon the generals, he was overlooked—which was proper, since it spared him the trouble of refusing. In an icy letter of six lines, the king conferred upon him the order of the Black Eagle. And when Stein, at the age of seventy, happened to be passing through Berlin, he was nominated a member of the National Council.

But the common people, both civilians and soldiers, appreciated what he had done. During the revolutionary uprisings a deputation of officers of the allied armies came to Frankfort to consult a professor of political law on the weighty question as to whether the laws of the empire made it possible to proclaim Stein the German emperor. The professor said yes, the people would probably have agreed, and the genius of history has certainly agreed. Only the princes themselves would have denied it with a smile, and, strangely enough, their opinion would have been shared by the Baron vom Stein.

Meanwhile, he was giving his daughter history lessons, which suggested to him the idea of collecting the incunabula of German history. He was now totally blind in one eye, and realized that he could not perform the work himself; but he superintended it, backing it with all his former energy, endowing it with money, employing scholars, and soliciting the aid of clergymen and libraries. The result was the Monumenta Germaniæ Historica. At the same time he procured greater freedom for the peasants in his own villages, doing here on a small scale what it had been impossible for him to accomplish for the country as a whole.

On the day of his wife's death (he survived her by a decade) he wrote a synopsis of her life, speaking of her husband as though he were referring to some stranger, and delicately attributing their earlier difficulties to the unsteadiness of his temperament and the vicissitudes of his career. Later he was disturbed by new "dissensions in the bosom of my family which in some cases agitated me profoundly and most painfully, and in the daily rounds of life frequently had a depressing effect."

So he resolutely turned his back upon worldly interests. He quoted the Bible more often now in his letters; and totally unlike most retired statesmen, he gradually gave up all mention of political matters. Yet when he wanted to have one wall of his dining hall painted, he chose for his subject the sorrow of the German army in Asia Minor when Barbarossa was dragged from the river in which he had been drowned. By looking at the soldiers, he wrote in his instructions to the painter, one should be able to tell that now, when on the verge of conquering the Holy Land, they have lost their leader "whose bravery had shone like a beacon to guide them through battles and storms; and now they stand forsaken, in the midst of a foreign continent, surrounded by traitorous allies and ferocious enemies." A profound revelation of disillusionment and torment.

One year before his death he was practically forced by a grateful king (since he was needed) to preside at seventy-eight over the diet in Westphalia. He was sick, but he ignored all his ailments and rose up with his former vigor. And he needed no bell now—for when he came stamping in with his cane, the whole room fell silent.

At the last, he emphatically opposed the revolutionary movement in Paris, Brussels, and Madrid. But the Greek struggle for liberty, a nationalistic revolution, brought the old gleam into his eyes again—and we may ask whether some remote corner of his heart was not revolutionary after all. Was it perhaps only by deliberate self-discipline that his impassioned temperament was kept within bounds? Or was it by reason of his deeply rooted ancestral feelings? Carved with his name on his tombstone are the words: "The last of his knightly race, which had flourished on the Lahn for more than seven centuries."

Since we must die, let us be brave.

BISMARCK

Earthly majesty is always akin to the fallen angel, who
is proud and unhappy, beautiful but troubled, and whose
plans and efforts, though vast, are denied success.

POWERFUL frame! How much was Bismarck indebted
to his physique, although he hardly ever came to actual
tests of fist and muscle! His body and his accomplishments were identical: the will of a giant vibrant with
the electric charge of magnetic nerves. He was like
those mastiffs of his which, precisely because of this
resemblance, he loved: strong and nervous, heavy and
somber, formidable and unrelenting towards an offender
—loyal to but one person, his master, yet devoted to him
until death. Bismarck was as powerful, as nervous, and
as dangerous as his dogs.

Like every strong man, he once saved his own life.
An assassin in Unter den Linden had fired one shot at
him and was about to fire a second, this time at closer
range. It would have been fatal, had not Bismarck seized
the man's right hand and hurled the weapon to the
ground. On another occasion, when he was younger, he
had plunged into the water after a man who was drowning—and for the rest of his life, among all the insignia
of honor which "go with the make-up of a minister,"
he took pride only in the medal commemorating this
rescue. Again, he saved Prussia, when the king was
about to yield to popular pressure and to abdicate, by
taking hold of the king's scabbard and literally shaking
him into a mood of self-defense.

None of these three equally important acts would have been possible without the assistance of his powerful physique. Wherever he went, he was the biggest man present. At a court ball, when he was in his twenties, his stature elicited the admiration of his first master. Emperors of the French and of the Russians, kings, princes, and princesses—all were impressed to see him stoop as he came through the door and then draw himself up again to his full height. Generals and politicians, most of them his opponents for one reason or another, were often astounded, and even terrified, by his build.

And yet his intimates, and sometimes mere government clerks, had seen the giant collapse, convulsed with weeping, tortured with despair, his features twitching and distorted. This is the other side of Bismarck, an aspect of him which the Germans readily gloss over, but without which the nationalistic side of his character could never have been effectual.

For while the spirit of history was still undecided whether or not to unite the German race after a thousand years of dissent, it produced a man whose own impulses were so rent that he alone was capable of coping with this other division. His own personal struggle, a restless oscillation between pathos and criticism, duty and power, flight and aggression, loyalty and vengeance, had its parallel for him in the condition of Germany; and this almost mystical, yet natural kinship gave him both the desire and the courage to battle for national integration. Almost unknown to himself, a powerful stream of emotion was flowing beneath the craftiness of the politician. This produced a vision, a kind of dream, which gave him consistency of purpose despite the seeming opportunism of his methods. And he could work only at white heat: rapidly, in barely eight years, Bismarck the Prussian forged Germany.

For Germany could not be subdued except by a man of emotion who, like the artist, was capable of casting his molten feelings into forms of solid iron. It was really an artist who shaped this realm of music into a state.

But he was also a realist; for this same soil nourishes a race of realists who attempt to balance their weakness for reverie and philosophy by a deliberate propulsion towards externals—their cult of action being, probably through fear, exaggerated into wariness. Bismarck was hard and realistic, with a keen sense of cold facts and an almost total indifference to principles. All during his thirty years of steadily mounting power, and even at the last when he was a dictator, he would ally himself with any party or any platform and oppose any party or any platform, purely as the occasion demanded. He hated passionately, lying awake far into the night. And the next day he would shatter his opponents like a bolt of lightning. But the very moment he had need of them, he would reverse his tactics and become conciliatory. It is absurd to ask just how far such a policy was pursued in the interests of his cause and how far in the interests of his personal power: for this man was a monomaniac who cared for no cause but his own and who felt that he alone could properly defend it!

Nevertheless Bismarck's *primum mobile* was neither the will to power nor the desire for fame—as to witness his long period of aimlessness in youth. At the age of thirty-five, when Bismarck the noble was taking his first steps into politics, Napoleon the parvenu was already emperor. He did not settle upon this career through any desire to be a dictator, nor any theoretical love for a fatherland which did not yet exist, nor through pride in Prussia, his more immediate home. But when he took trowel in hand and began laying stone upon stone, he was moved by the true artist's wish to produce order out of chaos, to give form to the formless—and along with this went a sound and thoroughgoing misanthropy which led him to ridicule the failures of his predecessors.

The German genius has always been either ideologist or artist. This people has never produced the pure *homo politicus*.

For this reason he was all the more violent in his opposition to the ideologists. He had little enough respect for philosophy, but he positively despised the pedants of the Frankfort variety, who had insisted, while the country ran riot, on examining in the light of ultimate philosophical principles every proposition laid before the assembly. A landowner from the Pomeranian backcountry, he placed a low value on city-bred intellectuals and professional men. He was self-taught, a political primitive; he stepped abruptly into the arena without previous experience or training, and also, of course, without party prejudices. Stammeringly, he hurled his doctrine of German unity at the astonished ranks of the diet until the king had singled him out. What could attract a sickly dreamer like Frederick William to this uncouth giant except that obscure element above and beyond the intellect which they had in common? Did this stranger arrive from his provincial estate with a fully worked-out plan of action? On the contrary, he had nothing but the vaguest notion of what he wanted, nothing but courage and the mutterings of anger.

For there was a heavy cargo of courage in this powerful hulk: a proud self-consciousness formed the ballast
for a vessel shaken with antinomies, and this alone assured it of a voyage without mishap. Bismarck's first
word to a king was a rebuke, as was also his last: March
'48, March '90. When not fighting, he was hardly more
than a misanthrope and a scoffer: his great energies were
drained by doubt, cynicism, and melancholy. But the
presence of an enemy restored them to unity, converted
them into action and purpose, and gave him self-reliance
by providing an external force against which his self-
reliance could be directed. And the nearer an enemy,
the keener his capacity for action. He fought with a
deeper devotion in domestic issues than against a foreign
foe. Bismarck hated the German politicians Windthorst
and Richter, but not Napoleon.

At bottom Bismarck was a thorough revolutionary. His first appearance as he came out of the oak
forests of his birthplace and threw himself with fury
into the narrow machinations of party politics; his attitude towards the kings and princes of his own country,
and later towards foreign kings and emperors; the bold
and simple No which he hurled at the political maxims
of his times; his insistence upon ruling without inter-
ference from others; his continual threat of resigning;
the splendid clarity, informality, and newness of his
diction—all these defiant traits of a freedom-loving
temperament belong to a man who, had he been born of
the submerged classes, would have advanced behind the
red flag.

He was not like Goethe, who needed order to encompass his own chaos: he was disharmonic through and

through, neither resting nor wanting rest. For it is not ideas, but emotions, which make the revolutionary; and the man who champions tradition with a fresh and terrorizing passionateness is often more revolutionary than a man who fights tradition with a calm pen or among the ranks of the many.

In reality, Bismarck created a new form of politics, in Germany at least. He revolutionized the methods of dealing with popular rebellions, founded the new school of diplomatic practice which openly struck terror instead of employing flattery and craft as in the school of Metternich. After a dinner in London, when he had outlined his program with astounding firmness, Disraeli, who saw him in the true perspective, said to his guests: "Take care of that man, he means what he says."

With these strong impulses to break the bonds of custom, with so much courage and self-reliance, such forcefulness and scorn—what kept him faithful to the old forms? What led him to decide socially against the future? What linked him with dynasties which had already begun to lose their meaning?

His blood. When he was being trained in the hunt, the old woodsman whose great-grandfather had served a Bismarck in the time of young Freddy called the boy "Herr Junker." He saw the inadequacy of his class, their degeneration and idleness, the futility and mismanagement with which many of his cousins fulfilled their inherited offices; and he saw the intelligence, industry, and pride of common citizens triumph over the mummified prejudices of the nobility—yet he constituted himself the guardian of his class and summoned his genius to its defense.

Above all else he defended the king. Not that he considered the king's blood to be better than his own: for more than once he told the Hohenzollern to their faces that the Bismarcks had tenanted the realm longer than they. But he saw in the king the apex of a pyramid which, if truncated, would seem odd, and perhaps even ludicrous. He was unwilling to imperil the hereditary prerogatives of his name; like the usual noble, the usual landowner, he was loath to relinquish any worldly possessions for theoretical reasons; he could never divorce himself from this sense of superiority which found its sanction in the very force of character behind it—and thus he gave unto the king that which was the king's.

For his house still flourished with manly vigor; the nihilism of an age of increasing transvaluations had not yet broken through his feudalistic code; and tradition was still powerful enough to extend its influence when aided by so faithful a scion. It seems as though this *Junker* inherited absolutely nothing from his mother, he was so totally lacking in any evidence of her bourgeois blood. Fifty years later—and Bismarck, with his temperament and will power, his fearlessness and independence, would have been a leader of the new era.

Thus he remained all his life a royalist, and grounded his work on dynasties. He himself asserted that his loyalty to the king was purely the result of his faith in God, yet this faith was forced to take strange shapes. He was a Protestant, highly unmystical, inveterately rationalistic. For years, up to the day of his death, he kept a prayer-book lying on his night-table; it was interleaved with blank sheets on which he jotted down the political ideas that came to him at night: truly a Bismarckian species of devotion.

In any case, no such transcendental reasons prompted him to show the least respect for other princes, and especially other German ones, even though they too felt that they ruled by divine right. On the contrary, he was scornful and heaped irony upon their heads. In the whole line of Prussian kings he loved no one, not even the great Frederick—and he cared still less for the rulers under which he himself had served. But he was bound to them by a feeling for feudal ties which must have been handed down through many generations, since blood alone can explain it. The noble granted fealty to his king through expecting fealty of his vassals. So great was the love of freedom in this revolutionary temperament.

The relationship always remained essentially one of equal to equal. And while he always observed the formalities, signing himself "most humbly" or "most obediently," he eyed the conduct of his master with suspicion and bit the golden chain when he felt its pressure.

At last he even bit the master's hand—and nothing shows Bismarck's latent revolutionary tendencies more clearly than the way he rose up at the first provocation against the one authority he had recognized, the king. The significant fact is not his going, but his way of going: every detail of this drama, in which a powerful old man was called upon to comply with the arbitrary wishes of a weak young sovereign, points to the imperiousness, the intransigence, and the thorough independence of his character. The hereditary nobility of his blood provided a rigid code which would not permit him to conceive of his work in terms of the German people rather than in terms of Prussian kings. But nothing, not even the faith he paraded so readily, could hinder another kind of nobility, the nobility of his temperament, from defying a prince by God's grace exactly as the young idiot deserved.

At times in the past he had ventured cautious criticisms or had, though always with the bearing of the liegeman, openly voiced objections when behind closed doors. But now, aroused like a mastiff, he broke into a rage against the master who had struck him unjustly. Bismarck's fall disclosed impulses which his inherited code had kept concealed for years. Only the lack of a great opponent, and the legend which the Germans built up around the mere pretext of a reconciliation, have been able to obscure for a time the violence of this outburst.

Yet even now he winced at the thought of open rebellion. Was youth all that this old man of seventy-five needed? Or were his royalist leanings still an unsurmountable obstacle? In any case, he did not go beyond farewell tirades in which he fired disturbing truths point-blank at his king and the other princes. Then he retired in fury to his den, hurling out stones which cracked the dilapidated royal masonry.

But the steel edifice of the state remained standing. For twenty-eight years Bismarck had governed; twenty-eight years after he was gone the old dynastic system collapsed—and Germany's enemies watched to see the entire structure fall into ruins.

But it held! Not a stone, except those which the enemy extracted, was loosened. Indeed, at the very height of calamity, skillful hands were at work making the pillars more solid than before. And it now became evident that whereas most Germans had revered the royalty as the very foundation of the empire, it had been merely a brilliant but unnecessary façade.

The survival of the state is the surest evidence that the important part which Bismarck assigned to royalty in his political scheme was purely a concession to his class— one might almost call it a weakness. For as the ruling houses fell and the empire endured, Bismarck's precautions for the future, despite all their baggage of tradition, were justified by their results. After the tempest, people looked about them and saw that the man who had done this was much more modern than he himself had ever hoped to be.

When the empire was founded at Versailles, amidst the medieval roar of victorious cannon, the golden mirrors in the Glass Gallery of the palace reflected only the forms of warlike princes; the industrious masses were elsewhere. When in the same hall forty-eight years later the empire was sentenced to atone and pay for its defeat, the golden mirrors no longer reflected a single royal figure. The last three emperors of Europe had been slain or deposed. Twenty-two German dynasties had been deprived of power—not by compulsion from without, hardly even by the natives themselves, but by corrosion, by the rust of an era which had served its purposes and was now ready for death.

Yet the documents which two humble citizens were called upon to sign at that momentous hour did not involve the destruction of Bismarck's work, but only of the work of William the Second. It was William who had fostered, and Bismarck who had opposed, all those policies which eventually involved Germany in war.

Foreign colonies and a marine were typical instances of all that the founder of the state had *not* wanted. Had he really raised the empire on the point of a victorious sword? Or had he not, rather, employed the sword purely as a means of overcoming Europe's resistance to German unity? Did he not, for twenty years thereafter, resist all the temptations of imperialism, all the enticements of militaristic expansion? And was it not Bismarck who, braving the anger of the king and all the generals at Nikolsburg, created the prototype of a modern peace: without cession of territory, without indemnity, dictated solely by the desire to restore friendly relations with the enemy as quickly as possible? Was Bismarck really of the past?

At the end he broods, despite protestations of homage, alone and in exile. When he is nearly eighty, and people try to argue him into the tranquillity proper to his years, he looks at them from under his bushy eyebrows and asks, "And why should I be tranquil?" The wife is gone upon whom he had lavished all the warmth which he repressed in his frigid dealings with the outer world. This woman had been his haven of retreat. All the yearnings for quiet, woodland, and home which troubled this restless, knotty character were embodied in her—even though his equally strong love of executive activity and political organization always kept him occupied in the service of the state. The more turbulent his career, the more peaceful his marriage had to be—and was.

He had a critical mind which readily turned to history and to literary composition; and he was by nature a woodsman and a huntsman, a rustic who resented all officialdom. His sojourns in the country, which he had accepted in his youth without thinking, were deliberately protracted in later years—for it was here that he derived the strength to breathe in ministerial chambers, in the closets of a castle, and in the halls of a parliament which he despised. This antinomy between the scene of his activity and the landscape of his heart never ended, for it was merely the symbol of a chronic indecision; and when, at the last, he had full leisure to enjoy the silence of his forests, he longed to be back in the turmoil which he had cursed for years.

This was his human lot. Bismarck was not happy by nature, and he knew it.

But he accepted life like a man, did his work with substantial materials, saw the vision of his thirties realized in his sixties, and for ten full years could look upon himself as the arbiter of the Continent. Yet he could never rid himself of the fear that all this might vanish overnight if he were not there—and in his last weeks his daughter heard him praying aloud for the future of Germany.

In a long coat, and a wide hat, peering out grimly like a Wotan, he could be seen, at the end, among the prehistoric oaks of his forests, walking about slowly and alone, between two mastiffs.

STANLEY

STANLEY

All I had to do was to free my mind from all else, and relieve it of every earthly desire but the finding of the man whom I was sent to seek.

STANLEY has been called a hero, a swindler, and an adventurer.

He lacked the fire to be a hero; even the most exaggerated reports could not have made him out to be a swindler; and he was still less of an adventurer, though he had the outward appearance of one. For he felt no attraction towards the unknown; he took no pleasure in surprise; and uncertainty had no charm for him. Everything that he did involved some thoroughly definite purpose.

Stanley was the first American in Africa. Both his weaknesses and his talents are wholly American.

The career which led to his romantic reputation as a man began with his disordered life as a child. He, John Rowland, was the illegitimate son of a maidservant who neglected him, and of a farmer who was killed in a public house. For eight years an outcast, he languished in the poor-house. At fifteen he became a shepherd, at seventeen he shipped to America as a cabin-boy. There he found a father, the merchant Henry Morton Stanley, whom he had seen reading a newspaper in his office and had accosted with the words, "Do you want a boy, sir?"

It is typical that he was not made heir forthwith to this father whom good luck had found for him, but instead got into financial straits, enlisted for military service, and one day earned money and rank for himself by an extraordinary piece of daring. During an attack by sea, the little petty officer swam under the fire of a fort five hundred yards to one of the enemy's ships and fastened a cable to the prow so that the ship—to the complete dumbfounding of the crew—could be calmly towed in by the foe. The next day he was an officer, with unusual pay.

His grim courage, backed by a strong constitution, had relieved him of poverty and obscurity. Had he been the born *condottiere*, at this point he would have taken his fate in his hands and perhaps have become a great American general. But he had other ambitions, and the means of carrying these ambitions into effect—although at present he was still unaware of them.

Another episode was needed to set him on the right track. During a pleasure trip in Syria he was taken captive—and when he got back half naked to Constantinople, he wrote an account of his adventures.

The plasticity, the suspense, and the vividness of these articles, which were published in an important newspaper, drew attention to their author. He was asked to write others. This, he felt, was the right tack. Forthwith he resigned as an officer and became a reporter. The greatest newspaperman in the world, Gordon Bennett, took notice of his work and sent him as a war correspondent to Abyssinia.

From this time on events followed one another in logical sequence.

After the fall of Magdala, Stanley ran first to the telegraph office and got a scoop on all the other papers by cabling to New York twenty pages of the Bible at the end of his report while his colleagues stood outside in helpless rage. Stanley became world-famous as an American reporter.

But it must not be forgotten that more than writing and lying are required to make a reporter of genius. Speed, courage, tenacity, discretion, patience, physical strength—during his next twenty years as his own reporter, Stanley demonstrated that he possessed all these qualities to a high degree. For he was by no means an author: he was a fabulous journalist. He never created: he merely recounted his experiences. What decided Stanley to go in search of Livingstone? His sympathy for an explorer, for a fellow-countryman, for a missionary? A passion for Africa, for adventure, for the Congo or the Nile?

He undertook the work precisely as Gordon Bennett had commissioned him: "No matter how much it costs, find Livingstone!" We Americans don't know what it means to be beaten. We'll show the world a brand-new work of art—we'll discover a white man lost somewhere in the thousands of square miles of the darkest primitive forests. If he is dead, we'll produce his bones. But in any case we'll find Livingstone. We'll give them something sensational!

His instructions might just as well have been to swim the Atlantic. But the records show that Stanley was the right man for the job. This was no anxious search-party sent out by the nation, by science, or the Church. The greatest newspaperman of America was sending his greatest reporter.

And he went, in fact, with American speed, and found what he had set out to find. "My mission to find Livingstone was very simple, and was a clear and definite aim. All I had to do was to free my mind from all else, and relieve it of every earthly desire but the finding of the man whom I was sent to seek. To think of self, friends, banking-account, life-insurance, or any worldly interest but the one sole purpose of reaching the spot where Livingstone might happen to rest, could only tend to weaken resolution. Intense application to my task assisted me to forget all that I had left behind, and all that might lie ahead in the future."

As is evident, he was going through the motions of the mystic. In any case, he was prudent enough not to mention why he set out for Ujiji, the very place where Livingstone was actually located. Stanley says nothing of the fact that the last news of Livingstone came from there, and that Arabian caravans in Zanzibar had reported Livingstone to be there.

This was the egg of Columbus, but Columbus did not stop at the egg. Nor Stanley. His tracing of the vanished missionary—as a feat and especially as a pretext for his brilliant book—brought him more fame than any subsequent journey; yet his really important exploit, the act of his career which made him immortal, came later.

The discovery of the Congo, less dramatic and far more magnificent than the relief of Livingstone or of Emin Pasha which preceded and followed it respectively, shows this American at the height of his energy. It was this trip which has been compared to the voyage of Columbus—and as an exploit it has been considered even greater. What plagues, mutinies, and perils this man survived during his nine hundred and ninety-nine days in the Congo, what he endured in his thirty-two battles with the natives—all this is unparalleled, and gives us evidence that any obstacle can be surmounted. For once in his life, Stanley was caught in the high winds of heroism. Following a river across a continent, to the point where it empties into the sea! Into the sea! This time Stanley did not find a human; as the greatest of his achievements, he found the sea. Had he been the man he mistook himself to be, he would have died now or retired to meditate. But he overlooked what extraordinary obligations this great act placed upon him. Had he died after this one great journey, he would have had fewer readers, but he would have gained in dignity.

A long life had nothing more to offer but two vast repetitions, a new trip to the Congo and a new search. Stanley went into politics and business without becoming either a politician or a business man of major proportions.

The English ministers, and even the merchants of Manchester, laughed at him. But the shrewd business eye of Leopold, king of the Belgians, detected the possibilities here—and before Stanley had reached London on his homeward voyage, Leopold sent two emissaries to meet him at the station in Marseilles with an invitation to Brussels.

Stanley found it easy to enter foreign service, since he was thoroughly international. For years this native Englishman had played the American, then changed his rôle at the appropriate moment. In the Civil War he fought on the side of the South, but after being captured and freed he transferred his allegiance to the North. Long after professing himself an Englishman, he took part at the Congo conference in Belgium as the representative of North America.

Heretofore this man had followed his journalistic impulse, for how had Stanley hit upon the Congo? Precisely as with Livingstone. "A little while after the burial of Livingstone . . . I strolled over [you hear the American?] to the office of the 'Daily Telegraph,' and pointed out to the proprietors how much remained shrouded in mystery in Dark Africa." Here followed an interchange of cables with America concerning funds to cover the expenses of the trip. By afternoon the expedition had been assured.

But now, when he was being sent by a king and a merchant, Stanley looked upon himself half as merchant and half as king. In short, he considered himself an instrument of culture. When men of action suddenly begin talking of culture, there is usually a mishap. Economically, he may have had a great deal of success: the whole concept of laying out a chain of stations along the Congo is a case in point. But he became ridiculous when he posed as the bringer of culture and salvation.

And yet his books are full of this posturing. What did it matter to this man of iron, however pious he was, what did it matter to the "Bula-Matari," the breaker of rocks, as the savages called him as he set them to work crushing rocks on the river bank with a sledge—what did it matter to Stanley whether the souls of negroes were saved? Was it not he who, with the conqueror's fist and the white man's gun, put the negroes to flight—he, the first American in Africa, a continent which explorers heretofore had penetrated with tears in their eyes? Yet, however different his feelings, he overloads his books with Christianity and humanitarianism.

Though he was determined to overcome all obstacles, this American did not have the slightest intention of

going out of his way to find them. (The cynical innocence of his coquetry with the mission is the only
typically English trait in this son of England.) His interests were extremely practical and rationalistic.

Prior to this second trip to the Congo, he asked the
head of the mission in Capetown whether he could charter the mission's boat at the mouth of the Congo.
"Never!" was the answer: for in view of his nefarious
past, they could not allow him the assistance of the
mission!

But what did Stanley do when he saw the tempting
boat on the Congo? He chartered the boat from the missionaries there, who had not yet had time to receive instructions from their superior in Capetown. He with-
held all suspicious mail, boarded the boat, and as he was
steaming off, allowed the gentlemen to have their letters.

He had a genius for the positive.

If the specialists did often vigorously challenge his
contention that the person who had been there should
know best, they may have been right in principle, but
were wrong in this particular instance. They tried in
vain to belittle his achievement. He solved the old problem of the Nile, it was claimed, by an accidental discovery which he himself had misinterpreted. A doctor in
Gotha, they objected, had described the bed of the
Congo quite accurately in theory, and Stanley had
"merely put it to the test."

Merely? When Galle in Breslau discovered Neptune
with the telescope, his achievement was hardly a tenth
as important as that of Challis in Cambridge and Lever-
rier in Paris, who had previously calculated by mathematics where the planet would be but had failed to see

it. But the man who settles the question of the Congo at Gotha has done nothing in comparison with the man who is first to follow it across the continent of Africa.

Furthermore, all that they attributed to good luck came purely as the result of Stanley's own merits. If he was fitted out like a prince, who induced the publisher and the king to invest so heavily in his expeditions? Never before was a traveler so sumptuously equipped. A quarter of a million to find Livingstone, more than half a million to find Emin. On his trip to the Congo, two hundred carriers, and provisions for barter sufficient to last him three years. And his supply of guns and merchandise, messengers and wagons, for his second Congo expedition was a marvel in itself. Livingstone, when he saw Stanley coming, called him a luxurious traveler.

Stanley needed all this—for he did not love these lonely uncharted forests. He admired them, but he never yearned to return to them, and he never did return. He loved the cities, the motion and confusion of crowds. He loved being a reporter. By his own testimony, he personally never suffered want throughout all his periods of hardship; and it is charming to hear him say of himself that even in the bogs and marshes of the primitive forests he shaved regularly each morning.

On his last expedition, for the relief of Emin Pasha, he repeated his first exploit, but with less success. This enterprise, for all its tests of courage and endurance, shows Stanley on the decline. For the first time in his life he made mistakes.

When hunting for Livingstone, he did not know definitely where he was, yet found him. Now when hunting for Emin, he knew his whereabouts precisely, but

for political and commercial reasons he chose a circuitous course, meeting Emin only after considerable
delay—and it ended by the rescuer appealing to the
rescued for assistance. And Emin, who was no more
anxious to be rescued than Livingstone had been, returned to his post.

When he came upon Livingstone he was like a prince,
at the head of a caravan which filled the old gentleman
with astonishment. But now, after frightful months
which left him half dead with exhaustion, he straggled
up to Emin with a handful of survivors in tatters. Emin
received him, surrounded by his soldiers, and offered
him the fat of the land: corn, honey, bananas, tobacco,
clothes of homespun, shoes made by the natives. Stanley had nothing to give him but thirty cases of cart-
ridges. When he went back to get his rear column, he
found the officers murdered or half dead, and more than
a hundred people lost. Tippu-Tib, the crafty Arab, had
not sent the promised carriers.

It would be unfair to hold him responsible for this,
yet it remains at least a *factum negativum*—the first in
his life.

He returned to Emin, whose own soldiers in the
meantime had taken him prisoner. They had decided
that Stanley, the exhausted rescuer, was an adventurer
who planned in conjunction with Emin to ship them to
the coast and sell them to England. Negro logic, but the
logic of the stronger.

Now followed, after Emin had freed himself, Stanley's greatest formal success. He landed in Zanzibar, to
receive the greetings of emperors and kings. It was his
greatest and most impressive triumph, and his last.

Stanley always wrote his voluminous travel books in a few months. His enormous energy was continually prodded by his desire to express himself at top speed. Now, after the Emin Pasha expedition, he wrote his thousand-page report in fifty days—and of all the accusations he refuted there, none of them had yet been laid against him.

It was not what he did, but what he wrote, that made him famous: these glittering, fascinating, haphazard books. In this way the world responded to his deepest, though hidden, motive for action. Here, we are assured by the initiate, the terrors of the virgin forests are immensely exaggerated. Even along a caravan route a thousand years old, horrors accumulate. In the heart of Africa paradise is discovered. Cartography is flouted, yet a mass of dates, figures, and names is assembled, and maps are drawn, although science treats the whole with skepticism. (As happened in another connection with Schliemann, the excavator of Troy.)

This may have been the result of one specific trait. Being a self-educated man, like every other American Stanley was a parvenu. With the parvenu gesture of greatness, he received his mother, whose name he no longer bore, only in private, and permitted her a few precious glimpses of the great metropolitan world. When the Geographical Society conferred upon him a gold medal, he answered with a speech which showed the perfect parvenu in his hour of triumph. He was mercurial in his attitude towards other people, being at times amiable, and at other times quite abrupt. In one of his books he inserts two pictures: Stanley before his trip and Stanley after, as in advertisements.

He was always the reporter, even when he became

confidential. As when he said that all women, white and black alike, were much nobler than "we men." Or when he confessed that he had been looking for a wife for twenty years, but had not yet had time to find one. Or again, when he announced flatly that on his first expedition he felt himself growing more mature.

Or in his picture of Livingstone: "When fatigued by his constrained position on the clay floor in that east-facing veranda, he would lift his heavy Journal from his lap, and, with hand to chin, sit for hours in his brooding moods, thinking, ever thinking—mind ever revolving the prayer, 'How long, O Lord, must Thy servant bear all this?'" Whereupon he was startled by a salvo of guns, and Stanley appeared, the messenger of the Lord (Gordon Bennett).

Yet there are also passages which betray the stammerings of a remarkable poetic feeling. He wrote on seeing the Tanganyika for the first time, as it lay deep blue at his feet: "And I? Well, I am so happy that, were I quite paralyzed and blinded, I think that at this supreme moment I could take up my bed and walk, and all blindness would cease at once." And when he came upon the Congo, his Congo, he compared it to the face of a promising child that was destined to be at once a great genius, a statesman, a commander, and a poet.

It was precisely this stylistic pastiche, this mixture of reporting, sentiment, and poetic description, which made Stanley's books so effective. No one before him had written of Africa in this manner. Stanley made Africa popular.

This fourth trip was his last. Soon afterwards, when he was nearly fifty, he married—having waited this long not because he had not previously found time to marry,

but purely because he had not previously won his bride.
He was denied her for a long while; but it could not be
said that he married her for money, as she was almost
penniless. The ceremony was performed with much
pomp in Westminster Abbey. The bride laid her wreath
on Livingstone's grave. Stanley had a Napoleonic feeling for the *beau geste*.

For a time Stanley contemplated a new field of activity. He ran for parliament. But he soon retired—perhaps because he was too domineering to work in collaboration with others.

He purchased an estate, and having grown gray, he
set to work now in miniature, laying out paths and
building barns, planting and draining. His wife named
the brook the Congo, and the woodlot the Aruvimi
Forest. He laughed, and accepted without protest this
bitter replica of his former career.

Nine years later he died, at the beginning of his sixties.
The bishop would not allow him to be buried in Westminster Abbey, the one place where he belonged. He
rests in a village cemetery, his grave marked by a large
rough stone with the inscription:

HENRY MORTON STANLEY
BULA-MATARI
1841-1904
AFRICA

If we compare Stanley with Livingstone, it is hard to
say which of them gains by the comparison.

Both were self-made men, the one beginning as a
cotton spinner, the other as a shepherd, sailor, and clerk.
The one was a missionary, the other a journalist. But

when they got down to work, Stanley remained what he was whereas Livingstone forgot the missionaries for his mission.

Both explored great rivers. Livingstone was a monomaniac in the grip of a misanthropic passion for the Nile, and he even had a peculiar love for its name. Stanley on the other hand was always actuated by some specific purpose.

Livingstone groped with a mystical urge towards enigmatic headwaters; Stanley broke himself a new path to an unpeopled estuary. Stanley was trying to fulfill a task; Livingstone was in search of Africa's marvels. The two men are alike in that they followed the two largest streams of a continent, the one going upstream to the source, the other going downstream to the mouth. Livingstone, loving Africa, wanted to explore. Stanley, loving his work, wanted to have explored.

Livingstone went for years without uttering a word. He wanted to remain alone with his savages, whom he loved as fellow beings. His wife traveled with him for twelve years, until she died in the wilderness—and thereafter he remained alone. When he heard that white men were near, he would retire deeper into the interior. It is amusing to observe the elaborate precautions which Stanley took to keep his expedition in search of Livingstone a secret, lest his quarry should learn of it in time to escape. Stanley drew a breath of relief each time he left Africa. Livingstone firmly refused to accompany Stanley to England or to the coast.

Stanley always sent word—and as promptly as possible. He was continually writing, whereas Livingstone hardly ever wrote. He was taciturn, and grew old and gray in the wilderness while maintaining silence. Stanley also possessed the great virtue of silence, but only when some important undertaking had to be kept in the dark. Livingstone's silence was philosophical, Stanley's was shrewd.

Stanley advanced by force of arms, a whole train of people surrounding him. He nearly always looked upon the black man as an enemy. But Livingstone, when a negro became angry, acted like a wise old gentleman who merely frowned to show that he was offended.

Stanley gives a famous account of their meeting, when he finally came upon Livingstone after an eight months' march: "As I advanced towards him I noticed he was pale, looked wearied. . . . I would have run to him, only I was a coward in the presence of such a mob —would have embraced him, only, he being an Englishman, I did not know how he would receive me." Stanley took off his cap and said:

"Dr. Livingstone, I presume?"

"Yes."

"I thank God, Doctor, I have been permitted to see you."

"I feel thankful that I am here to welcome you."

Livingstone records the incident in his journal: "It was Henry Moreland Stanley, the traveling correspondent of the New York 'Herald,' sent by James Gordon Bennett, junior, at an expense of more than £4000, to obtain accurate information about Dr. Livingstone if living, and if dead, to bring home my bones."

The seeker: young, ambitious, optimistic, thoroughly pleased with his job. The sought: an old explorer, skeptical, mature, misanthropic, kind-hearted, eternally restless. The messenger of God, and the messenger of America.

Soon after this Livingstone died, alone in the primitive forests, at the heart of Africa. Black men brought his body to the coast, but England buried him in Westminster Abbey. Stanley died near London fifteen years after leaving Africa for the last time. He died well off, with wife and child at his bedside. But England refused to bury him.

Which of them should be ranked the higher?

From the standpoint of drama, it could only be Livingstone. Yet if I had the palm to award, I should lay it upon that rough stone on which is inscribed: "Bula-Matari."

PETERS

Yet I lacked spirit.

COURAGE and the hunger for achievement, will to power and the awareness of superior faculties—these are the elements of his success. It is absurd to call any one but Carl Peters the founder of a German colonial empire.

But he lacked the monomania of the discoverer. He loved neither the country that lay before him nor the country for which he labored. He loved only himself, and placed so high a value on himself that he could never bring himself to give up one thing for another. These are the elements of his failure.

Both stories—the founding of the colony and the life of the founder—are thoroughly German. An instructor in philosophy goes forth and conquers a piece of Africa for his country, which has hardly any foreign possessions. A poor German job-hunter, who has written a Schopenhauerian work on "Free Will and Cosmic Will," is suddenly at the age of twenty-five transported as though by magic to a London villa, and becomes a rich and elegant "independent gentleman" in the leading nation of the world. The son of a German pastor becomes an English "man of the world"; yet by the same token he becomes a European, learns to love England passionately, finds a career open to him in India, but cannot bring himself to renounce philosophy.

When his rich uncle died, he became half a business-man. The two elements intermingled, and he was con-

fronted by the formula: philosopher or farmer. His
relative in the ministry was scandalized that he could
not decide between the study of epistemology in Berlin
and the marketing of swine in Illinois.

He could never turn definitely away from one thing
to another: he always wanted them both. He went back
to Germany and began negotiations with the university
—yet at the same time he hoped to carry out certain
London plans for gaining access to the gold deposits of
Zambezi. His idea was brilliant, but unfortunately it
was pure theory. The year 1883 was really the "historical moment when Germany could appropriate Africa."
There was no British South Africa; the Boers were victorious; there was no Rhodesia, no Congo Free State;
and from the Zambezi the continent "rolled out" to the
north and the south. Yet Germany had no fleet.

But young Peters wanted to accomplish something,
no matter what. At twenty-eight he was the first
German to form a colonial syndicate. But disastrously,
he still wanted to do two things at once, still vacillated
between business and philosophy. He organized a company and raised funds with considerable skill—but at
the same time he thought himself capable of writing a
thesis: "To What Extent is Metaphysics as a Science
Possible?"

As a result, immediately after launching his colonial
project in Berlin, he left to devote himself to metaphysics. And in the meantime his associates did as they
wished, converting a vast scheme of national proportions into a petty land speculation. He was compelled to
return in haste, and begin again at the beginning.

He now decided on a wild gamble. Since Bismarck
was impervious to schemes involving territories over-

seas, and his councilors kept repeating "For God's sake, hands off Africa!" Peters concealed his new plan from the government, which had interfered with his Zambezi projects. He also kept it a secret from his investors, and suddenly went on his own responsibility to East Africa. Followed by the shrill mockery of the whole German press, which he misled for safety, he had to take a round-about route for Trieste—and the disciple of Schopenhauer shipped secretly in the steerage for Zanzibar. As soon as he arrived there, a consul read him a decree of the German government, which in the meantime had discovered his real purpose. He was warned that he could not lay claim to protection for a colonial empire, and that the government would not stand sponsor for his personal safety.

Yet his great energy drove him forward. Speed was an important asset. Count Pfeil was also a courageous man; Gustav Nachtigall was under the protection of the government. But no other German, before or after Peters, conquered Africa as he did.

What sort of man was this, who made treaties with the sultans and secured the surrender of a territory the size of South Germany? Neither a soldier nor a hunter, neither an adventurer nor an aristocrat, but a man who had no understanding of technical matters, who had never gotten free of his admiration for England, who was without experience, without arms, almost without money, and was accompanied by a single friend. Yet in five weeks' time, despite the warnings of the government and the ridicule of the press, he laid the foundations of a German colonial empire. In comparison with this, how absurd the secret conclaves seem which later caused his downfall!

He returned. The ninety-year-old emperor gave this thirty-year-old self-made man the imperial letter of safe-conduct for lands which Germany had not previously known the name of. The high point of his career.

Now he needed money. Fifty millions boldly spent, and then everything would be assured. Stanley won over the king of the Belgians by schemes which were financially sound. Rhodes organized a company in Africa to furnish the money for his plans. But Peters could not shake off the "suggestion of national charity" which he had needed at first but now would gladly have exchanged for credit at the banks. He felt that in this matter too, Bismarck had the last word, but he knew the old man's dislike of overseas territories.

In his memoirs Peters inserts the significant sentence: "I had to convince the prince himself, and then all would have been won. Yet I lacked spirit." Here we see at a glance all the contours of this character. And two years later, when he felt the need of autonomy for his new venture, once again he failed to approach Bismarck. "I regret now that for a second time I could not bring myself to face the prince and lay out to him the advantages of my plan." Perhaps had he done so, all subsequent mistakes might have been avoided: there would have been a mercantile administration instead of the assessorial one, and the antagonism of certain domestic political factions might have been prevented.

This lack of spirit can be traced to the fact that his impulse to act was purely one of self-love and did not involve any spontaneous attachment to the work at hand. He overvalued himself so greatly that he did his work first and procured the official sanction afterwards.

Had he been an uncultivated man, a genius in the rough, a giant with the strength of a bear, we might admire the simple directness of all this. But he was a small, not very appealing man with eyeglasses—a philosopher and an Englishman—who wrote well and was thoroughly acquainted with the machinery of government.

Two years after occupancy, his group, the German East Africa Company, had control over a section as large as British India. The main thing now was to establish satisfactory relations with a government which was still undecided as to whether it wanted this territory or not. But Peters irritated people by playing the outsider. And not being genius enough to win them over in spite of this after the manner of Bismarck, he got entangled in the wheels of this machine, which in Germany is always guided by some privy councilor.

The cabinet was a mass of intrigues. Each department of the government did its share in attacking this irksome upstart who had neither military nor judicial rank to excuse him for his genius. If Peters had shown as much skill in handling the Germans as he did in handling the Africans, he would never have fallen. In a tight diplomatic situation he made an excellent treaty with the sultan of Zanzibar, although he was well aware that his best argument was his personal influence with the sultan. Why could he not do the same with the German councilors?

Now they refused to appoint him imperial commissioner, although this appointment was necessary to his plans. They put off this matter "until he had shown positive results"—and in the meanwhile he had to get along the best he could as general consul. Then, immediately after he concluded the decisive treaty which formed the basis of Germany's entire holdings in East Africa, he was recalled. A typically German story.

"I showed in those years, it was said, that I did not fit in with our bureaucratic system. That is possible; but the question is: Does this speak more against me or against the system?" And Peters forgets that at the head of this system there had been a man who, though much more untamed than he, did nevertheless tame himself.

Now he was uprooted. He made mistakes. He lost his sense of proportion. Since the world did not value him as highly as he deserved, he was compelled to value himself more highly than he deserved. His attitude in the Emin Pasha expedition was both magnificent and silly. He was seized by the mad desire to hurl himself against the gigantic machine, although he had no sound means of resistance. Formerly he had carried out his plans in opposition to a whole world of powers. Now he forgot that there is a great difference in this world between an uncrowned king and a deposed one; forgot that the legitimate would avenge themselves when he outdid them; forgot that power in Africa did not guaranty power in Berlin.

Once again he showed enormous energy. In the year 1890 he really made Germany a power on the Nile, founding the province of the upper Nile and, since he himself had no governmental authority, relying on Emin's troops for support. He was searching for Emin when he heard at Usoga that Emin had been relieved by Stanley a year ago and had gone off with him. He now tried to salvage what he could. On the twentieth of June Emin declared himself willing to place Peters' recent acquisitions under the protection of the emperor. Ten days afterwards the treaty between Germany and England was signed—and all further action became pointless.

Could he oppose the power of the empire? What could Peters do with his hundred guns if Germany and England were in agreement? When he was about to leave the coast, an English admiral confiscated his weapons. He was now in a certain sense outlawed. Wissmann advised him to throw over the whole scheme, but Peters answered:

"Would you, under similar circumstances, abandon the expedition?"

Wissmann: "Of course I would!"

Peters turned away in silence. He was now beset by demons.

This treaty did not provide that Zanzibar should be relinquished in exchange for Helgoland, as is commonly supposed. Zanzibar never had been German. But German influence there was now replaced by English influence. And if the German guaranty of Zanzibar's independence was annulled in the interests of England and this concession was purchased by the transference of Helgoland, this was only possible because of the fact that Peters had established German power there four years previously. Thus, by superb irony, a man who had nothing to do with the fleet and who worked at the equator unintentionally became the originator of a German naval base: the Anglomaniac gave Germany a bulwark against England.

In a touching passage near the end of his memoirs, this deeply embittered man discusses the importance of

Helgoland in case of war. If the experts in the marine, he concludes, thought that Zanzibar and Uganda were not too high a price to pay for the acquisition of Helgoland, "then I would console myself with the thought that my years of toil, pain, and danger at least helped my people to strengthen its defensive position on the sea in Europe."

Nevertheless he remained in England until the war. The German missionaries and the press, who could not get over it that some thieving negro or other had been hanged in the shadow of the Kilimanjaro for having been the rival of his German master, martyrized Peters quite undeservedly. During the war, which he looked upon with mixed feelings, he died, embittered by his premonitions of the future, for he knew the impregnability of England and the weaknesses of Germany in the colonies.

Shortly before the war, he set foot on the African coast after an absence of twenty years. But the empire for which he had acquired this land gave him no official welcome.

A typically German story.

RHODES

Take care always to remember that
you are a Roman. . . . Have a care
you are not too much of a Cæsar!

IN his bedroom, which had been kept unchanged, lay a copy of Marcus Aurelius—and this passage was marked. Outside, beyond the large windows, stretched the heroic landscape of Capetown, with its Roman pines.

Stanley, the ambitious discoverer, was impelled by a desire to set new records. Peters, the daring politician, could not devote himself whole-heartedly to his work. Both were, from the standpoint of nationality, uprooted. But Rhodes was more Roman than any Englishman had ever been: realistic, tragic, and unmusical; a judge of men, a republican and a diplomat; unerotic, irreligious, educated; a romanticist of distinction, a genius as colonizer, an imperialist to the point of madness.

He was big and broad-shouldered, with observant, gray-blue eyes. His mouth alone broke the regularity of his features, promptly registering the variations of every thought and feeling. A friend has described it: "At its best it expressed determined purpose—at its worst, well, I have seen storms of passion gather about it and twist it into unlovely shapes."

Like Peters, he was a minister's son and well bred. He was a diligent student at Oxford. He came to South Africa as a consumptive, searching for health and finding diamonds. He returned to Oxford in order to finish his studies, and then came back to Africa. At thirty-two he was still unknown; at forty-four he had fallen; at forty-nine he was dead.

At Kimberley he looked about him and saw ineffi-ciency everywhere. Each operator was mining diamonds on an absurdly small scale with his own limited resources. The walls of the mines frequently collapsed; the negroes were continually stealing; the market was low and un-stable. Rhodes succeeded, where all others had failed, in bringing these people together, in consolidating hun-dreds of individual operators into a single company.

When he had amassed a fortune, he went into politics —not from vanity, like the "magnates," but from pas-sion. He did not marry. He felt no particular need of a male heir. He applied himself to his work and finished it within a decade, laying the groundwork of a railroad the length of a continent and organizing a colony which is healthy and prosperous, and as large as Germany plus the old empire of Austria-Hungary. It now bears his name.

There was never another man in Africa so purely the man of brains as he. Rhodes demonstrated that even savages can be brought under control by the use of brains. He learned the languages of many tribes and bargained with them. Stanley and Peters wrote well. Rhodes talked.

Like a Roman, he was an orator, but in modern guise. He persuaded people, he wheedled them into accepting his point of view. Not by deception, but by suggestion. "To be fair with you," he began when he wanted to convince some one, and that was a kind of frankness

which no one had expected. He knew that every man
has his price—he merely asked how much.

People, corporations, or governments—he never quar-
reled with them, he persuaded them. He was an actor;
after he had spoken at a conference, he knew how to
take his seat with firm emphasis, as though to say, "What
objection could possibly be raised!"

During the revolt of the Metabele, he went into the
stony wilderness of the Matoppo Hills with three companions, all of them without arms. He waited for weeks
until the natives came, then he showed them that he was
defenseless. They were astonished. He asked them what
were their grievances. They gained confidence and told
him. He promised them help. This parley lasted for five
hours. And as they were leaving, he said, as though it
were an afterthought: "Now, for the future is it peace
or is it war?" Then they laid down their sticks in front
of him, as a symbol of surrendered arms. The uprising
was over, and the Metabele were his friends. Armed
blockheads, subdued by sheer brains. When he withdrew,
he characterized the episode to one of his companions
as "one of the scenes which make life worth living."

In the same way he bewitched Jameson, the physician.
Jameson was healthier, and therefore bolder. He was
Rhodes's right-hand man.

The German, accustomed to a narrower set of living conditions, is surprised when he hears that a consumptive student from Oxford and a practicing
physician collaborate to found a colony, then succeed
each other as prime ministers, and finally, when one of
them has died, the other brings about the consolidation
of four states.

Only one man, old Kruger, refused to be persuaded—

and for this alone he wins our admiration. Had he been tractable, and given the settlers the franchise as Rhodes insisted, there would have been no war. But the old man refused, thus becoming the instrument of a vast historic process.

Like a Roman, Rhodes knew all that he needed to know, and no more. His library contained copious information about Africa and colonization. Naturally he was a Darwinist, and despised all abstract discussion. When the conversation took a turn towards metaphysics, he yawned.

Like a Roman, he considered the useful and the beautiful synonymous. He himself designed the plans for a public bath in Kimberley, a lion house in his park, and a high school in Capetown, guided in each instance by the use to which the structure was to be put. Like a Roman, he protected the arts on a large scale, and near his own house he built a "poet's cottage"—where, by the way, Kipling spent many months. He allowed the public free access to his gardens, and on Sundays often retreated to his bedroom. He assisted the farmers generously.

He had in his library modern biographies of all the Roman emperors. Also there were long rows of volumes on the emperors written by Latin authors. These were set up in English especially for him, from originals hitherto untranslated.

He loved maps. In all the rooms of Groote Schuur, his country house, he had hung maps of Africa which could be let down on silk cords. These maps were a source of inspiration to him: they started him dreaming and planning. When his friends in Capetown were bored of a summer evening, they went after Rhodes and brought him to his maps. In pursuing one idea, he said, you came upon another; when you got to the Zambezi, you were already on the Tanganyika.

Like a Roman, he could recognize no political boundaries. The governor had said: "I think you should be satisfied with the Zambezi as a boundary." Rhodes answered: "Let us take a piece of note paper and let us measure from the Block House at Capetown to the Vaal River; that is the individual effort of the people. Now let us measure what you have done in your temporary existence, and then we will finish up by measuring my imaginings." The whole idea of the Cape-to-Cairo railway was pure imperialism. He called it, in the words of one of his adherents, the "vertebræ and spinal cord which would direct, consolidate, and give life to the numerous systems that would eventually connect the vast central highroad with the seas."

Like a Roman, he thought that the power of his people was unlimited. Justice, Liberty, and Peace—by his code—were the highest products of evolution, and so, if a God existed, His noblest attributes. The English-speaking race was the type of race which did then, and was likely to continue to do in the future, the most practical, effective work "to establish Justice, to promote Liberty, and to insure Peace over the widest possible area of the planet." Wherefore: "If there be a God, then what he would like me to do is to paint as much of the map of Africa British red as possible, and to do what I can elsewhere to promote the unity and extend the influence of the English-speaking race." This atheist becomes positively religious when thinking of the empire.

With the solemnity of a Roman, he questioned one of

his engineers as to whether the spray from the Victoria Falls would ever splash the train.

"That would depend," was the reply, "on the way the wind was blowing."

"But if it blew the right way, would it?"

"Certainly it might, and probably would," was the reply.

"Oh, that is delightful," he exclaimed.

His friend had spoken of "storms of passion" which gathered about his mouth and twisted it "into unlovely shapes." But did Rhodes have passions? Towards the end of his life he drank a great deal, because he was suffering. And if he also drank before this, what of it? It was the usual thing in his environment. At times he was interested in women, but these occasions were brief and unimportant. On the whole, he lived so much alone that in all South Africa there is hardly a story current which links the name of this much-hated man with a woman.

His house is a man's house. Everything is somber, substantial, and wainscoted. Nothing is light, graceful, or colorful. A certain self-consciousness or love of ceremony led him to put in his room the table and chair of Van Riebeeck, the popular old governor—and the seal of Lobengula lies on his table.

But he did not even have the passion of the curio-collector. The Phœnician hawk which was unearthed in Rhodesia is kept under glass. By way of ornament, the theme is repeated in wood throughout the structure. A few hunting trophies—and otherwise the house, though rich and comfortable, is without embellishment.

In his will he specified that this house should be the seat of the prime minister of the Union of South

Africa, a union which did not exist at the time of his death but which he had talked of twenty years before its birth. By the irony of fate, eight years after his death the union did become a reality, and the premier did live in Rhodes's house—and the premier was a Boer.

Yes, this Roman had one passion—Napoleon. He seldom spoke of him, but a hundred documents and biographies lie on his shelves, well thumbed, and with no Empire bookcase. In his bedroom there stands a statue of General Bonaparte; above his bed hangs an engraving of the emperor crowning himself. "Have a care you are not too much of a Cæsar!" Marcus Aurelius warns near by. At times he spoke in the Napoleonic style: "It is inevitable fate," he said, speaking of Central Africa, "that all this should be changed; and I should like to be the agent of fate."

His own inconsiderateness and lack of passion made him forget that others felt differently about things. An Austrian captain, who once took him down to the Cape on a specially chartered ship, told me how Rhodes found him one day on deck looking very depressed.

"What is the matter, Captain?"

"Yesterday in Mozambique, no news of my family!"

Thereupon Rhodes looked him straight in the eyes, and exclaimed with a mixture of scorn and anger, "Captain, you are a baby!" Captain was over fifty.

His enterprises were his passions—his two enterprises. There hangs in his house a flag composed of two sections: above, is the crescent of Egypt; below, the springbok of South Africa—and laid across the two is the Union Jack. That is the railway.

He devoted half his fortune to this railway. He carried it as far as Salisbury and Victoria Falls—fifteen hundred miles. Before the war it was in process of construction as far as the Tanganyika, which is crossed on ferries. From Cairo it already reached by rail and ship southward to Lake Albert. All that was lacking was the section between the Albert and the Tanganyika, a stretch of three hundred and seventy miles. Meanwhile, it is already possible to go by rail and boat—though not without some difficulty—from the Cape to Cairo.

The unfinished section had to traverse a few hundred miles of Belgian or German territory. That irritated Rhodes. He visited the emperor—dressed in the famous summer suit which the Germans took as a show of arrogance. He asked the emperor for this strip of land which he needed for his railway. But he did not offer enough in return, and the plan fell through.

It is preposterous to compare the Cape-to-Cairo railway with the Siberian railway. The latter cuts across an inland country, the former will have junctions all along its length, for Africa is after all an island and a very regular island. The railroad is not being constructed to provide a land route in place of a sea route. For by land it would require at least the seventeen days now necessary to carry the English mail from Southampton to Capetown. Its extraordinary commercial importance lies in the fact that it will tap the interior. Rhodes imagined England extending the whole length of Africa. Soon, by reason of the railroad, this will be a fact.

His second and greater enterprise he loved so much that he even built his house facing the "hinterland." From his windows in Capetown he could not see the ocean. There was nothing on the ocean for him.

The magnates, of course, did not understand him in

the least. Old Beit found it absurd of Rhodes to want a
colony, but was perfectly willing to let him have one
if he insisted.

In Rhodes's behalf, Jameson led north the five hundred
men who set out to take over what is now Rhodesia.
They were not soldiers, but prospectors, farmers, and
adventurers. Jameson negotiated the first treaty with
the sultan Lobengula. Then the British Government issued to Rhodes a charter for a prospective organization
which is now briefly designated as the Chartered Company.

In his house, under glass, hangs the escutcheon of the
first British Chartered Company. I read there:

MERCHANT ADVENTURERS 1896

Rhodes's company, organized with a capital of one
hundred and twenty millions, has never paid dividends;
but it has suppressed for England, without any assistance from England, two native uprisings.

In the famous night-session, during which Rhodes
brought about the fusion of all the diamond mines, he
compelled Barnato, his only rival in Kimberley, to allow
the excess profits of the mining company above a certain
per cent. to be paid over to the Chartered Company.
How great must his power of persuasion have been
when in exchange for a seat in parliament he could
force this concession from a vain man to whom it must
have seemed absurd. Shall I take these millions which
belong to me and pour them into an unknown territory
that pays no dividends? Thus, roughly, ran Barnato's
thoughts.

Those years marked the preparation for political
catastrophe. The English in the Transvaal demanded

rights that were refused them. Everything was Boer, except the gold in the mines. Whereas no one could induce old Kruger to grant the English the prerogatives of citizenship, he commandeered them for service in the suppression of local uprisings. A "reform committee" of financiers fanned the fire in Johannesburg. The English needed a little prodding. All this had a pronounced effect on the new colony of Rhodesia.

Rhodes was both prime minister of the English Cape Colony and director of the Rhodesian Company. These two important offices were linked all the more effectively by the fact that the same vigorous personality managed them both. They were the symbols of both his commercial and his political interests, the symbols one might say of his general and personal ambitions, his nationalism and his passion. This symbolic duality was the cause of his downfall.

He knew of everything. Despatches which were later brought before the House of Commons show that he was in agreement with Chamberlain on the matter of rebellion. He advised the committee, although as an English minister he dared not take any official cognizance of their meetings, and above all dared not be present in person. While the English farmers were gathering under the leadership of his friend Jameson to attack Johannesburg by surprise and force concessions from the Boers, Rhodes, who was the guiding spirit of the enterprise, was officiating as English minister at the Cape hundreds of miles away.

The reform committee did not do its work well. The English in Johannesburg had few weapons, and even these few were not properly distributed. When Jameson suddenly appeared before the city with eight hundred men from Rhodesia, armed with maxims and cannon, only a small troop came out to his assistance. But the Boers brought cannon from Pretoria. Jameson surrendered and was sentenced to death along with the leaders of the committee. But he was merely imprisoned in London for a short time, while the magnates purchased their freedom by the payment of twenty-five hundred pounds each!

Jameson loyally took all the blame upon himself, but Rhodes had lost, for Chamberlain thought: Had it succeeded, then too there might have been talk of pardon!

Merchant adventurers, 1896.

Since the rebellion was a failure, Rhodes lost both the portfolio of the ministry and the directorship in his company. The government restricted the privileges of this company, and appointed its own commissioners.

Now after his defeat Rhodes became really great. He went back to work in the north. He interceded in the uprising of the Metabele and made peace with them as we have already described, without weapons and without office. After that he spent a year in the Matappos, in the heart of his colony. Then, when he went to England to answer the charges against him, his trip to the Cape became a triumphal march led by this defeated genius through South Africa. Like Danton, he faced the government in London with the thought: They won't dare!

The Boer War was not yet ripe. But as his trump card Rhodes could lay before the House the telegram which the German emperor had sent to Kruger; it showed the problem in the light of international politics.

During the South African war he remained in the background, serving merely as an officer at Kimberley.

A few weeks before peace was declared he died, still under fifty. This was eight years before the establishment of the Union, and surely less than thirty years before the completion of the Cape-Cairo railway.

Rhodes had left instructions that he should be buried in the Matappos, far up in Rhodesia. His former enemies, the Metabele, cremated him after their custom like a chieftain, slaughtering fifty oxen, dancing their grave dance, their lament piercing the night.

Their leader said: "Our great chieftain Umsiligazi, the father of our nation, has lain buried here for many years. Now the white chieftain will go to join him."

His grave clings in a vast, lonely wilderness of rock. I never saw a grave more befitting an emperor.

After several hours' journey by automobile, one travels on foot up a rough path, over a gigantic rock, and then across a flat cupola. The rocky surface grows smoother: the syncopation abates, leading us into a different movement, a *maestoso*. We pick our way upwards, now without a path, continuing across the cupola of stone. A few enormous bowlders lie at the top of the cupola, black against the light, like fallen thundercaps. As we mount, the landscape mounts with us, curving away into the infinite.

Words fail. Even if I did not know who lies here, I should feel that this could be no ordinary person, no mere adventurer. The man who dares to bed in such a rock earns our admiration by this one bold thought alone. At the last the way is very steep; a streak in the stone shows the course of the cables by which the black hands lifted the coffin of the man who, in Capetown fifteen hundred miles to the south, selected this very spot, at the crest of the cupola where those bowlders rest, peculiarly rounded, their bases worn away by the action of stone upon stone.

The surrounding landscape seems in the African light to stretch away as far in the distance as though seen from the peak of Mont Blanc. The hills of the Matappos, which are in reality very low, circle about like gigantic mountains. And the barren rock continually suggests the forms of animals. Are not those out yonder like the backs of some prehistoric monsters? And these, off here to the right, like some living creatures, cowering inert? Then of a sudden, in the midst of this glare, we see a lunar landscape: craters and slopes lie about us, curving and contorted. Further beyond, on all sides, the African steppes stretch away until they are lost to sight.

"Here lie the remains of Cecil John Rhodes."

The gray plate covers a vault which was blasted out of the rock. I put my hand near it, and could feel without touching it the coolness which came from this plate and from the grave beneath. Yet it was glistening in the African sun.

No wife, no son, no garland.

No human being for a hundred miles, no tree. No flora, no fauna. The rock is seldom crossed by the shadow of an eagle.

Like a chieftain he rests here, the son of a London pastor. So Napoleon might have rested.

WILSON

Justice.

On board the *George Washington,* June 28, 1919, towards midnight. The ship is crossing the Atlantic, but is still near the coast. The President, who left Paris this afternoon, on the day of the signing of the treaty at Versailles, is standing alone at the stern. He is pale and melancholy: sickness and the responsibilities of recent years have weakened the long lines of his formerly athletic body. It is evident now that he is in his sixties. His narrow lips droop heavily and wearily—like boats riding at anchor after a voyage. His hair is almost white. He is looking back towards the distant lights on the French coast, the last sign of this perilous continent. His expression, which had once been gentle and contemplative, seems hardened; he betrays resentment and scorn. He is thinking:

You were victorious, Europe; I return as though in defeat. Soon all America, too, will turn away from me —and I, who held the destinies of entire nations in my hands, will sink back into powerlessness, the laughing-stock of my contemporaries! Why be deceived by one's desires? My new League is, to be sure, one of the main points of the treaty. The League has been founded, and will perhaps some day become what I had hoped it would be. But the new dawn which I wanted to bring to this continent has not yet arisen. All these people are in darkness, as I stand here now in darkness—and there is no unerring rudder to steer them through their seas as this stout ship is being guided!

It is the same ship that brought me here. On the December day when we landed, was I sure that my plans would be successful? When I told my friends that I feared the struggle after the war more than I had feared the war itself, my good friend House assured me that everything would be all right, and my wife smiled at me encouragingly. The papers called this ship a new *Santa Maria,* when it had brought us to the train at Brest, prepared for the discovery of a New World within the Old. When we drove through the Champs Elysées, throngs gathered about our carriage, and on the Arc de Triomphe was emblazoned in gold letters: "Hail to Wilson, the Just." I became uneasy, and as I turned to beg a glance of encouragement from the companion at my side, I was pierced by the old, gray eagle-eye of Clémenceau, who was sitting behind me and studying me as though he were already seeking out my most vulnerable spot.

Ah, this continent! Though I cannot say that our own is any better. When I think of it, it is hard for me to decide which of the two has done me greater harm.

(He begins pacing back and forth on the promenade deck.)

How will a biographer treat this matter? What would I myself have said, if I were writing Wilson's life as I wrote Washington's? Has any other individual in modern history, without conquest or tyranny, aroused such expectations? For ten days prior to our landing, the pretty lad in the blue uniform was kept running up and down the steps to the wireless station. In Asia the Armenians called for help; in Russia, the Ukrainians; the Germans sent assurances of their change of heart; the

Jews were knocking at the door of their new father-land; Persians complained against the oppression of the British; the Koreans were resisting the Japanese; Albanians, Chinese—all were pleading for justice. Every one was begging for help against every one else—and it was as though millions of sufferers depended upon me alone, for I had found the one word that could fit all their individual desires, I had found a universal formula to encompass what each demanded singly. America, Europe felt, does not expect to profit by this peace, though America alone has made it possible; America has not intervened to procure material advantages for herself, but to restore satisfactory order.

And now who is satisfied? Not even the crowd that shouted at noon today among the playing fountains of the park at Versailles. They shouted merely because they wanted to shout—they were merely drunk at being relieved of their suspense. They shouted at us as we—how do you say it?—we "Big Four" were coming through the portal of the *Roi Soleil,* which is neither sunny nor kingly. Sonnino, next to me, looked pale and gloomy. Clémenceau, who got most of the glory, was not enjoying it. He was smiling, but I could see that he was thinking of Tardieu's article in the morning, and of the wave of public feeling which might turn against him at any moment. Lloyd George alone was laughing, laughing with two sound rows of teeth—and he shook his seductive locks, this sly old fox, as though he believed everything that he wanted the people to believe. But it was a sorry lie, and for a moment I thought of the poor German emissaries: they were after all the only two men in Paris who had no future disillusionment in store for them. . . . How did it all happen?

(He enters the open door of the saloon and steps up to the life-sized portrait of Washington.)

If I only knew what this silent man thinks of my mission! He was kindly and wise, and he was in the thick of the battle—yet in the end he was happy, and no other name eclipses his in the eyes of his people! He knows his people and their weaknesses. He would be just; he would be the only man before whom I could lay my case. Well, George Washington, why are you smiling there in your golden frame? I am too little of a Don Juan to invite you as my guest. But if you are minded at this ghostly hour to have a conversation with me, I am perfectly willing—and I am ready to go as far as you like!

Washington (steps out of the frame): How do you do, Mr. Wilson! Here I am.

Wilson: Welcome on board your own ship! Have a seat, Mr. Washington. Unfortunately, I cannot offer you anything. The kitchen is closed, and alcohol is now prohibited.

Washington (slender, elegant, bold, brown-skinned; is wearing a heavily decorated and beautifully braided general's uniform, with lace at the collar. He looks sprightly, and almost gay. His loose gray hair flutters as the vigorous movements of his head punctuate his speech, which is masculine and shows the social ease of cosmopolitan breeding. His light blue eyes rest benevolently on the pale, disillusioned features of Wilson, who peers through his eyeglasses with intensity, and at times with an expression of pleading, at his first and greatest predecessor): Don't go to any trouble. I had much to put up with in my day.

Wilson: Yes, to be sure, soldiers never escape that.

When I see you so lifelike before me in your beautiful uniform, I almost forget that you were ever a politician.

Washington: I should be very sorry if my outfit distressed you on this day of peace. But unfortunately I am no longer in a position to change it. It is the same one that I wore when I reëntered New York one dark November day after eight years of war. Be thankful, Mr. Wilson, that you got off with two years. During the whole time, I never once saw my home on the beautiful Potomac.

Wilson: I love Mount Vernon—and not merely because we too come from Virginia. But principally because I can feel there the noble breadth of your life in the country, and I can understand how such active management of his estates would prepare a nobleman for national administration. Many times I have envied you this.

Washington: And I have envied you the humanistic quiet of your beautiful university. There one can find repose, and has an opportunity to study the political systems of other peoples and to profit by the mistakes of one's predecessors.

Wilson: We have always looked up to you with unconditional respect.

Washington: And you have chosen to write of me in the same way. I am much obliged. When a man has been dead for a hundred years, people want him to be canonized. They are entitled to idealizations. I have noticed with satisfaction how you have tried to convert our old Puritanical Constitution into a—a more Cæsarian one.

Wilson: Behind your polite smile, you seem to be

making sport of me when you say that, Mr. Washington!

Washington: Not at all, Mr. Wilson! Only I thought that you wanted to exchange confidences with me—or did I not hear you correctly?

Wilson: Then you will not hold it against us if we attempted to metamorphose gradually the ideal republic which your generation founded a hundred years ago as colonials and nobles, but which must now be adapted to the needs of a population of one hundred million. If we tried to centralize the power into the hands of fewer men, we have in recompense increased their responsibility. My ideal would be a statesman who was tribune of the people and dictator simultaneously.

Washington: You have combated the corrupt tactics by which your financiers are trying to undermine the health of our state. That requires courage—and for this work please let one of the founders of the state take you by the hand.

Wilson: On such a heart-rending day as today, your encouragement is invaluable. Often during the war I asked myself: How would Washington have acted?

Washington: I did that, too, as a spectator. At the outset when, instead of obeying your English blood, you compelled yourself to maintain neutrality, you undoubtedly chose the only way of avoiding a civil war. For as you once said, we are not a people, we are the makings of a people. Furthermore, you had to gain time —and you needed an army before you could attack. Perhaps you could have increased the national army even sooner—

Wilson: Impossible! No one wanted to become a soldier, not even in a war against Mexico! The time when

people thought first of weapons and later of money and
business was already coming to an end in your era; and
Lincoln also had a great deal of trouble in recruiting
his men.

Washington: I know it only too well! My mercenaries
came when they wanted, and left as soon as I failed to
pay. Yet I would never have secured peace without the
aid of the mailed fist—and I made the profoundest discovery of my life when I found that one cannot enforce peaceful political ideals without recourse to arms.
You are smiling, Mr. Wilson? And perhaps you are
thinking of that Prussian baron whom I borrowed from
King Frederick in order that I might school our young
democracy with the help of this old *Junker*?

Wilson: Am I to assume that you approve of those
precise military forces which we set out to annihilate?

Washington: I am glad that it is over with, for I was
always a republican, and I was never more dreadfully
shocked in my life than when a certain faction during
the war proposed that I be given the title of king. But
although I never attempted wars of conquest, and was
content when we had gathered together our thirteen
lambkins, yet I was always decidedly in favor of preparedness; and during my last years, when my strength
was waning, it was not without reason that I placed such
hope in a new army.

Wilson: You are to be envied!

Washington: You, a pacifist, find that enviable?

Wilson: To be one's own general, and thus be able
to apply this atrocious power at the exact point where
it is needed!

Washington (laughing): Of course it is atrocious! I
too would rather survey the land in peace, as I once did,

than traverse it in war—and no negro was ever scourged
on my estate. But without war, by purely ideal demands, we should never have gained our freedom—and
we should have acquired no greater unity than a people
ever does acquire by peaceful means. The unarmed are
looked upon as weaklings. As to whether it is possible
to pull through today with an idea alone, you are a better judge of that than a man in so old-fashioned a uniform as mine.

Wilson: An idea, Mr. Washington? Of course, at the
beginning, after the Germans sank the *Lusitania*, I tried
to quiet our citizens with an idea when they were crying for vengeance. A nation, I maintained, could be so
much in the right that it need not resort to force in
order to gain its point. And although, as you have said,
my English blood—and likewise my upbringing as a
pastor's son and my education as a professor—made me
revolt against the despotism of that militaristic state, I
still resisted the pressure of war with all my strength.
For when a nation is not bound together by the tie of
blood, when two factions, each of them numbering
millions, are living and working side by side, neutrality
is the only course, regardless of our desires. Would you
as a statesman have acted differently?

Washington: I have admired the calm with which you
exposed yourself to the charge of cowardice and even
preferred to sacrifice Bryan rather than give in. My
reservations, if I may call them such, come at a much
later date. And the national army, which I was the first
to consolidate in a modest way, you have expanded to
enormous proportions, giving it its first voyage and its
first victory overseas.

Wilson: You are being polite, General! If I happened to have the rank of Commander in Chief, that was merely because your Constitution imposes this office upon me, however painful it may be to a civilian. But as you know, I was not victorious in the way that you were; I was merely instrumental in the victory of others. Meanwhile, you are wondering how one can at last be driven to war and still advocate a peace without victory? You marvel that during my campaign in 1916 I stumped for peace while the halls in which I spoke were guarded by the military? In a word you, like my opponents, are dissatisfied that I wished to reward a victorious country with nothing but an idea instead of securing money and privileges in exchange for its sacrifices!

Washington: I have nothing to do with your opponents. They wanted you out, and to get you out they slandered you. But although I too would probably have prosecuted the war, I have never quite understood your own reasons for doing so.

Wilson (gesticulating more vigorously): Behind me was an unsure country, shaken by conflicting emotions, and repeatedly aroused by the stupid and insane acts of the German navy; and in front of me was an indignant Congress which shouted for war at first, but later grew frightened at its own uproar. You know these difficulties—

Washington (smiling): This institution, which we established, was abusing me even in my old age, when a marble statue of me was already standing in the public square. The facts of history develop a kindly patina, until the nation and its heroes are thought to have been in perfect accord. As a matter of fact, every statesman has considered his own nation ungrateful. You, as a student of Kant and Rousseau, must have been completely disorganized by the turmoil of war.

Wilson: I was not! You are wrong, Mr. Washington! There is not a single word of pacifism in any of my books! In contradistinction to Kant, my way to peace is by means of protections and punishments. My League guards right with might. It was for this reason that I could call it the aim of America before we entered the conflict! For it was only in this way, by showing the world our growing preparedness, that we could escape the odium of weakness or cowardice when we counseled arbitration. Otherwise we should have been in the gruesomely comic situation of missionaries who, when under attack, merely cry out the name of their God, as though He were minded to intercede.

Washington: Perhaps He is. Cannons are necessary merely in case that He is not.

Wilson: Since I was by no means sure of Him, I built cannons and ships.

Washington: You are not—a believer, Mr. Wilson?

Wilson: I—believe in the progress of reason.

Washington: In our day, before making decisions, we prayed and fasted.

Wilson: I do not fast, but I do not shoot either.

Washington (smiling): *Pas trop mal pour le lendemain de Versailles!* You were speaking of the League?

Wilson: The masses were waiting for a slogan. You know the feeling: when they look at you questioningly, attentively waiting for the right word. Prussia's tyrannical policies were looked upon everywhere as an obstacle to peace. In order to suppress them, we had to destroy all possibility of their recurrence. It was necessary that all nations be compelled to accept peace. That was the aim of the first League for which, long before we entered the war, I became the spokesman, making its principles popular enough to awaken a dream in the hearts of a hundred million people and to form an ideal in their minds. When I first proclaimed the principles of the League, I did so to make the people ripe for war. While I was pointing to eternal peace in the clouds, I was asking Congress for troops and ammunition—and yet no one accused me of inconsistency. The whole country, down to the last cowboy in Texas, understands me—for we are all living in a League of Nations.

Washington: And what did this cowboy think of Europe?

Wilson: Washington, he thought, founded the first League of Nations with thirteen states; now we are forty-eight and still do not war among ourselves. Why not force upon Europe, with its endless broils, a similar kind of unity! For he knew nothing of all this palaver about the divergent historical development which each state on this small continent has behind it— and thus nothing short of indolence or cowardice could prevent him from applying such principles. And in our own case, are not some states more jealous than others of their "historic conditions"? Did you not have nearly as much trouble with South Carolina as Lincoln did? And could one really go so far as to assert that because the different peoples of Europe are territorially segregated, it is harder to unite the states of Europe than the states of America, where the different peoples intermingle? A tenement with a hundred rooms may house twenty different families which do not even know one another. Yet they can live peaceably under one roof so long as each family has its own apartment independent of the others.

Washington: On our slave plantations there was continual trouble. I have often thought of that in considering these European peoples, who are mostly in subjection. You are quite right.

Wilson (excitedly): And yet, from the light in your eyes, I suspect that you have an objection to make.

Washington (smiling): I have two, in fact—and I shall state them. Your basic idea was good, and will prove practicable. If I remember correctly, we once wrote something similar in our statutory laws—although I have not had occasion to reëxamine them for quite a while—

Wilson: "That, to secure these rights, governments are instituted among men, deriving their just powers from the consent of the governed; that, whenever any form of government becomes destructive of these ends, it is the right of the people to alter or abolish it."—Proclaimed more than ten years before the great revolution in France—and every child in America today knows it by heart. "We, the people of the United States, et cetera . . . do ordain and establish this Constitution for the United States of America." What have I done but lower the anchor of our ship of freedom in the seas of Europe! Did not our best minds, Emerson and Whitman, preach and sing the same thing? I did not deserve the credit for a new thought, nor the discredit of pure ideology, when I wrote as the cornerstone of the new peace the proposition that government should be only by consent of the governed. That is older than America: we were merely the first to make it a reality.

Washington: And we all applauded you when you cited one after another the views of the founders of this state: Hamilton, Jefferson, the two Adamses, and also myself. But—

Wilson: But?

Washington: But I suspect that you aroused your opponents by claiming that America, with its enormous resources, wanted to be the servant of nations, and not their mistress. When you made this moral exhortation, did you not have in mind the Americans of my time rather than of yours—and further, were you not seeing them with the patina of history upon them? When our armies took the memorable step across the gangplank to fight and bleed in Europe, their desire to help Europe was a minor aspect of their psychology. Aside from their love of adventure in general, they were impelled primarily by a feeling of rage against a ruler in whose name their noncombatant kin had been sent to the bottom of the sea. And if our brave lads did set out to annihilate the German concept of power, which was symbolized in the military helmet, in your zeal you have probably overlooked the fact that although the Germans were probably the most heavily armed nation in Europe, they were not the sole advocates of militarism; and in combating an evil principle you were forced to accept the assistance of allies who were not governed by overly pure principles themselves. I always loved France, yet in later years I drilled a new army as a protection against her—although I patched matters up with her satisfactorily before the close of my life. It had to do with young General Bonaparte; and the thought of this great soldier—if you will pardon me—is very appealing to me.

Wilson: France! Do you see those last fading lights there in the East, just beneath the constellation of Aquila? I will never set foot again upon that coast, with its vengefulness, its craftiness, its timidity, and its greed!

Washington: Of course you were deceived; and if we compare the peace terms which you signed today with the fourteen points which your allies had pledged themselves to accept as the basis of negotiations, we will be painfully reminded of that scrap of paper by which the German unmasked himself with such drastic consequences in 1914. Except that perhaps some of these points were so abstractly worded that they could be easily circumvented. In times of need, in times of fear and suffering, people make extravagant promises which they honestly mean to keep. You remember the "earthquake love" which broke out at the time of the fire in San Francisco? People planned to build an ideal city, but within a month all this Christianity was forgotten, and every one was busied with his own affairs. For this reason, perhaps it would have been advisable when terms were being agreed upon, if the powers had not only declared themselves against secret diplomacy, but had specifically abrogated all the secret treaties in which the new allies had made one another all sorts of pleasant promises.

Wilson: At Mount Vernon, on the threshold of your venerated home, we tried to make it certain once again —as was fitting on the anniversary of our national independence—that we are the guardians of the old idealism. Earlier I had proclaimed peace without victory, in order to prevent the collapse of Germany; but by now the Germans had become so unreasonable that my abstract principle was more difficult to maintain. Yet I still believed that our own position was unambiguous, still believed that America wanted nothing for herself; I thought that we still held to the terms of our intervention. In any case, we always called ourselves an associated power, in order to keep a freer hand. But when I announced to the world that there would be no more secret treaties, this was also intended as a warning to our allies. Do you know, Mr. Washington, that at this time Lansing had no precise knowledge of the London agreement? Will you believe that as Secretary of State he was kept in the dark concerning compacts which were later to form the general basis of the peace? Thus the blame cannot be laid to Lansing, but to our defective diplomacy, which is even worse in its operations than that of Europe. For our practice of recalling our foreign representatives every few years, just when they become familiar with conditions abroad, is one of the major shortcomings of our system.

Washington: Quite so. But could you not, on the basis of your fourteen points, have attacked the London agreement in Paris?

Wilson: I declared it null and void! But consider the uproar it caused. Our agreements were made prior to yours!—cried Italians, Rumanians, Japanese, and half a dozen others. And the so-called major powers, the same men, or the replicas of those men, who had signed this treaty three or four years ago, reminded me of their oaths pledging them to secrecy. And they pointed to Trotsky's scandalous publication of Russia's secret treaties. Trotsky was thoroughly in the right, I said, when he exposed those predatory compacts before the whole world. But each day I became more deeply entangled in the web of secret alliances; each week they got a stronger hold upon me, until they threatened to stifle me. By the time I had been in Paris a month, I had found pitiless corroboration of all my forebodings during the voyage over. I had come alone to state the terms of a new order—and no one would assist me, not a single one of those people who had greeted me like a god! Thus it became a struggle.

Washington: We observed with satisfaction the departure of the Italians. We decided that you were going to establish one of your points in the matter of Fiume.

Wilson: That is how it looked from the outside. But if you only knew what took place behind the double doors of the council chamber! Later, I shall write of it. Even after our intervention, even in the course of 1918, even during the conference itself, these forbidden treaties were being extended. England had made sure of her rights in Persia and Turkey; Italy had been won over solely by the promise of Dalmatia; Rumania, in addition to other morsels, was expecting the Banat, a fact which, furthermore, had to be kept secret from Serbia. Oh, if you had only been present at these meetings, and seen Bratiano and Vesnitch shouting at each other on one side of the table, with Clémenceau and Pichon trying to calm them on the other, and all of them piling lie upon lie! With Japanese unctuousness, the Baron Makino called such treaties an "exchange of views," while getting for himself the guaranty that the islands north of the equator would go to Japan. Otherwise he would not have produced his submarines. When they were cutting up Turkey, some spoke of "arrangements." And while I was sitting there with my well-known point concerning Turkey, some Arab chieftain to whom England gave the title of King was flourishing his account of what the Allies owed him. The one idea of every single minister was to bring home for his voters a piece of land which would look very pretty on the maps in the show-windows—or at the very least he hoped for a mine or a pipe-line.

Washington: The spirit of peace! Then it was practically impossible to make the conferences open to all —as you provide for in your scheme for the League—so that the lesser states might be able to form a block in opposition to the major states?

Wilson: That was decidedly impossible, President! Though they were allies, they hated one another! France, which had formerly detested the Prussian Clausewitz, now adopted his theory that peace is the continuation of war. I on the contrary wanted scientific inquiry to form the basis of all transactions. I advocated frankness and exactness—but all the others were for strategy and diplomacy. They wanted the old method: I wanted a new spirit.

Washington: And that is the point, Mr. Wilson! A new spirit! You know Lincoln's life better than I; and you are aware that this great practical mind, as a leader of genuine Pharisees, was only able to conduct the war against the South by making it a war against cotton instead of a war in behalf of the slaves. You know that he permitted slave-breeding in the border states, and disapproved of his generals' method of raising troops by offering freedom to runaway slaves, so that the real opponents of slavery opposed his reëlection. By this circuitous route Lincoln fulfilled a political ideal, created a new spirit—whereas this could not have been done through sheer goodness of heart. Is it possible, when such principles as yours have been suddenly proclaimed, that the corresponding spirit should arise forthwith to meet them?

Wilson: Did Washington do any differently? At one stroke you compelled the uncultivated populations of several crude states to become the citizens of a new order! The question is like the question of marriage: must love exist at the start, or can it develop afterwards?

Washington: If it is to develop afterwards, it will do so more readily among crude and uncultivated people than among refined ones. For that reason we found it easier to create a new spirit in our era than it would be in yours. Such ages of scientific method, as you call them, are much too discreet. Well, did they at least accept the method?

Wilson: The first time I proposed sending experts into one of the contended areas, do you know what Orlando, the so-called champion of freedom from the south of Italy, exclaimed? "If we did that, we should be setting ourselves up as judges. We must appeal directly to the people concerned!" That is my own opinion, I cried. And on another occasion, when England and France were wrangling over the boundaries of their so-called "spheres of influence" in Asia Minor, I asked to the dismay of every one: Do the gentlemen know whether these spheres of influence are agreeable to the natives?

Washington (laughing): I would have given my past life to have been there! It must have been a show for a dramatic poet, or for the immortal gods themselves! But how did the gentlemen act at such times?

Wilson: It depended on the person and the situation.

Clémenceau would point to photographs of the dev-
astated regions or to his statistics of ravished women.
Once, in arguing about the Rhine border, he told me
to my face: "You are pro-German." Some time later,
when I had calmed myself by a ride in the Bois, and had
begun expounding my principles again, he gripped my
two hands and said: "You are a great and good man!"
And that was the way he felt at the moment; for there
is something feminine about him—and whereas he has
been called a tiger, he might better be called a tigress
who is protecting her young. Resourceful and highly
trained in everything that had to do with politics, he
was swayed by a truly passionate love for his country.
But when he was not getting his way, he would set the
press against me, as I learn from a document which
reached me through certain channels and which I have
on board here in my large chest full of such papers. But
when he threatened to resign during the crisis in April,
I capitulated, for I knew that he would be succeeded by
Tardieu or Poincaré, both of whom were accusing him
of laxity.

Washington: And Lloyd George?

Wilson: He acted with incredible elasticity, contriv-
ing as speaker and strategist to ally himself with every
camp. He accepted "in principle" everything that I advocated, and then challenged every particular instance.
Or he would merely shift his vocabulary. When I refused to hand over a piece of Turkey to the Italians,
he asked himself forthwith, "But what is Africa for?"—
and suggested that "indemnities" be paid for refusing a
claim which was in itself unjust. I am not certain
whether the Italians deceived him more during these
six months than he deceived them, or vice versa, but I in-

cline to believe the latter. He was always crafty enough to act as though he saw no breach between us—and often when he did back me it was owing purely to his distrust of France. But when I fell sick and everything was at stake, he abandoned me forthwith—and the only way I could frighten him was to send a cable ordering this ship back to France. For he really was afraid. First, he was afraid of his constituents, to whom he had made too many promises; and he was afraid of the Germans, since they might refuse to sign after all. Yes, they were superior to me in eighteenth-century tactics—in intrigue, corruption, and espionage. I never felt this more strongly than when I lay sick and watched the sentinel walking to and fro in the sparse little garden in front of my window. "You are a prisoner!" I thought, and then listened again to the sounds of the consultation in the adjoining room, until Colonel House would come in to ask my opinion on some important subject.

Washington: Mrs. Wilson always gave you advice?

Wilson (emphatically): Always! Did you not have similar assistance in your day?

Washington (hesitating): I—hardly ever had occasion to call on my wife, in war or in peace.

Wilson: Do you consider such influences harmful, Mr. Washington?

Washington: I would not go so far as that. But—in the last analysis, women are women, and are highly susceptible to the influence of environment.

Wilson: We all were! Seven and a half million corpses calling from the earth for vengeance; twenty million cripples; four years of murder, rapine, destitution, and lawlessness—and this had created a psychosis which could not be healed within a few scant months. Balfour was perhaps the only man who had intelligence, calmness, and humor enough to remain composed and reasonable—but he was a skeptic, and I needed men who had faith.

Washington: Or men who had power. As I listen to you this warm night out here on the water, and see you standing before me pale, feverish, and disillusioned after your struggles, I am more convinced than ever that a pure and simple world-peace in the grand style can only be established at the point of a victorious sword. You had slain one dragon, but the other still breathed out poison and hate. And your one big mistake was in your failure to recognize the mighty foe in peace who stood beside your mighty foe in war and who was your ally in name only. Heretofore every true benefit to mankind has been imposed upon them by force. I forced the acceptance of national unity; Lincoln forced the emancipation of the slaves, a great many of whom had no desire to be freed. Perhaps your military power was not great enough to back your League and your program of disarmament.

Wilson: The army! That was the worst difficulty I had to face in the whole issue. Even before I landed on this coast, the military party had defeated me. Before I could get here they had stretched the terms of the armistice far beyond measures of precaution and had rapidly occupied whole provinces. Now, when the principal danger was over, and things were going along smoothly, why should these influential gentlemen quietly retire? If only as a matter of self-preservation, they despised my ideas, since these ideas interfered with their profession. But since they were continually trying to stir up new wars, half my strength was consumed in trying to frus-

trate these new schemes. An English general erected a
White government in Western Russia; an Italian, on
his own initiative, began advancing in the Adriatic and
in Asia Minor; even an American led the Czechs in the
coal districts; every week brought some new advice
from the general staff proving that Central Europe
could only be saved by a new war.

Washington: And Foch? There's a man whose hand
I should like to shake! Is it true that he goes to mass
every morning?

Wilson: If he does, he receives no divine inspiration
there. For this great army leader is as low-visioned as
any Prussian general. When he wanted to lead the
Americans into Poland for use against the Bolsheviks,
the favorite bugbear of the militarists, I interfered and
said openly in the conference that the military party
had been responsible for the stupidities of 1815 and
1870. Despite their undeniable bravery, these men have
such an intense fear of Germany that they were even
willing to renounce some reparations in the interests of
safety. "The German Rhine must be France's battle-
cry," said the Marshal. He called the Rhine "a prominent campaign base for counter-offensives" which he
could not dispense with; and he literally spoke of the
League as a "permanent military alliance between the
three nations and America." Consider how I felt when
they were saying things like that! They blocked every
attempt to assist Germany; and when we did manage
to hold the Marshal in check at Paris, his ilk in Budapest
and Vienna were playing the same game, and by their
advance upon Hungary created the Red episode there
purely in order to suppress it.

Washington: When I compare your experiences with my own, it seems better that politicians should become generals, as happened in my case, than that generals should become politicians. The latter condition, which did so much harm in Germany, is now being taken over by the victors, along with other demolished Prussian vices. And so you were left totally without support?

Wilson: My sole allies, the workers of the world, were divided, since I had the peculiar misfortune of being the only man in Paris who fought with equal zeal against the militarists and the Bolsheviks. It was a moral solace to open the "Labor Herald," which printed for a solid month in gigantic letters across its first page: "Don't be wangled, Wilson!" But the people on the streets rallied around me, claiming that I had found the right words to express their longings. When Jaurès' murderer was shamelessly acquitted, the workers of Paris passed in an unending procession through the avenues, carrying red banners with the words: "Down with Clémenceau! Vive Wilson!" At the time I was lying sick in my room—and the incident was quite painful to me as a guest when I heard of it. Fortunately he did not witness the incident either, for he was still suffering from the effects of the anarchist's attempt to assassinate him.

Washington: Strange. I was a soldier for so many years, and escaped without a wound—but the two matadors of the Paris conference lay on their backs, one brought down by a bullet, the other by excitement. Yes, culture has progressed in the last hundred years. You should be glad that you didn't share the fate of Lincoln.

Wilson: That is still a future possibility—for this ship is now bearing me home, and you have mentioned with bitterness the ingratitude of nations.

Washington: You expect to be greeted with a revolver, Mr. Wilson?

Wilson: In Germany there is a legend that the people stabbed the army in the back just as it was on the point of victory. This is untrue, but it is a splendid metaphor, and is derived from a beautiful saga of the Germans. When I first read that, I felt that it applied to me.

Washington: Would that I could deny what you are saying. But what I heard—

Wilson: —is only a part of it. In reality, our people, or their representatives, have already sunk the dagger into me! It began in the Senate at the time of the armistice. A President of the United States crossing the water on official business? These men agreed that conditions were bad—and yet I was merely trying to improve them. But no international affiliations! The Monroe Doctrine is in danger! Europe accepted my principles during a period of stress. But America, as soon as she had gained her victory on my terms, flatly repudiated them. The new elections had given the opposition a majority in Congress. Lodge demanded war indemnity from Germany, with a substantial part of it for ourselves. Johnson exclaimed that we should work for the good of America and let mankind take care of itself. Borah opposed the hundred-million-dollar expenditure which Hoover, who is an intelligent and honorable man, required to feed the starving peoples of Europe. During such wrangles as this I embarked. They immediately inaugurated a campaign against the League of Nations. While I was making the discovery in Paris that my

Allies were my mortal enemies, my own countrymen were banding together in opposition to me. They pointed across at me, immersed in the affairs of Europe, and said: Let the fool go, for there is no one behind him! They tried to pull me two ways. There was nothing for me to do, if I was to rescue my ideas, but to turn back after three months.

Washington: A frightful decision! To leave the battle at its height in order to combat another enemy in the rear!

Wilson: You understand! When I came home, half America was exclaiming: "He is betraying our national institutions! Washington in his farewell address warned against entangling alliances. For a hundred years America has prospered because we never allowed Europe to meddle in our affairs and we never meddled in the affairs of Europe." Of course, I answered. And it is because every specific alliance is dangerous that we want a universal League, hoping to widen the Monroe Doctrine into a world doctrine. But they demanded that new clauses be inserted, including the right of withdrawal. The guaranties of French safety, which Clémenceau repudiated as being much too weak, seemed to America much too strong. I was forced to make concessions. I hurried back on this ship to Paris. Do you know how they greeted one member of my party?

Washington: Tell me!

Wilson: "*Bon jour,* your League is certainly dead now!" For as soon as I had gone, they set up their golden calf again. They had renewed the armistice by making fresh demands of the Germans which were most revolting, and had actually made plans for a new congress to follow the signing of peace, when they could discuss the

League of Nations and "other such general topics"! I began the battle again, but my four weeks' absence and the continual allowances I had to make for America weakened my position. And added to that, Lansing! He was sober, timid, conservative—a pure nationalist who was my opponent from the very outset.

Washington: I thought that you had a friend in Colonel House?

Wilson (embarrassed): Such an excellent man—with all the qualities that I lacked. He was good-hearted as only a man from Texas could be; he was a judge of men, and was not ambitious; yet, however confident he was of his ability, he was not strong enough. The news of Trotsky's new army; the Italians' threats of leaving; the desperate desire to make peace as quickly as possible; and besides, certain private distresses—

Washington (evasively): You have been through a great deal, Mr. Wilson. You had to compose your notes of warning to Germany beside the death-bed of your first wife. When the world fails to recognize you, you try to find quiet in your own conscience. You have nothing for which to reproach yourself.

Wilson (springing up): You are wrong! I am almost broken by self-accusations! Do you want to know everything? Even during the war I should have given my attention to the matter of the secret treaties, since Lansing did not! I should have let Lansing go because he opposed national self-determination! I should have been less satisfied with my one-sided manner of thinking—oh, I know what there is to be known about Wilson!—I should have sought the advice of others, and should have received members of the press in Paris! I should not have dared to return! And when I did travel,

I should have gone back and forth in an aircraft, making all the trips in twelve days instead of in thirty! I should not have weakened under the strain: I should have been twenty years younger! Yes, younger! I should have taken into account the *unimaginativeness* of Europe's statesmen, and should have realized that they are not the real representatives of the people, with whom alone I wanted to make arrangements for the new League! And when everything went wrong, I should have left with my party in April despite the charge of desertion, and should have let the whole conference go smash rather than sign that stupid, brutal treaty this noon, in the atrocious Mirror Room of that Roi Soleil who was the one person most suited to stand godfather for these hundreds of articles!

Washington (rising): It is one o'clock. And even though the Constitution of the shades is much more realistic and less romantic than people in this world usually imagine, still it is time for me to be getting back in my gold frame. Every one knows his own shortcomings best, but you have gone to the extreme. You judge what you have done from the standpoint of what you wanted to do. We from beyond, who differ from you so slightly, have learned how slow is man's progress towards betterment, and we rejoice at every slight gain. You need not inquire about the sources of my knowledge; but let me match your list with one of my own! I will say nothing of all that you were able to accomplish despite the opposition of Italy and the other states —and I will speak only of Germany, which was after all the main subject of our discussion.

Without your intervention the war with Russia would have been resumed; sooner or later Germany would have become a battlefield, and would probably now look like the north of France. Without you, the Allies would have made the Rhine the boundary of Germany, would have flatly confiscated the Saar and all of Upper Silesia, would have proclaimed the Rhine in revolt and occupied the Ruhr. In a word, they would have dictated a peace after the manner of the Germans at Brest-Litovsk. Without your three years of proclamations and your brave six months of struggle, a League of Nations would never have been established. And even though it is still frail and has not admitted the important enemies of the Allies, it will soon exert a decisive influence upon its members, and within ten years will be strong enough to delay over-hasty actions like those of August 1st until an angry world has grown calm and amenable to reason. You have set up a new code—you alone in this era—alongside the fascinating but dangerous code of the Russians. You have formulated a secular goal, an aim which is at once practical and ideal, a beacon towards which the best minds and the youth of this continent may turn! And in the future, when the United States of Europe becomes a reality, people will call Woodrow Wilson its founder, just as they call me the founder of our "League," although I did nothing but take the first steps. For you were the first to convert the dream of poets and philosophers into a political program and to defend it with physical force. Just wait for one more century, and your grandsons will be astonished! And now go to bed, Mr. Wilson, and have a pleasant sleep!

RATHENAU

A man must be strong enough to mold
the peculiarity of his imperfections into
the perfection of his peculiarities.

The door of his imposing house was narrow, so narrow that two people could not enter it at once. The pleasure of companionship and the grace of love were kept from him and from his home. But this curse of loneliness, which nature placed upon him, was responsible for the distinction of his writings and of his acts.

I do not know who may have loved him; he himself loved no one but his mother. Women sought in vain to attract him. And though he may have mustered up a little warmth now and then, at heart he remained alone. Not that he was a stern philosopher who could not smile and who avoided women in the salon. But he admitted no one into the recesses of his soul. The door to this temple, like that of his house, was too narrow.

In this hyperborean field which lay about him, the laws of magnetism ceased to function, as in that other fantastic area about the North Pole. In this thin air only two forces could live and work: intellect and the will to power. And as the waves of these psychic gases, which he was continually absorbing throughout his lifetime, circled about him, all his other impulses—all feelings of kindliness, friendliness, and good humor—were more and more thoroughly obstructed. Finally, when he felt that he was totally steeled and impregnable, in order to breathe still thinner air he climbed the Gaurisankar of his dreams—and perished there.

119

"To act is easy, to think is hard; to act according to our thoughts is troublesome." Few Germans have understood the full import of this only half mystical beginning of Wilhelm Meister's indenture. And fewer still, among this nation of "poets and critics," have been able to think and act at once. Rathenau, who was a German politically but not racially, was able to do this. While broadening his palace of knowledge and thought, he worked ceaselessly at the tower of action which he had erected in one corner of the palace. It did not suffice him to know all that this century has to offer, and to encompass the entire thesaurus of the Occident within the confines of a single human brain. He was also ambitious to become skilled in every field of action—and he actually did succeed in mastering everything to which he applied himself.

He knew how to paint portraits, how to design his house and mix the stucco for it, how to construct turbines; he was a judge of wood carvings; he could attack Montaigne, strike a balance, transform factories, write verses, negotiate treaties, and play the Waldstein sonata. He attained, not genius, but a certain degree of expertness which usually made him superior in any one field to a person who had devoted himself to that field of activity exclusively. We could say with justice that his specialty was the world as a whole, for the variety of his interests was astonishing. Rathenau, who wanted to be a genius, was perhaps the most talented intellect of his age.

Capable now of both thought and action, equally at home in matters of logic or of daily routine, in science and in poetry, and equipped to handle both his own per-

sonal problems and large social issues, he was thoroughly
aware that such a nature brought with it a crystalline
coldness. He felt how this enormous wealth of intellect
and knowledge was piled up like geological strata, without chemical fusion; and he might have succumbed to
his abysmal loneliness had he found no method of synthesis. He might have departed, leaving a touching
posthumous diary to the world—and thousands of kindred spirits would have reached for this cynical and
unhappy document, as they do for the books of Pascal
or Weininger.

But a vital urge kept him at work. He was determined, in a life almost joylessly clear, not to surrender
before he had obtained the one enjoyment which could
satisfy his strong ambitions. With the gigantic search-
light of his egocentric intellect, he projected the image
of his own destiny upon his century, receiving back
from the epoch and its shortcomings that which was
native to himself. He felt constrained by mechanisms,
even though they were mechanisms of the highest type;
in all his efforts, in all his sovereignty over his contemporaries, he never forgot his obstructions; yearning for
warmth, soul, and salvation, he laid the blame upon his
century and explicitly denounced the soullessness of old
Europe as the basic cause of all modern suffering.

Despite this genesis of his doctrines, they are right.
Except that we are taken aback by the violence with
which Paul rages here, and we suspect that behind it
all there is a Saul who was never conquered and who
was constantly seeking concealment. A man of the
purest, highest intellect, he desired to be healed of his
ambitions, and yet was forced to employ the intellect
in justifying this mystical urge. What a drama! But

nothing more than a drama. When we hear him preaching of the dangers of the utilitarian, of the temptations of the demon of numbers, of the annihilation of soul through property, we may believe that we see in his books evidences of the new Savonarola holding the mirror of vanities up to his times; but when we turn back and find that this prophet was skilled in the subtlest branches of economic biology, even readers wholly unacquainted with the author become impatient. And the beginning of doubt is the beginning of certainty.

As Goethe has said, the public is always wrong in detail, but never in the whole. Despite his vast public of acquiescent readers from all nations, Rathenau was never able to establish a belief in his personality as a moral leader; though this thinker had many to admire him, no one loved him. These are facts which have their foundation in the depths of his being, and from which his doctrines arose as though in mute protest.

Even during his lifetime this inherent justice exerted a frightful influence upon his destiny. This man seemed to possess all the good things of this world: health and liberty, knowledge and money, intellect and culture; one evening of his conversation would repay a long journey; yet despite his great gifts, he was friendless and was betrayed the most readily by those who called themselves his friends. He was perfectly aware of this, and at rare moments spoke of it with bitterness.

Though from the empirical standpoint his opponents were nothing but heartless scoundrels, from another angle they were more in the right than they suspected. For had he not betrayed himself? Did he not feel the vulnerability of his "undogmatic Christianity," the

feebleness of his "directive force of the soul," the flac-
cidness of his "social solidarity"? As a critic of his age,
he was inferior only to Nietzsche; as a seer of the future
he was unsure. This mixture of love and hate with which
he pursued the capitalistic system that gave him birth
caught him much the way Strindberg was caught in his
attitude towards women.

Not that he resorted to display and prodigality. His
house and his manner of living were both quiet and distinguished, and in the best taste. He was a Crœsus without passions and without collections. He never spent
money lavishly; occasionally he bought a beautiful picture, or a rare tapestry, or expensive books. Nor did he
ever succumb, like a miser, to the intoxication of mounting sums. To artists and deserving young people, he gave
financial assistance from his own funds. But although
he proclaimed his doctrines in totally anti-capitalistic
terms, and had formulated sound measures against inheritance and other causes of accumulated wealth, he
spent his life in the atmosphere of corporations and
banks, thinking in the language of stocks and dividends,
and never abandoning this field for any other.

His enormous, continually growing fortune, for
which he had neither direct nor indirect heirs and which
he finally neglected or forgot to dispose of in accordance
with his vast social schemes, was his substitute for
power, becoming the means of power at one remove.
This gave rise to misunderstandings which alienated both
camps, the capitalistic and the socialistic. While managing one of the largest businesses in Germany in a purely
capitalistic manner, he was attacking this system in his
books. And while advocating universal sympathy for
all mankind and a religion of goodwill towards all, he

remained more aloof from the workers in his own industry than many a hard-headed employer who looks
upon labor purely as a commodity for exploitation.

We do not ask that as a prophet he should have gone
about with a beggar's cup in his hand. But this conflict
between his preaching and his practice, this tendency
to follow in the concrete a course which he condemned
in the abstract, should finally have been brought to an
end. He should have broken with the mechanistic system he was attacking—but instead he remained among
the leaders of this system.

"The secret of the personality is: strength from weakness." That is one of Rathenau's unconscious, all-too-
shrewd disclosures. He always wrote attacking personalities which could affirm themselves amorally. Indeed, he
even attacked Nietzsche with the priestly words: "The
master of this black art has been praised as a superman."
A new evidence of suppressed motives. As a matter of
fact, no one ever willed himself more emphatically than
Rathenau; and with his great endowments he was certainly the man to make his ego, if he ever brought himself to it, an asset to society. Yet because he would not
admit this to himself, or at least wanted to conceal it
from the world, people could not understand him; and
even his most scurvy opponent who was repeating some
vulgar accusation against him was to an extent justified
if we look at the matter from this standpoint. Lassalle
admitted to himself that his genius alone could meet the
problems at hand, and he spoke of passing in triumph
through the Brandenburg Gate. Rathenau, lacking the
least trace of simplicity, had no one in the world to

whom he could even have secretly confided his will to power.

Must we not pity him? With what an expression did this man look into the mirror when he was alone again after an evening in society? For several hours he, who had been neither *poseur* nor *causeur*, had felt the strength of his intellect. His countrymen, who listened to him with skeptical curiosity, and foreigners, who followed him with suspense, had been affected by his beautiful barytone voice and his splendid German diction. In an endless flow of comparisons taken from the entire range of life and history, he had made judgments which were deeper, more independent, and better grounded than most of the opinions expressed during the conversation. Perhaps there had been a young man present this evening who listened in astonishment to find what mastery can lie in speech and knowledge. With the same familiarity he had spoken of China's future policies and of the preparation of this *chateaubriant*, of the new opera and of the new loan, of the latest discoveries in Egypt and of the latest contributions to the molecular theory—not merely grazing the surface of these topics, but going into them at length.

But now he stands alone before the mirror and thinks: Will B finally cause the overthrow of A? And if he is beaten, will C use his influence with D in my behalf? He really ought to be well disposed towards me, but he hates me. They all hate me. If I were a dictator for one week, for three days, I could settle the whole affair with the two emissaries in a couple of hours. Abroad they have confidence in me. They know that I always give warning. The time is coming nearer. Soon it will be here.

He had given warning, for years. From the first day of the war he had foreseen the danger and explained it. At the close of July he had written admonitorily. To one friend he said: "Do you not catch the false note?" He had said to us repeatedly: "Woe to us if we are victorious! It would not be possible to breathe in this country!"

But when the great crisis was at hand, he came to the rescue and attempted with considerable success to make the catastrophe serve at least as a way of procuring internal reconstruction. Naturally he would have gone with the Emperor—as nearly every one did or would have done. Now he went with Germany, in that he organized the nation's raw materials—although the idea was not originally his own. Now for the first time one end of the rope was thrown out to him—and none of the regular officials suspected how vigorously this ambitious expert hand would take hold of it. When one person has done something, what is easier than to say, that another person in his place would have done the same! This much is certain: that Rathenau displayed unheard-of energy, transforming the entire economic basis of Germany, and really neutralizing the effect of England's blockade. If Ludendorff's service was in the beginning good, Rathenau's was better.

He had hardly taken the first steps in this important contribution to his country's defense before the officials began muttering and decided to "substitute" one of their own men in place of the Jew. Then he waited for four more years, until the republic needed him again. Now he felt that his hour had come. Beginning as an adviser, he gradually moved to the fore, until by the close of 1921 he had the country in his own hands: a

pious Christian had recognized the worth of this resolute Jew and accepted his cautious guidance. He should
have remained in this position, governing indirectly, for
as an avowed leader he was totally unacceptable to the
Germans. And Rathenau knew this.

Nevertheless he accepted the official leadership. Now
at last he possessed the external symptoms of a power
which he had been wielding for months. The Genoa conference was approaching. Forty nations would gather
about one table; a world congress would carve the names
of the most important emissaries in the eternal archives
of history. Rathenau wanted to feel, and even needed to
feel, that he too would sit at this horseshoe table, and
be Germany.

And this happened. He did not merely sit at the table:
he shone—because he was one of the cleverest men at
the conference, and his broad European attitude showed
the world for the first time that not all Germans were
alike. He returned home with a great moral victory; the
entire public applauded, since this was the first national
treaty which seemed to restore Germany to activity.
It was spring, and he had reached the apogee of his life.
June came, and he gathered the leaders of new Germany
under the old oaks by his office. That evening Rathenau
was probably happy.

A few days later, while in his car, he was shot. He
sprang up, saw the murderers for a second, and then was
gone—without pain, without consciousness. This man
whose life had seldom been happy met a kind of death
which even the happiest could have envied him. The
signs of a reversal were already at hand; he could not
possibly have resisted the discontent, envy, and intrigue

of powerful opponents from all camps longer than the
end of the year in which he had openly assumed control. He would have returned to the daily routine of his
business, with his evenings and his summers devoted to
his output of criticism. And he would have beheld petty
brains at work destroying all that he had attempted to
construct. The curve of his hopes, which heretofore had
mounted steadily, would have risen no higher. He was
through. And he was spared the spectacle of all this by
a shot from the gun of a cowardly assassin.

This same shot was his atonement. The manly courage with which he had faced the threatened attack for
weeks, his feeling of a destiny to be fulfilled, had canceled off every petty act of this highly problematic character. His unfriendly friends bared their heads, for this
man had been in earnest. His friendly enemies pointed
to him as a model. A whole great people, which had
never known him, suspended work for half a day in
his honor. The German republic gave him such a burial
as Rome gave to its dead Cæsars.

Once again the door of his imposing house was
opened: the door which was too narrow during his lifetime to admit any one who loved him, and yet which
was wide enough to make room for the oak coffin of the
lonely dead.

LENIN

LENIN

One technical expert is
worth twenty communists.

BLEAK and gray, in a cramped, stuffy street, a high
narrow laborer's house peers through a dozen pale windows. The blue lake of Zurich, with its restful villas and
its trim old parks, seems far in the distance; yet it lies
but a few hundred paces off, surrounded by a wreath
of blue, white-capped mountains, cheerful and pure,
free and sunlit. Looking through the window above the
near-by inn, however, one sees nothing of all this,
nothing but the weird face of another house, equally
gloomy. In the one-windowed room which the exile and
his mate occupied for two years during the war, there
are two wooden beds and two crude tables. Manuscripts, books, and newspapers are scattered everywhere; and the odor of tea and tobacco is augmented by
the heat of the little iron stove.

Eight months after his exile had ended, Lenin was sitting in the Kremlin at Moscow—the Kremlin, which is
fortress, church, and palace. Like a new czar, endowed
with absolute powers, he was at the focal point of that
very country which previously persecuted him and
condemned him. Vast halls and galleries lay at his dis-
posal; there were gurgling baths and brilliant music,
and a legion of servants to fulfill for him the dream of
the poor tinker in the comedy. But being compelled by
political symbolism to live here, he selected for himself a couple of rooms on one of the inner courts, living-

rooms of medium size—and here, with his intimates, he lived, ate, and slept. Not a single one of his mortal enemies, not a single report from among the hundreds spread by his adversaries, has ever dared assert that this man needed, desired, or used anything beyond the barest necessities.

To remain cold and collected when at the height of power, a man must be devoted to a pure idea. He must be a realist, and immune to fantasy. This is part of Lenin's secret, the first key to his success. For Lenin is certainly the most thoroughgoing, and the coldest, fanatic of our times.

For fifty-two years he was in perfect health. As outlaw, in hiding, in flight, in exile; in the daily routine, in the turmoil of congresses; in ambush, defeated, countermarching, decamping; and finally, at the helm—he was always healthy, always confident, always nervy, smiling, hopeful, and totally fearless. This man had no conflicting passions. He was driven by one single passion, the idea of his mission. He liked to hunt and to travel; he was on friendly terms with animals and children. He was naïve without being sentimental. Though crafty as a peasant, he was not underhanded. He was good-natured, yet ready to employ the most extreme measures against any one who resisted or interfered with his ideas. Cheerful, modest, without vanity or pretense, he was as Draconian as any dictator in the interests of his cause.

In his cool workroom in the Kremlin, which was bare except for a few maps, this undersized man with the freckled, somewhat fawnlike face would sit opposite a visitor and blink one of his oblique Tartar eyes—eyes behind which irony and pugnacity seemed to lurk—

until the other eye would appear to acquire a sharper vision. When he was most unassuming, when he talked little and listened carefully to what was being said to him, he was all the more certain to get his interlocutor under his control. With his unfailing health, his ability to dispense with sleep, and his broad laughter, in any transaction he would always prove to be the more untiring.

This physique, which gave him his energy and his endurance, and his care-free laughter—this is the second key to his nature, and to his success.

The third is to be found in his cold scientific precision. As a critic of his age, of his friends, and of his own acts, he was consistently the clear-minded historian. He was like a doctor, observing with professional interest the pulse-beat, the temperature, and other such symptoms of a crisis. An indefatigable student of himself and of the movement in which he was involved, he never, literally never, let himself be carried away by the enthusiasm of the moment. And at crucial stages, when his colleagues became elated or enraged, deriving new strength from such sublimated drunkenness, Lenin was subjecting the situation to a sober analysis.

This grim aspect of his temperament gave rise in turn to two traits, one of them dangerous, the other fruitful.

As a pure intelligence, he believed in putting things to the test. He became an experimenter, feeling no more need to justify his purposes to himself and the world than the doctor who resorts to the vivisection of animals. Both desire human happiness at whatever cost, with the one difference that in Lenin's case the victimized are of the same species as the benefited. But since Lenin, on assuming this frightful responsibility towards his fellow men, courageously and unselfishly placed his own life in jeopardy, the absurd charge that he was a monomaniac working for his own personal gain failed to tell against the armor of this fighter. "I know a pair of eyes," Gorki says of Lenin, "which have been for ever numbed by the burning sorrow of the Terror."

The dangers of such experimental statesmanship were partially neutralized by another, half-naïve and half-cynical, aspect of his scientific procedure. Since he planned without passion, he was open to whatever compromise might seem advisable at the moment: he had no sympathy with theoretical objections to such a course. "It is childish," he writes, "to reject compromise on principle. . . . One must simply know how to analyze the circumstances and the concrete conditions of each issue." And in all justice his friend Lunacharsky dared call this man, whom all Europe thought deluded, "a genius at opportunism."

In fact, Lenin might be compared to Lloyd George, as the greatest political realist of his day. And while trying to realize Tolstoi's social scheme in Tolstoi's country, he was in a deeper sense his opposite. Equally inartistic and un-Christian, this atheist—an opponent even of positivistic philosophy—wanted to introduce in his state the advocates of the Great Revolution, in which he resembled his western predecessors.

Also, he lacked many characteristically Russian traits. This realist had neither the romantic nor the metaphysical leanings of his colleagues. In compensation, as Trotsky has said, his peasant-like craftiness was heightened to the point of genius. Even his opponent Axelrode backs up the suggestion with a statement of his own:

"Lenin has about him the smell of the Russian soil."

Further, a certain immoderation, such as characterized Ivan and Peter, seems to have a racial origin. And Lenin recalls Peter the Great also in his determination to arouse the people from their state of lethargy, to enforce his belated discoveries upon these Orientals, and by an Occidental system transform them from the most backward to the most progressive members of the white race. Both, under the impetus of European idealism and nationalism, tried to telescope whole centuries of development—and for this reason neither procured much more than an astounding façade. "What is communism?" asked Lenin, and then gave the superbly grotesque answer: "The Soviet Republic plus electrification."

In 1870, half a century after Marx, Lassalle, and Bismarck, Vladimir Ilyitch, who is now known as Lenin, was born on the Volga. He was of the lower middle class, a social status which his father, who had become superintendent of several public schools, attempted to outreach by acquiring the rank of national councilor. During his boyhood the assassination of Alexander II took place; and as a student of law at Kazan he felt the results of this anarchistic attack, sharing with his comrades such resentment and impatience at their slavelike life under the knout as might be expected of so obstinate and freedom-loving a temperament. His elder brother was his teacher and his ideal. He was the first translator of Marx and Hegel, and initiated the younger Lenin in these authors. The brother planned a conspiracy in Saint Petersburg against the new czar six years after the last assassination. But he, with the other conspirators, was arrested in the street on the morning

set for the attack, was brought to court, and hanged.
This was the last attempt at terrorism.

Lenin was seventeen. This cataclysm, whose reverber-
ations were heard far out in the provinces, in the quiet
of his home, must necessarily have one of two results:
either it would definitely banish all thought of rebellion
and active resistance from the boy's mind for ever; or
it would make him the avenger of his brother, whom he
had loved and from whom he had received the most
decisive features of his education. His courage and his
love made him rise to the occasion; but being cool and
intelligent, and having the horrible warning of his
brother's fate as an idealist, Lenin realized that success
could not be obtained at one stroke, but must be carefully prepared for over a period of years, perhaps during a whole lifetime. Thus, by the logic of history, the
brother of Russia's last destructive terrorist became
Russia's first constructive socialist. Marx was his
brother's will and testament; Lenin saw in Marx the intellectual weapon which might succeed where the bomb
had failed.

Yet Marx brought him a second antagonist.

Whereas, in the orthodox revolutionary manner, he
would have struggled only against the crown, he now
learned to recognize another opponent in the bourgeoisie, whose moderate reforms and restricted liberal-
ism enraged him. Now, with a new solution to the old
problem, he set out to study the nature of that class by
whose strength alone the revolution could succeed, and
for whom alone it should be fought.

For years he traveled through Russia, studying the
laborers—the peasantry he knew instinctively—taking
endless notes on both the intimate and social aspects of

their lives. He was a scientific investigator, much like Zola, who at about this same time was collecting data for his "Germinal" in the mines and huts of Belgium. But in lieu of a novel, Lenin wrote pamphlets and flyleaves; and while a student, he was also an agitator, trying to awaken in his auditors a feeling of responsibility which might later spread of its own accord through the entire laboring classes.

Unlike the most of his comrades, Lenin did not begin as a theorist, a writer and a speaker, but as an investigator of the human soul in its direst straits. He did not, like Marx, construct a system in his study; nor did he, like Lassalle, suddenly become a champion of the laboring classes when this seemed a likely method of obtaining personal advancement. By systematic observation, substituting deliberate study for the painful experience of the born proletarian, he gradually trained himself to understand the masses. Though he was often deceived in the case of individuals, Lenin was infallible in judging the desires and motives of the masses—for out of thousands of experiences with the individual, he acquired a feeling for the type.

His first banishment was from the university in Kazan. Now he was looked upon with suspicion at the capital and throughout the country, moving under the surveillance of those same police whom, though they were now his oppressors, he was later to place under a surveillance equally strict. Forty years after the founding of the first German labor union, and at a time when the German socialists were already a formidable power in the Reichstag, he and his friends attempted with much misgivings to take the same steps in Russia. As a result the first strike was organized. But it was suppressed, and Lenin was again banished, this time to Siberia for thirty years.

This Siberia, which we usually imagine as being a much more desolate place than it seemed to many of the political prisoners, was for Lenin a kind of intellectual health resort. His confinement was in reality a period of recovery. Here he met men who thought as he did, Martov in particular, with whom he talked and planned. Though different in its motives, this period resembled in its results Luther's confinement at the Wartburg—for it was now that he worked out the details of his schemes. His first book appeared under the pseudonym of Tulin. It was plain, almost simple, and sparse in pictures and metaphor; but it was clear, as were all his subsequent volumes. This forcible removal from the field of action had taught him a lesson. He saw that the revolution must be prepared for even more cautiously and quietly than before, by beginning abroad, on the periphery, to educate "revolutionary experts," men who were revolutionaries by profession and not mere enthusiasts, idealists, or dilettants.

"Let our comrades," he writes, "permit the use of the rigorous term 'technical expert,' for when I speak of inadequate preparations the accusation applies also to myself. I have worked with men who set themselves very high and difficult responsibilities, yet we suffered painfully from the feeling that we were but amateurs. The more ashamed I am to confess this, the more bitter I feel towards those sham socialists who fail to realize that we dare not lower the revolutionary to the level of the amateur."

For the first time, Lenin was jeered at by his own

party. But he was certain of his course, and was an inborn autocrat—so that his opposition to the moderate radicals quickly developed into a hatred which soon overshadowed his hatred of the Czar.

Return from banishment. The circle of his opponents grew narrower. He withdrew from the social-revolutionary faction, which wanted to placate the liberal bourgeoisie on the grounds that their assistance was necessary. The party was split at the congress of 1903 because Lenin demanded that the statutes should obligate each member not merely to a financial contribution but to active participation. Although this looks like mere hair-splitting over a paragraph, it was in reality the decisive test of adherence. The minority wanted to pledge money and sympathy and go no farther; but Lenin with the majority showed his fist—literally—on the platform. The shadow of a dictator was cast against the wall of the assembly room. And now the protestants separated from the orthodox, who believed in salvation by works alone.

Lenin found himself abandoned by the friends of his prison days, by Axelrode, Martov, and even the personally honored Plechanov, the old leader. Trotsky called him the "destroyer of the party," but he made a further remark, revealing that mixture of admiration and jealousy which one of these antipodal minds seems to have felt towards the other. "Lenin," Trotsky wrote at that time, after the congress, "came to the conclusion that he is the iron hand, he alone. And he is right. By the 'logic' of martial law, on which he insisted, he had to predominate."

Lenin met this separation from his old friends in a pronouncedly personal manner. His work and his life were one. In his next articles, he heaped curses upon these "renegades, crooks, and traitors," although they had lain for years in the prisons of the Czar for the same cause as he. And he also attacked Kautsky, the purest of them all.

October 1905, the great strike led to a street fight. The guard shot into a procession of workmen—and the first Soviet Council was organized spontaneously in the factories, exactly twelve years before the erection of the Soviet Republic. Yet where, at this moment, was Lenin, who had played a prominent part in the preparations for all this?

Precisely where General Bonaparte was until evening on the 18th Brumaire—which is to say, invisible. Wearing a false beard, he stood in the corner of a gallery listening to the various meetings called to discuss the common cause. To save his life, his party had forbidden him to show himself. So he stood there in his disguise, forced to maintain silence, yet stamping with impatience to enter the discussion and take part in the work. Nevertheless he was discovered, and had to flee a third time. He went to Finland, was tracked down again, and then escaped to Paris, and later to Cracow. All this time he was writing and publishing, using the thinnest possible paper in order that it might be more conveniently smuggled into Russia. . . . What had this attempt at rebellion taught him?

As a scientist, a biographer or a sociologist, he collated all his data, to discover for himself and others how they should modify their tactics in the future. Why had the soldiers shot into the crowd? Because the soldiers were sons of the peasantry. Therefore, the land must be taken from the feudal owners and transferred to the poorest peasants. Here again, the formulation of a new political procedure was the result of psychological considerations rather than of economic ones. And here again, he was almost alone.

Yet while his demands grew stricter, he became more willing to accept even the humblest ways of putting them into effect, and he angered his friends by this growing elasticity which had transformed him into a politician. Why boycott the Duma? Was it not a forum of public protest? Still more comrades dropped away from him. Stubbornly, Lenin accepted his isolation.

The World War brought at one stroke the highest expectations and the heaviest disillusionment. Perhaps in those momentous days no one had more to lose and waited with greater tension than this little band of genuinely European intellectuals who saw their hopes shattered. For when the International went up in smoke, that meant to them the first, and perhaps the most frightful, explosion of the whole war. Every one, forgetting the Red Flag, ran to his national colors. Every one forsook the comrades to whom he had commended resistance against the martial rulers of their own country.

Lenin, with a very small group, pulled himself together after this blow, renounced the vacillating attitude of Tcheidse, scorned Plechanov's patriotism and Krapotkin's anti-Germanism, and promptly issued (September 1914) an international program which shows the broad outlook of the European:

"It would not cause us the slightest distress to see the overthrow of the Czar, since his barbaric government holds the greatest number of nations in subjection. The sole watchword of this war should be the formation of the United States of Europe. Yet we must impress upon the masses the fact that this watchword would be pure sham and nonsense without the overthrow of the German, Austrian, and Russian monarchies. In order to deceive the workers more successfully, and to deflect them from the one real war of liberation—which is to say, from civil war—the bourgeoisie of all countries is attempting to increase the respect for 'its' national war by patriotic lies calculated to convince the people that they are seeking victory in order to 'free' all nations except, naturally, their own."

These words, which contain not one jot of communism, were shouted above the battle courageously and despairingly for the common people of all nations to hear. And they show a man who, in the midst of the tempest, descried sooner than most the haven of refuge. For thirteen months he sat with such thoughts in the stuffy room in Zurich and in a few other Swiss lodging-houses which were little better. He had very little money and a very restricted field of influence. Yet he was watching and preparing, and gathering together an advance guard in Kiental and Zimmerwald.

Finally, on February 17, he heard the hoped-for news from the East. The Czar overthrown! But by whom? By our mortal enemies, the Democrats?

Lenin was in a fever of impatience. He and his little circle of Russian émigrés were not so much interested in returning to their country as in the battle after their return. After three centuries, and then again after three decades, the hated power had collapsed—and at this time of all times they were detained abroad! For Milyukov was doing all in his power to prevent the entrance of his dangerous opponents. Lenin sat in the café in Zurich and read, "The new government will continue the war"—and yet he could not get away. England refused him passage! Who could help him?

Friend Ludendorff, who could do everything, and who had now thought out a fabulous scheme. We must inject into the enemy the bacillus of pacifism, the General decided—and accordingly he began negotiations with these insane Russian sectarians in Berne. Lenin pricked up his Tartar ears. When Prussian royalist generals become psychologists, he thought and laughed his broad laugh, there is something in it for us Russian revolutionaries. He made an offer, concealing nothing. His terms were granted, and before boarding the train for Germany he announced his plans and his expectations in a letter to the Swiss proletariat.

Not a single boastful word, not a single anarchistic phrase, not the least hint of excitement on the part of this man who after twenty-five years of waiting was on the verge of success. A historian was speaking, a scientist: "Certain circumstances will transform us for a time, possibly a very brief time, into the leaders of the revolution in Europe. Russia is a very backward peasant community where socialism cannot be directly or immediately victorious. But if we deprive the landed proprietors of their enormous wealth, this peasant community can become a mighty force in the general revolutionary movement." All of which is very measured and cautious, like the diagnosis of a physician.

At the same time, he frankly told the German military party what fools they were: "We are anything but absolute pacifists, and will not abstain from war when we consider war necessary to the victory of socialism.

Although we are obliged to take advantage of this speculation on the part of a nationalistic government, we do not make the least concession to this government in the matter of our policies." At the same time he publicly declared, as spokesman for all those who were returning to Russia, that they went home with the hope of "inciting the proletariat of all countries, and especially Germany and Austria, to revolutionary warfare against their own governments!"

Yet Ludendorff, the besieged Trojan, built his own Trojan horse, snapped the door shut with a know-it-all expression, and sent his tightly plugged train through Germany, to release the passengers on the opposite border of the country three days later. It was not Lenin alone who laughed on this train. The laughter of all his comrades confined there was as Homeric as the horse. The traveling expenses of this trip were paid by the passengers, but the experience was at the cost of the sender.

The Finnish station was jammed with people. The radical faction of the capital received the returning exile like a savior. In the Czar's reception room at the station, his intimate opponent Tcheidse greeted the little man with the shabby cap: "The revolution bids you welcome, Lenin!" From without came the strains of the Marseillaise. Lenin, standing in his automobile, passed slowly through the milling throngs, calling out a few sentences to them, simply, like a peasant, yet with a voice of bronze. Today for the first time no one saw him laughing. Fate was hovering above him. Somberly, grimly, he foresaw victory.

"I shall never forget the scene," one of his opponents has written, "for it astounded not only me, a heretic, but all the men of his own faction as well. I had not expected anything like this. All sorts of people, from all quarters, seemed to have been drawn here." No radical doubted but that this man alone was their leader.

Soon after his arrival he announced his program in the "Pravda": to fraternize the soldiers at the front; to renounce all conquests; to accord full power to the soviets of workers and peasants; to combat the government which was continuing the war; to socialize all property; to consolidate all banks; to get control of all food supplies; to establish a new international.

Up in the palace the government wrinkled its brows, for it felt that the enemy was in its midst. Czardom was a moldy, superannuated system—but here came a new one, the future. At the first workers' congress the eight hundred delegates remained silent at Lenin's metallic speech, and remained silent at Kerensky's feverish answer. "I will not be the dictator that you seem to want," he called out to Lenin. Lenin sat below, stroking his chin, and wondering who would be the dictator.

In July, after the congress, in which he had remained with the minority, he was forced to hide again. Then he was ferreted out, and had to flee this time to Finland, as he had done twelve years before. This was three months after his arrival in Petrograd. Again, with his scientific instinct, he retraced his own steps: he wrote on "The State and the Revolution." He subjects his various phases to an attentive critical analysis. But when he comes to the events which he had recently passed through, he interrupts his report with a rather strong bit of humor. He was, he said, "interrupted by a new political crisis, a disturbance at which we cannot help but rejoice. The second installment of this pamphlet will probably be a long time in appearing. But it is pleasanter and more important to take part in a revolution than to write about one." In the fall he returned again with a forged permit, and stood again on the gallery. He found Trotsky, his more interesting rival, at his height. The party was stronger, and the peasants were clamoring for peace, as Kerensky had decided on a new offensive.

But he could be held down no longer. This time he changed his mask, shaving and wearing a wig to escape detection. In this disguise he took part at the central session. He felt that the hour which most of his comrades had ceased to hope for was near. This seemed to him the time for action. Standing on the platform, half unmasked, but still with his false hair, intensely agitated, and breathless at the thought of being so near to attainment—Lenin stirred his comrades to action, and forced the uprising of October 24th.

During the five years that Lenin was in power, he became more and more the dictator in domestic issues, though he developed into a pronounced politician in his treatment of foreign affairs. When he felt endangered, with the aid of his sailors he disbanded the Constituent Assembly. Yet in the summer of 1919 he said to Gorki: "The astonishing thing about it all is that no one has yet taken it into his head to show us the door."

Yet for this very reason he was shifty in his foreign policies. In January 1918, in opposition to Trotsky, he used his influence with the Central Committee to force the acceptance of Germany's oppressive treaty of Brest-

Litovsk, asserting that "workers who lose a strike do not thereby betray socialism." At this time, when all his colleagues were against peace, Lenin proved his statesmanship. "You cannot make peace with the Hohenzollern?" he said during the meeting. "You are more stupid than a hen! She can't step over a circle of chalk, but at least she can accuse some one else of drawing the circle. But in this case we ourselves have drawn the circle—and you would not go beyond the formula. We employed this formula to arouse the masses. Now you demand that we remain loyal to it, even to the extent of failing on principle and allowing the capitalistic governments to triumph!"

Objections. Wrangling. Lenin said: "Now is the time when the muzhik must set foot on the land we have given him. Do you not see that the muzhik has voted against the war?" When and where did he do that? asked Radek. "He voted no with his feet: he ran away from the front!" And Lenin was justified by the subsequent course of history, since the treaty of Brest was soon canceled. He always dealt with foreign nations in this way, purely as the situation demanded, and regardless of any breach between theory and practice.

He had to carry his country safely through the three invasions of five expeditionary units, and through a blockade of three years' duration. Yet at the same time, although he had not even had previous experience in local politics, he began slowly and patiently restoring a vast nation to order after an almost fatal calamity. Yesterday—literally—he was still a revolutionary of the underworld; today he was a leading statesman. At the same time he was disavowed and scorned by the majority of his comrades in all countries, who did have good reason to resent a foreign dictatorship which had lasted for years. But as our aim is simply to sketch the figure of the leader, we need not decide here the historic question as to whether the ruins of Russia are derived from the war, the revolution, or the general blindness. It is enough to observe that a nation of enormous size was permitted to skip half a dozen stages of evolution and to adopt a new system in close accord with its oldest traditions.

And this much is certain: Lenin was the first man to show his party that a good statesman defeats his opponents by taking over their tactics. He even favored the Taylor System as a means of reducing all work to a minimum of movement, although this was the ultimate and most barbaric refinement of the economic code which he was combating. "At whatever cost, the Soviet Republic must make use of all important scientific and technical improvements. We do not need *élan*; we need the measured tread of the iron battalion."

He employed French and German monarchists as technical advisers. For his passion—the idea of a boyhood friend who was still with him—was the electrification of Russia, both in the rural districts and in the cities. "A single technical expert is worth ten communists," wrote Lenin.

So they set to work and tried it out for a year or more—and from day to day the situation grew worse.

But before the year was over, Lenin had new ideas as to what was possible and what was not possible. Turning his back resolutely on theory, he was first to advise the communes against socializing more industries than they could manage. Likewise he was first to demand of the worker an "adjustment of wages in proportion to the total output." And one day, to the surprise and horror of most of his colleagues, he suddenly made a speech in which he insisted that measures were being forced through prematurely, and that the party was headed for disaster unless the economic policies were reversed and new measures adopted. He advocated a tax on food-stuffs, the payment of which would entitle the taxpayer to resume private business. He pointed out that military communism had been required by the war, but that now new methods were demanded. "Yes, the petty bourgeoisie will rise again, and even capitalism. This fact is undeniable," Lenin went on, while his comrades blanched. "But why shut our eyes to it? We must simply steer in the direction of state capitalism! The way to do this is to grant concessions to foreign nations. But in order to make these concessions of advantage to us, and to prevent their becoming a menace, we must consider the matter of relative strength when allotting and apportioning them, since the ultimate decision rests in battle."

A third encounter with Trotsky, who wanted to stick to the pure idea. The third victory for Lenin, the experimenter, who was always in search of new methods and would allow no theoretical principles to interfere.

Thanks to this naïve elasticity, he worked out his own technique of government. We might call it the equalization of responsibility and absolutism.

Entirely dependent upon himself, unable not only to organize an office force but even to dictate to a stenographer, he would appear in person—with the complete frankness of a man who had only himself to blame—before the peasants of some village and say: We made a mistake, and we were beaten for it; we will correct the mistake in such-and-such a manner. And since every Russian is a born confessor, they respected his self-criticism. The workers, moreover, who had long since ceased to believe in heroic redeemers, were encouraged by his frankness to participate in decisions affecting themselves—and thus they learned to think politically.

But while asking that every one should enter into the discussion, Lenin demanded "unconditional subjection to one single will," saying that "the only possible system is that of personal dictatorship." He had a consistent reason for this. This revolutionary, who had been responsible to his party for every move he made during the last thirty years, hated the collegial form of government by which Occidental administrators have learned to shift responsibilities; and though he wanted every single official to be elected by the people, he demanded total compliance on the part of the constituents and total accountability on the part of their representatives.

So the principles by which this man ruled always merged into the traits of his character. And contrary to Marx's theory, the pure but relentless will of the leader influenced his country's development—though to be sure the results often differed somewhat from the intentions, when ideas were put to the acid test of reality.

One day, after three years of office, he was shot on the street by a woman who was a fanatic like himself, and who was perhaps a victim of the Soviet or the wife or the sister of such a victim. Lenin's sound constitution saved his life, but the bullet had impaired this sound constitution.

He lay in the Kremlin for a year at the point of death, barely able to rise. His friends announced that he was exhausted: this man who had been all bustle, fight, and pluck was exhausted. From seventeen to forty-seven: thirty years of deprivation, flight, persecution, flight, exile, flight—internal and external struggle. Then, after a sudden victory, three years of superhuman toil, with battles raging everywhere against powers multiplied a hundredfold. At fifty with a bullet in his body—his resistance was gone, the flame of life had weakened, and a used-up man lay on his bed. Legend quietly gathers about him. "In this gruff politician," Gorki wrote, "there flares up at times the light of an almost womanly tenderness, the dream of a future happiness for all. . . . His private life is such that in a religious age people would have made of him a saint."

Lenin had courage and intelligence, faith and integrity; and with such qualities behind his enormous vitality he was able to hold a steady and unwavering course. Possibly, under the circumstances, this course was a wrong one—but it does none the less serve as a pattern. It demonstrates to us that today—as has been true of the past and must be true of the future—the will of one man, if he is guided by a consistent purpose, is capable of shaping the lives of millions. Considering him as an idealist who attempted to put his concepts into practice, we find his career a model of courage, independence, and unselfishness.

But he has paid for this with his life. His laughter is now definitely silenced.

LEONARDO DA VINCI

Once I have learned how to die,
then I shall know how to live.

His life was a dialogue with nature.

Often this dialogue may have been obscured by the silence of his eternal loneliness; at other times it was revealed in brief notes, in comparisons, deductions, observations, and notations. Frequently it attained expression in formal works—yet with a few exceptions these too remained fragmentary or soon lost their power of survival. Since he valued things purely as experiments, and since neither ambition nor jealousy nor the sheer feel of mastery could induce him to mirror himself in his works, nothing now is left but a few tables, a painted wall, a few dozen drawings, and the diaries with their 5000 pages or so of notes.

These papers, the documents of an essayist, were soon as thoroughly enshrouded in legend as the works of a mystic. Mystery seemed latent in these reliques of a creative life—and the less tangibly his life was revealed, the more readily it took on the compensatory veil of mystery, as with the life of a prophet. Later generations told of his riding through the streets like a prince, on a white, gold-bridled horse, wrapped in flowing silks, and preceded by the laughter of beautiful boys, his pupils and minions: a symbol of the artist in the heyday of that era.

The truth is simpler and deeper. The life-long dialogue between himself and nature exacted of him a profound loneliness—for this sort of dialogue is not only a dialogue; it is also a monologue. In these countless musings of his note-books, which almost seem as though they had been washed up from alien shores and which whole centuries have labored to decipher, he admonishes himself repeatedly: "Remember . . . wrong! right! mistake! . . . That is a beautiful possibility, worth further investigation! . . . How then would you account for the presence of gravel on high mountains? . . . And do you have all the necessary anatomical data?" And in order that his dialogue with himself and nature might be made less accessible, he resorted to mirror writing.

For Leonardo was both a student of nature and a prophet—and this duality of his character produced marked contrasts which had an important effect upon his work. Without his scientific eye—his observation—he would never have become the greatest pathfinder of the new Occident. Without his mystical gaze—his vision—he could not have used his knowledge to make himself, we might say, the prehistoric discoverer of all that a later era worked out patiently and laboriously. For a thousand years, there has been no other prophetic temperament except Goethe so richly endowed with this intellectual duality, this pliant realism. Leonardo occupies the relatively easier position of groping prophetically into regions not yet explored. Goethe, likewise an observer and an essayist, but with the mania of the genuine collector, was better able to coördinate his discoveries. And although he too left very little finished work behind him, the thousands of pages of notes have rounded themselves off into a consistent interpretation, so that his results become more tangible. Goethe produced more, and carried more of his works through to completion. In many-sidedness Leonardo remains un-matched.

But as his work was never assembled or completed, his endowments were much greater than his results. He did plan to collect his notes into books, arranging them by subject, such as a treatise on water, on mechanics, on painting, and so forth. The whole was to be called: On the Things of Nature. But his curiosity drove him rest-lessly on from decade to decade; a roving and vigorous pioneer, he had none of Goethe's resignation, restraint, and punctiliousness. Thus the tangible results were few, everything remaining in the stage of theme and hypoth-esis. Like a sportive god, this genius took up the works of nature one by one, looked at them, and laid them down again—and thus Leonardo himself remained hardly more than a sport of nature, almost without predecessors, and wholly without successors.

He preferred to be know as an inventor—and he did maintain his interest in inventions throughout his entire life. As a young man he wanted to raise the baptistery at Florence and set it on a new base of marble. At thirty he offered his services to the Duke of Milan as an in-ventor, to construct for him pontoons and chariots, gal-leries and mortars. Then he built tanks, testudines with a double covering, dray-horses inside the shell and em-brasures in the cope. At the same time he applied him-self to the problem of canalizing the Ticino and con-necting it with the lakes. At fifty he wanted to trans-form Florence into an ideal city, planned the canaliza-tion of today, and proposed streets with an upper and lower level connected by steps, the upper level for promenade, the lower for commercial traffic. He invented modern chimneys, self-closing doors, and roasting spits turned by currents of warm air.

Meanwhile he renewed an old plan for canalizing the Arno from Pisa, to do away with the silt deposits in the river by the use of embankments. In his old age he laid out a network of canals in France for the Saone. Four hundred years later, the Ticino, the Arno, and the Saone are canalized very nearly as he had proposed.

In countless drawings he designed hydroplanes and the first parachute, diving bells and the submarine. "Why not describe my way of remaining under water? Because of the evil nature of men who would destroy their enemies on the bottom of the sea by boring through the hulls of ships and drowning the passengers. But what I disclose here cannot do damage: The mouth of the tube through which I breathe would reach above the water, sustained by cork or inflated skins." He tried to use steam as a means of propulsion, designed the first steam cannon, made powder, constructed a glass oven and a still. He built machines for sawing, spinning, shearing, washing, pottery-making. He constructed artesian wells, all sorts of mills, scales, the concave mirror, and the pendulum.

These were all inventions of a self-taught man who began at thirty teaching himself Latin and mathematics. For this reason he was the enemy of all the academic humanists of his day, who looked down upon him "because I am not educated,—I, an inventor!" And he felt scorn, most often a gentle scorn, for all sophists and philosophers. For an experience, an empirical experiment, always marked the starting point of Leonardo's dialogues with nature.

While planning the flying machine: "In order to learn how to fly, you must first understand the winds. And the winds are explained by studying the undulations of water." Instead of theorizing with the humanists over the problem "Is warmth a substance?" he drew his conclusions by comparing the weight of an object when at white heat with its weight when cold. He observed the accelerated motion of a falling body and found the law —which he was not looking for—two centuries before Newton. Employing engines of war to lift weights, he constructed the block-and-tackle, and was the first man since Archimedes to record the principles of the lever. In drawings which he made for the study of difficult problems in physics, he developed the law of the conservation of energy. When wandering over the Maritime Alps he discovered mussels on the mountain tops and founded the science of paleontology—then, he added what he knew of stratified rock, of fossils, and of tidal movements, all of which brought him back to astrological studies of an earlier period.

Like golden fish, laws leap out to him unbidden from the cascades of his experiments. Before Galileo he discovered the law of virtual velocity. He stated the principles of gyration and the vortex, and the law of communicating vessels. He was the founder of hydrostatics and of the entire science of hydraulics. He understood the undulatory motion of the sea, and applied its principles of transmission and reflection to sound and light; he measured sound-waves, explained the echo and the vibration of overtones four hundred years before Helmholtz and Herz. Before Goethe he inaugurated comparative anatomy in a book with red chalk drawings of bodies which he himself had dissected; he compared

the tongue of the woodpecker and the jaw of a croco-
dile with the corresponding parts of the human body
and indicated a common prototype. He explained the
eye as a camera obscura, recognized the functions of the
lens and of the retina and the mechanics of sight. All
medieval piety and traditionalism had vanished. The
first man of a new era, Leonardo had faith solely in experimentation. He, and not Bacon, was the founder of
the experimental method.

Yet while these *human* eyes were seeing and recognizing everything that nature put before them, he also
possessed the clairvoyance of the *prophet*. In the midst
of matters totally different, he suddenly wrote down in
large and solemn letters: "*Il sole non si muove.*" And
there is a jotting elsewhere: "In your teachings you
must show that the earth is a star, like the moon: in this
way you will establish the world's splendor." Written
fifty years before the book of Copernicus, and without
explanation or proof.

Like Goethe, he observed and recorded everything
that his eye lighted upon: the chimes in Siena, the foun-
tain of Rimini, the form of the carts in the Romagna.
And again like Goethe, his diction and his thoughts
mount suddenly to distant heights. Leaving the mathematical formula, the business of numbers and roots, he
would soar gradually into the air of metaphor, like a
hydroplane rising from the surface of the water.
"Weight, by its own nature, perishes when it reaches
the desired position. . . . Weight is material and force
is spiritual. . . . If force yearns continually for flight
and death, weight yearns for perpetuity. . . . Propulsion results from the death of motion, and motion from

the death of force. . . . Force is born of restraint and dies of freedom—and the greater it is, the more rapidly it is consumed. . . . Whatever resists it, it expels with violence, wishing to destroy the very conditions of its existence, and in victory causing its own death."

From this high pantheistic outlook he then drops lightly back to the mechanics of the physical world which he had, we might say, begrudgingly abandoned. Again and again, however, the inspired accents of the prophet interrupt the concise conclusions of the investigator. He was the first to explain with exactness the function of the pupil—then suddenly, in the midst of his notes, he adds: "O great necessity! With the highest wisdom, compelling all effects to participate in their causes! Who would believe that such a fraction of a second could encompass the transformations of the universe? Thus human thought rises to the contemplation of the divine."

This scientific nature-worship betrays the dual aspect of his character. He angrily derided the necromancers, spiritists, and ghost-seers of his day. "Take no miracles on trust; always look for causes. . . . Those who avoid the absolute certainty of mathematics must live in confusion and will never be able to silence the endless clamor of the sophists." Words of scorn flare up at the mention of alchemy, the music of the spheres, and *perpetuum mobile*. He laughs at monks who live on long-dead saints. The deluge was for him a purely geological phenomenon.

But the same pages contain fantastic prophecies which he has heard, half burlesqued and half allegorical accounts of plagues, disasters, and crucifixions. He described at length a giant in Asia Minor—where Leonardo never traveled, by the way, despite the legend. One day he painted on his tablets imaginary azure-blue cliffs and valleys, grottoes and rocks; and the next, on Monte Rosa, he explains the blue color of the sky in a manner which was to delight old Goethe three hundred years after-wards. Goethe, who understood Leonardo profoundly, wrote of him (in a remote passage) : "As an artist who perceived and apprehended nature immediately, think-ing of the phenomenon itself and penetrating it, he al-ways found the truth."

And suddenly, without any connection, there breaks forth from Leonardo's monologue the boldest sentence which ever mortal man has cast to the world: "I am discovering for mankind the first or perhaps the second reason of their existence."

Despite this constant interplay, he did not seem at all disturbed, as Goethe was, by this double life. On the contrary, it produced in him a state of equipoise, as his life, his portrait, and his art testify.

The vicissitudes of his era had some effect upon his career: he rose, fell, and recovered. But aside from this, his outward personal life was uneventful, and his inner life too was lived without irruptions. One single day of his many years is wrapped in secrecy, and it in turn conditions all his secrets. This is the day of his birth.

In a century of famous bastards, among the hills near Empoli, fate chose a certain young traveling Florentine as the man who was to make a peasant girl the mother of a genius. No one knows her name or her history. The young man, later a fashionable lawyer in Florence, married her off with her child to some unknown peasant. He was the father of nine more sons, legitimate and forgotten—and she perhaps bore several more children.

After his rightful father adopted him, she must have fallen almost completely out of touch with Leonardo, for not a single one of the many entries in his note-books indicates that he knew his mother. Also, he received nothing from his father—and in later years he entered into litigation with his brothers over the inheritance. Finally he provided for them in his will. All the details of his race are lost; but one thing survives, the name of the village. And so a maid brought this poor place immortality: Vinci resounds through the centuries because Leonardo was born there.

Until the age of thirty he roamed, unknown; like all the artists of his time, he was looking for a prince to whom he could offer his services and who would give him in return the protection of his house. Then he found Lodovico Sforza, the powerful Duke of Milan, called Il Moro. In a high-sounding document, Leonardo offered himself particularly as an expert in military engineering and an inventor of weapons. He also wrote that he could build houses and conduct water, that he knew how to model in marble, bronze or clay—and finally that he could paint and play the lute.

Yet the Duke first commissioned him to do an equestrian statue in honor of his brother. After this, with a few interruptions he kept Leonardo engaged for the next twenty years on all the things in which the Florentine—since he passed as a Florentine—had boasted his abilities.

When the King of France conquered the Duke and threw him into prison, Leonardo promptly transferred his allegiance to the victor, merely writing on the cover of one of his diaries the words: "The Duke has lost country, property, and freedom; he could not complete any of his plans." Alongside is a passage: "Rhodes has in the interior 5000 houses." Some one had told him this on the same day.

For sale to any master who could pay the price, like every *condottiere* of the age, he now went over to the man of the hour, France's ally—for this was just after the turn of the century, when Cæsar Borgia was at the height of his power. Leonardo became "general engineer for all fortifications." After Borgia's campaign the city of Florence, which was at war with Pisa, sent him into the field for the purpose of diverting the course of the Arno from Pisa towards Livorno. But corruption and stupidity defeated him, and he attempted unsuccessfully to live again in Milan, from whence he was recalled by Florence.

A niggardly republic, however, could not suffice for Leonardo; he needed some generous prince if he was to pursue his work unhampered. So at this moment fate sent him a more powerful patron whose wishes the Florentine councilors had to respect: for the next few years, until the beginning of his sixties, Leonardo was engaged in the service of the French king at Milan. Then political upheavals again deprived him of his haven. In the war between the pope and France, the son of Il Moro regained his father's duchy of Milan. Leonardo again took sides with the opposing party, and went to Rome, where Leo Medici, the friend of genius, had become pope. By his mechanical artifice, which he palmed off as alchemy, he enthralled the handsome decadent Giuliano, the pope's brother. But Raphael continually threatened to eclipse him.

Once again history took a turn in his favor. King

Louis was succeeded in Paris by King Francis, the
nephew of Giuliano. Being determined to despoil his
ally Italy of everything transportable, he also took with
him the old enchanter who might still produce almost
any sort of mechanism. With a title and a good salary,
he established Leonardo in a castle of the Touraine, and
here, at Cloux, the aging man spent his last years in
perfect freedom and without the slightest feeling of
homesickness for his fatherland.

As he surveys the whole of life, he encompasses both
belief and doubt, humility and pride, in the profound
words: "Our life is subject to heaven, but heaven is
subject to reason."

His life was uneventful in an age of great unrest, and
clement at a time of pronounced inclemency. He was
consistently successful in living the sort of existence
which he preferred. For he was interested in the contemporary situation only insofar as it affected his shelter,
food, and security; he felt no attachments of friendship or politics. Consequently he placed his ability at
the service of one Mæcenas after another, with the
complete and naïve cynicism of his century. He had no
desire to enter the combat; he wanted to be an observer.
While engaged as a military engineer, his feelings were
wholly pacifistic. He arraigned men for their warlike
frenzy, but finally assembled all his impressions of the
horror into a single work: "The Battle of the Standard."
It is immaterial to him who conquers and who is defeated. And while drawing with punctilious fidelity the
body of his patron's assassin as it swung on the gallows,
he wrote no damning epitaph on the margin, but a list
giving the colors of the hanged man's garments.

When in the pay of Sforza he designed the statue for a Sforza; and when Il Moro was defeated, he altered his plans for the same monument so that it might suit the commander who had defeated Il Moro. He left Milan at the time when his master of the last twenty years was about to fall and lose his realm. For after all, what did he owe the Duke! While the Duke's fate was in the balance and no one knew what would happen next, Leonardo was studying winds and waterspouts and investigating the nature of sea waves. "For kindly nature sees to it that you may find something to learn everywhere in the world."

Then in the service of Florence he depicted the severest defeat of Milan on the wall of the Hall of Council. Three times he transferred his allegiance to the victorious enemy. He knew how to use tact and flattery with rulers whose goodwill involved his own well-being. He appealed to the naïve taste of the young French king on his entrance into Rome by making a comical lion which took a few steps forward and then opened its breast with its paws, allowing the Bourbon lily to fall from its bosom. By this absurd invention, it seems, he won the king's favor and bettered his own position.

He advised young artists to remain polite when being censured. He, who scattered the profoundest bits of wisdom throughout his notebooks couched in succinct epigrams, outlines half a dozen letters to his master accusing his assistants of frivolity. Even in his sketch-books he takes precautions, and they do not stop at mirror writing. When writing against the eating of meat, he is afraid "to say more, since it is not permissible to speak the truth."

Yet in all walks of life he was borne up by his sense

of dignity. "The master gives commands; the slave carries them into effect." That is the form in which his pride sanctions the essayistic nature of his work. He never gave his patron the proper title, but addressed him as Signore. With the intense pride of a man at peace with himself, this rebel wrote in the midst of a thousand revolutionary jottings: "I will let the crowned books stay, because they contain the highest truth."

Handsome and well-groomed, obviously careful to preserve a distinguished appearance, he loved the body and laid emphasis on the matter of dress. "Coarse people of bad habits and shallow judgments do not deserve so beautiful an instrument, such a complex anatomical equipment, as the human body. They should merely have a sack for taking in food and letting it out again, for they are nothing but an alimentary canal." For such fastidious reasons he disapproved of sculpture; he did not like to "be forced to stand, dusty and dirty, while the painter sits comfortably and quietly at his work, using beautiful colors and a brush as light as a feather. He can dress as well as he pleases; the room is filled with lovely paintings, and often there are musicians sitting about, and people to read aloud." Similarly he was fond of animals and would not eat them. He bought caged birds in the market and freed them immediately afterwards.

In youth he may have affected and exaggerated these natural traits. He may, when he had money, have ridden on horseback through the streets with friends and servants, to give the people a display and give himself the feel of splendor. But in the countless jottings to do with money and expenditures which keep turning up in his diaries—and most of these go back only to the beginning of his thirties—there is no mention of horses and luxury. Even the handwriting, which is precious and fantastic only in the oldest books, becomes plainer.

In his fifties he rescued from the vicissitudes of war his entire wealth, 600 gold florins, the savings of seventeen years, depositing it in the savings bank at Florence, drawing sums from time to time, paying debts and lending to friends. Everything definite which we know about his public and private life indicates that during the latter half of his career, the period in which all his intellectual and artistic achievements took place, he lived a quiet, comfortable, and ordered existence, much like a distinguished stranger, for "only by being alone can you belong completely to yourself."

But when it was to his advantage his public dealings were strained and undependable; he acted as a Bohemian towards every one who commissioned him to do work. Neither a sense of duty nor a desire for fame could drive him to complete a work, so that he hardly ever abided by his contracts; and since none of his contemporaries understood him, and least of all his biographer Vasari, no one who gave Leonardo a commission was ever satisfied with him.

Churches and individuals with whom he contracted to finish a painting within a definite period of time would give him gold florins, lodging, and wine as advance payment; he would begin work, and then he would not like it, or he grew bored with it; he would go away, and they would complain about him or even bring action against him.

When the city of Florence gave him, in his fifties, an important commission "for a beautiful work" to decorate a wall in the Signory, the city fathers were cautious

in dealing with this untrustworthy man: they bound
him to an agreement whereby, if he had not finished
by a definite date, he should refund his monthly pay-
ments and surrender the cartoon to the city. But when
the citizens paid him his gold in copper coins, he began
to grumble. He could no longer lay eyes on the gigantic
picture, which he was endangering by new technical
methods; he wanted to return to Milan; he took leave of
absence. The gonfalonier threatened him with a fine if
he did not return. The matter came to court—whereupon the King of France appeared *ex machina* and the
wishes of his majesty prevailed.

He often got into difficulties with Il Moro as well.
The remarkable thing is that they were on good terms
for so long. A ruler who had risen to power by force,
who feared a similar violent end, who was continually
harassed and was continually making demands; a philosopher who was always equable and observant, but
who was an inveterate experimenter and never brought
his work to completion. As the equestrian statue, the
"great horse," continued to remain in the stage of trials
and models, the Duke hired another artist. But when he
did not paint the *camerini* of his castle, and finally failed
to finish the Last Supper in Santa Maria delle Grazie,
their relations became strained. Already, for some time
past, the Duke had assigned him, instead of money, the
income from certain city gates and water rents which
he was to procure for himself as best he could. "The
painter made somewhat of a row today, and on account
of this he has left," the Duke writes, but the painter
notes: "First the benefices, afterwards the work, then
the ingratitude, and finally these unseemly scenes." Yet
they became reconciled—just as the Weimar Duke much

later was to quarrel and become reconciled with his factotum. The Duke restored him to favor, gave him money, and a vineyard besides.

He took what was given him, and asked for what he needed. But in his book there is the murmur of his monologue: "Oh, do not place a low value upon me, I am not poor. He is poor whose wants are many."

There was no place in this life for passion. Leonardo moved through the *Secolo appassionato* with the perfect composure of a philosopher. His genius and his beauty, his association with the nobles, and the universality of his achievements put him in touch with the interesting women of his country; but none of those humanistic feminine epistles in which the society of that time discussed matters of love mentions his name, and there is no love story connected with this most fascinating of all Renaissance artists. In keeping with his narcissus-like monologue and his reserve, and with the sweetness of the characters in his paintings, he might be expected to show a predilection for male youth—and as a matter of fact there are documents and anecdotes bearing on Leonardo's interest in young boys.

Few of the records of his earlier years are dependable; but we do have reliable evidence that he was tried for the corrupting of an unruly boy and was only partially acquitted. And when his diaries, amidst all their macrocosmic and microcosmic questionings and answers, sketch the arabesque of his life, we see emerging everywhere from his pages those blond heads which his drawings and paintings have immortalized. For the most part they are students—and what curly locks this one has, and what a loquacious fellow that other one must have

been. Between mathematical calculations of the pendulum, along with drawings of sluices and basins, we
can decipher how at Rome, instead of polishing his concave mirror for him, they ran off with the Swiss guards-
men of the pope, or on a bird hunt, or to a drinking
bout. And then again, immediately adjoining: "Ask
how skating is done in Flanders."

Generous, hospitable as an oriental, he gave the beautiful lads what he had, made them presents of his best
pages, which they signed and sold. And when they
stole from him, he stood for it, acting as though he had
noticed nothing. But he devotes an entire page to a list of
the things which a certain Giacomo pilfered from him
and his friends, and to an account of what this boy had
cost him in clothes, shoes, and belts. And along the edge,
in all clarity, we read: "Thievish, deceitful, selfish,
greedy. . . . How much does the boy cost me?"

As he and they grew older, most of them gradually
drifted away. Only two—Andrea Salaino and Melzi—
remained with him, as comrades, helpers, and friends.

And suddenly, in the later monologues he writes:
"Intellectual passion drives away all lusts."

Leonardo's art flows from the sources of this sublime
eroticism.

Since painting was by no means a monomania with
him, or even a predominant interest, he could at some
other period in the history of art have become a musician, even had he not constructed instruments of silver
and excelled as a flute-player. The truth is that no other
painters painted so musically as Correggio and Leonardo,
the two most delicate eroticists of the south.

But there is still a closer path from scientist to painter:

the path of observation. For his pure experimentation was no less pronouncedly visual than his painting. In this also he resembled Goethe, whose visual perceptions disturbed the equilibrium of his genius for twenty years and struggled to make of him a painter. Leonardo was always searching for pictures, precisely because he was searching for knowledge. Constantly, in his youth and in old age, he was seen with a sketch-book in his belt. When he began his work on anatomy by listing four ways of registering emotions through movement and expression, here the scientist was almost a painter. And when, according to the testimony of a contemporary, he followed odd-looking people halfway across the city in order to get their features accurately, here the painter is very nearly the scientist.

There is a passage in the monologues: "Giovannina, fantastic face, lives in Santa Catherina, in the hospital." To paint a character from the Bible, for an old man, a beggar, or a shepherd, he would go to the public squares and the drinking dens, where he would be most likely to meet such persons. And he would draw a type or an animal from observation a hundred times before turning to his picture to fix it there for all time. He is said to have brought home peasants from the market and got them drunk in order to draw them. At the same time he was looking for laws; while studying the facial traits, he recorded the transitions in the closing and opening of the eyelid, the wrinkling of the nose, the pouting of the lips, in laughing, sneezing, yawning, cramps, perspiration, weariness, hunger—always he looked for the cause behind the expression which he was painting.

While Michael Angelo, at times even under the same roof, was covering enormous walls with the colossi of his imagination, giving them their ultimate form and leaving them thus to glitter or pale through the centuries; and while Raphael's skillful eclectic fingers were at work to capture the absolute in beauty, Leonardo was the essayist, the relativist, a tester and a player. He declined to paint alfresco or in tempera, since he could not interrupt such work for "the sublest reflections," as he called them.

For when he painted, he must be able to abandon the oil picture suddenly whenever he felt a change of mood and the desire to study some aspect of nature elsewhere. From a cloister near Florence, which had ordered a Madonna of him and had been waiting several months for its completion, an ecclesiastic writes: "He is applying himself passionately to geometry, but he can't say a good word for the brush." Once—by the report of a Milanese, who saw him busy on the "Last Supper"—he painted the whole day, beginning at sunrise and standing on his scaffold without food or drink. Then again, he would not appear for days, or he would sit before the canvas for a couple of hours, silent and meditative, and then would leave again. Or he came into the church at midday after a ride on horseback, heated and excited, touched one of the figures with two strokes of his brush, and vanished.

Since he was a pure intellect, and only occasionally attempted to reduce his observations to pictures rather than to laws, he never wholly mastered his medium. As an inventor, his struggles with matter were victorious; as a painter he was continually in retreat. It is as though the technologist in him refused to govern the musical precincts of his art. To be sure, he was continually immersed in the problems of his material. For his "Battle of the Standard" at Florence he mixed the coarsest stucco as a ground, lit a coal fire beneath it in order to dry it out; the whole began to sweat, his work perished beneath his hands—but he promptly turned his back on it and left it.

By his experiments with the ground-colors, he ruined a Madonna for a gentleman of the Vatican. And when as the first step in a work for Leo Medici, he began preparing the varnish by an involved process of distilling oils and herbs, the merry pope said: "Alas, you will never finish. You are thinking of the end before you have begun!" Similarly, he left both the principal works of Milan in an unfinished state. Even in his own days the "Last Supper" had begun to vanish into the wall as the result of one of his obdurate experiments with the mixing of oils. The gigantic statue, which stood in clay for years in the courtyard of the Castello, was never cast because he insisted that four furnaces should first be constructed for smelting the bronze. New wars intervened; Il Moro at times lacked money and at times interest. And so nothing was left of this work, on which he had been engaged intermittently for sixteen years, but a dilapidated model which drunken marksmen later demolished with their arrows.

"Without sound theories," he wrote to himself, "one cannot manage well in the hazards of painting." As an artist, Leonardo the technologist was a victim of his technique; but it seems that he was a willing victim, for since he always had a vision of the completed whole he could readily interrupt the incomplete experiment. Even the few pictures from his hand which we call completed, he himself considered to have been left in an unfinished state. "The desire obstructed the work," said Petrarch.

And yet he loved this art more than all others; and after several pages of reasons why painting is supreme among the arts, he concludes with the proud exclamation: "We, in our art as painters, dare call ourselves the grandsons of God!"

A single opponent arose in this battleless life. While the era was replete with the artistic rivalry of the cities, the jealousies of the patrons, the intrigues of the schools, Leonardo in his private diaries never once criticized his competitors for fame. Without time or country as he was, the battles of the artists did not excite him any more strongly than the battles of Italy's duchies and republics, and these did not interest him at all. Through all sorts of factional broils, we see him living and working in peace, like a distinguished stranger.

Only one man, his great antipode, could have aroused him to emulation. And the Signory of the city in which they both were reared actually did call them into the lists together. It may have been more than an accident: it may have been the design of some Florentine senator to bring Michael Angelo and Leonardo together by having them paint the two walls of the great Council Hall. At least Leonardo took it in this way, even if we do mistrust a banal artists' legend connected with the statue of the "David." For here, and here only, in the "Battle of the Standard," this painter of shimmering mystery, this composer of secular rhapsodies, this sensualist in the grand manner, has plunged into the subject of motion— apparently to compete with the master of motion. He amassed an egregious tangle of fighting, tearing, shrieking men and beasts, enraged, ominous, and distorted to the point of madness.

Yet while the bathing soldiers on Michael Angelo's
wall stretched their naked limbs, Leonardo clothed all
his warriors. This melting flesh which he painted elsewhere was not made for war—so he felt—but for
pleasure alone. On the other wall the painter summoned
all his art in the rhythm of the arms and legs; but Leonardo laid chief emphasis upon the expressions of the
men's and horses' heads. Each an extreme of its type,
the painter of bodies and the painter of souls placed their
works opposite each other. Both works have been lost;
yet after half a century there was enough of Leonardo's
visible for Cellini to prize it as "the school of the entire
world." And the drawings of the old soldier and the
young soldier, their faces distorted with shouting, still
stand like watchmen turned to stone before this sunken
garden.

They could also be compared as sculptors, although
in this instance too their principal works remained incomplete. Michael Angelo's tomb of the Medici has survived only in fragments, and Leonardo's tomb of Tri-
vulzio only in sketches. Both found the same symbol of
sovereignty: both had slaves in chains bowing at the
feet of their heroes. These two masters, one of whom
bore within him a tragic human world and the other
a smiling realm of the gods, had this one melancholy
thought in common.

For this realm is a landscape projected from within.
And whatever visions he captured, whatever dreams he
converted into art, whatever magic figures he drew,
stemmed from that world. They seem to live in thinner
air; midway between knowledge and desire, their passions are intellectual passions. "Art," he writes in his

monologue, "creates the illusion of a divine beauty whose natural prototype has been destroyed by age or death."

And his realistic studies, the results of unceasing observation, though they were apparently intended merely as literal copies, carry us beyond accuracy. The counterplay of observation and clairvoyance which made Leonardo significant as an inventor, was of constant assistance to him in his art, where it has so pronounced an effect at decisive moments. For is not this transformation of a thing seen into an internal vision the very nature of art? Is there a better combination of endowments than an eye which can rest lovingly and understandingly upon the objects of nature, noting with greater and greater sharpness and silently recording the fluctuant connections between one detail and another—and a human heart, filled with an internal, ever-youthful melody, and veiling every clear perception with its own peculiar tonality? Given this—and the resultant record will be at once accurate and inventive, humble and independent. Even the most singular reflection of nature will, under such circumstances, reveal the stigma of the type, and yet in the copy of a flower done by an artist we can detect the evidences of a Divine intervention.

Leonardo drew a stone-cutter, a crow-bar, a dredging machine—and though these were without landscape, sky, or people, their wood and iron, their stone, wire, and plaster seem nothing less than living muscles, pulsing veins, and glowing flesh. The shadows play so musically along the cold and murderous edges of a cannon that no one who knows the madonnas of this master could fail to recognize the same hand here.

He would select the budding twig of an oak, or a forget-me-not, treating it in isolation as the Japanese artists of his day were doing unbeknown to him, and the result would be flooded with the same inward warmth and would envelop the observer in the same sweet redolence as the warmth and redolence of arms, breasts, and lips. The piece of a garment, laid sketchily across a thigh, a slight bit of material hardly amounting to more than a few folds, is so full of feeling that one might draw the face of the woman to whom this thigh is a part. Anatomical studies divided into squares and robbed of all illusion by the system of printed numerals in the corners, essays in proportion totally devoid of esthetic purpose, peer forth from the depths of the soul and live their own secret life independently and in defiance of their maker's will. None of Leonardo's great masterpieces brings us so close to an understanding of his processes as these studies whose unintended magic puts them beyond the sketches of every other master.

How each the Whole its substance gives, each in the other works and lives! Like heavenly forces rising and descending, their golden urns reciprocally lending. How these faces stream from the pages to make new harmonies with one another! There the elder Jacob, sketched for the "Last Supper," looks down, handsome in his fright, upon a castle drawn small in the corner, and seems of a sudden like a spirit, a great angel, who is calling upon the sleeping inhabitants of these towers to awaken. Alongside a hasty design of the "Last Supper," the mathematician had drawn circles in conflict with angles—and one cannot tell whether the mirror-writing on the bottom of the page applies to the magician at the table or the magic of the circle.

At times it is thought that this man lived by the laws
of contrast, and that he would have failed had he not
brought opposites together. In this way he put caricature next to beauty, not that a grotesque effect might result, but in order to make the marvelous still more un-
forgettable by emphasis. All these noses and mouths,
hydrocephalic heads and hunched backs which he jum-
bles in among his lovely youths are products of his perception, but also of his vision; and since they did not
originate in either mockery or madness they mean to us,
as they did to him, merely the observance of peculiar
accidents of nature.

Everything on this earth which has aged partakes in
Leonardo's work of the nature of caricature, and scru-
tinizes critically the heaven of eternal youth which lives
in his imagination. Thus he puts two profiles on a page,
each a separate study, unrelated to the other—and the
old man, with his seven hard lines as profile, seems to
be saying to the charming youth: Do you know that I
was once like you, and that some day you will be like
me?

To get the answer, we have but to place the portrait
of himself in old age alongside the superb version of
earlier youth.

Nine paintings are now recognized as his own. All the
others are doubtful; and since neither the Vienna picture nor the two in the Biblioteca Ambrosiana, neither
the Madonna Litta nor the Leda are up to his level, we
are willing to accept this verdict. Of the nine authentic
pictures, the "Jerome," the "Annunciation," and the
"Madonna Benois" are second-rate, and the "Adoration
of the Kings" is hardly begun. There are left not more
than five pictures which completely represent for us

Leonardo as a painter: the "Virgin of the Rocks," the
"Last Supper," "La Gioconda," "Saint Anne," and the
"Saint John"—while we might also recognize among the
authentic works of the master the brother-piece to the
"Saint John": "Bacchus." All these five or six pictures
were painted late in life: the "Virgin of the Rocks" and
the "Last Supper" in his forties, "La Gioconda" and
"Anne" after fifty, and "Bacchus" and "John" about
sixty or later. Except for the "Last Supper," all of Leonardo's masterpieces are in the Louvre.

All these pictures are pervaded with the same melody.
With the exception of the "John," each of his characters
arises from the same landscape, this dream-landscape of
greenish lakes and white waterfalls, of brush-covered
islands and cliffs magically blue. These are nocturnes
lighted by an unseen aurora. But his people are not native to these places; the veil-like garments of these delicate, placid creatures could not shield them from the
tempests which lie sleeping in such grottoes. It is purely
the symphony of the dream which binds man and landscape, man and man.

For they all resemble one another, much as though
they were brothers and sisters. And then again they resemble the figures of the drawings, even when the drawings are not preparatory studies for the paintings. "A
figure is not worth noting," he writes once in his monologues, "unless by some gesture it expresses the passion
of the soul." This sign-language is utilized most power-
fully in the "Last Supper," his one major group. Here a
dramatic moment heightens the expression of thirteen
men, although their agitation and the absence of women
take from the work the flower-like repose which elsewhere is so profound an aspect of the Master. This com-

pendium of emotional expressions is robbed of its full
effect as much by Christ's reproof as by the partial dem-
olition of his figure. It stands quite alone among Leonardo's works; even if we include the paintings by him
which have perished, it could at the outside be classed
only with the "Battle of the Standard." And the picture
cannot readily be grasped as a whole, but must be viewed
as a series of events.

That passion of the soul, which is the subject of his
meditations and which figures in all his paintings, is a
knowing passion. There is no suffering in Leonardo: he
painted Christ as a Wise Man; and we can more readily
understand why Leonardo left Him incompleted in the
"Last Supper" if we look at a faded, obliterated drawing
of the Thorn-crowned King in Venice. And there is no
innocence in Leonardo: the "Virgin of the Rocks" is a
fallen angel—and the other angel beside her looks out
knowingly at the observer. Neither Saint Anne nor her
daughter, nor the Christ child, nor even the John of the
"Last Supper," to say nothing of the others, show evidence of that high innocence which possessed the Um-
brian painters and which even Raphael sometimes mastered.

Yet Leonardo's figures are not worldly like the saints
of the Venetians. Rather, they live far removed from
strong light; they live in the regions of the intellect.
But they all understand love, and this is the passion of
the soul which their creator demands of them.

The same kind of love stirs in both his men and his
women. On a page of profile sketches of girls and boys,
one cannot always be sure of the sex. The heads of John,
Philip, and Matthew in the "Last Supper" could be the
heads of girls, but the angel in the "Virgin of the Rocks"

could very easily be a boy. Bacchus, and above all the
John in Paris, are pure hermaphrodites. It is not until
the men grow beards, as with the elder Jacob of the
"Last Supper," not until a wealth of love-nights has
compressed the mouths of his women deeper into the
flesh of the cheeks, that the sexes are differentiated; but
even then they retain in common an element of spontaneous sweetness which speaks through the browless,
long-lashed, ever-knowing eyes, through these always
lightly trembling lips.

And yet, in the midst of their sensuousness, these same
figures have a super-sensual trait in common: it is the
modicum of knowledge in their pleasure, the sadness of
dreams fulfilled. It is the trait of a bewitching melancholy which sets Leonardo's creatures apart from all
others, and raises them above all sensuous painting, even
above the charming figures of Correggio. All of them
remember their master's self-admonishment: "Decipi-
mur votis et tempore fallimur et mos deridet curas."

He seldom painted men at their prime of life; they are
either youthful or aging. The virile type is never prominent. But he did depict mature women, since they did
not affect him erotically: in particular as the Gioconda,
as Anne, and in the red chalk drawing of the duchess
Isabella d'Este, who belongs among his immortals.

The Gioconda, on which he is said to have painted for
four years, and the Isabella, which he may have drawn
in an hour, are the two of his women most distinct from
each other; and precisely because even these have some
unescapable trait of kinship, we recognize the one man
author to both. La Gioconda is more suggestive, and
stranger—made more attractive by the landscape behind

her hair, by the ironically sweet language of eyes turned
almost full upon us, by the charm of lips inured to love,
and by her calm assertion of experience.

Isabella, ten years younger, with more race and less
personality, generally firmer, more seclusive and expect-
ant, turns from us, despising the unknown observer at
whom the other woman had smiled. With her averted
glance, and her powerful but immobile features, she is
less captivating. But this queenly neck, caught in a single
line, this tumble of metallic hair which crowns her like
a helmet, the clarity of her eyes and the boldness of her
posture—in short, the entire freedom of her splendid
figure, speaks less of the painter than of his era; and
more thoroughly than the most famous pictures of
women of that time, it preserves for subsequent centuries a type of high-strung womanhood firm in her
grasp on life.

Between them, and perhaps beyond them, soars the
figure of Saint Anne. Related to La Gioconda, superior
to her though hardly older, she sums up in her mature
smile all the spiritual adventure and love-enchantment
that has ever been painted; and as she looks at her daughter and the angel, there seems to be more retrospection
than hope in her contemplation of the generations. This
painting, the "Gioconda," and the "John," which are
now assembled on the walls of the same high room, ulti-
mately contain all that the prophet sank into human
picture.

In the "John" he seems for the last time to recapture
the vivacity of his youth. With a mouth which might
have belonged to La Gioconda's eldest son, with such eyes
as might have tried to fascinate the mother, with breast
and arms which seem more natural to a woman in eve-

ning dress than to a man, he dares to point upwards
with his voluptuous finger, thus in the name of his
Master promising Bacchic beatitude to those who have
already enjoyed such, here below.

He was an old man when he painted this youth. He
was then living in his old castle, attended by a servant
and the oldest of his favorites. He was living like an enchanter. To be sure, he was called court painter to the
King of France, who honored him in his letters as *"notre
très chier at bien aimé Léonard,"* collected all of Leonardo's work he could find, and even tried without success to remove to Paris the wall on which the "Last
Supper" was painted.

Yet the master lived in seclusion. As weathered as
the hundred-year-old Faust, he spied himself again in
the mirror; and though he copied himself imperturb-
ably, he wrote in his diary: "O Time, devourer of all
things; envious old age, which destroys all! When Helen
saw herself flaccid and wrinkled in the mirror, she wept
and thought: How have I twice been the cause of
plunder!"

Finally his right arm was lamed, and he devoted himself exclusively to invention. A Spanish cardinal found
him in the midst of his dissections and compounds,
retorts and machines—and when permitted to look
through the manuscripts the cardinal wrote: "If all this
were to see the light of day, how great our delight and
our profit!" Now the old man, near the close of his
career, tried to collect and order his material. He did
bring together a few treatises, but it was too late: the
constant experimentation of a lifetime could not at the
last be hastily assembled into the systems which he had

always despised. When one has been consistently a learner, one does not become a teacher in old age. It was too late, and it was also too early, for he was still constructing and planning unceasingly: now, in accordance with his earlier ideas, he wanted to build embankments for the river near him, drain the swampland, and reclaim areas now lying under water.

Then he felt that his strength was diminishing. He apportioned his property among his friends, dignifiedly put all his affairs in order, and in the spring when he felt that death was near, the dying prophet wrote in his monologue:

"Man, always festively awaiting the new spring and the new summer, complains that the longed-for things are slow in coming, and fails all the while to notice that he is longing for his own end. Yet precisely this wish is the true quintessence of the elements which feel themselves imprisoned in the body through the soul and wish constantly to return to their maker. But I would have you know: this same wish is also the true spirit of nature, and man is but a cosmos in miniature."

SHAKESPEARE

Lascivious grace in whom all ill well shows,
Kill me with spites; yet we must not be foes.

SHAKESPEARE's life is hidden in darkness. For all the efforts of the scholars, it is still hardly more than a legend —and the dozen dates, letters, and documents that we do possess give us a silhouette rather than a portrait. As in the case of Leonardo, the records of his private life are missing, although there are biographical clews in Shakespeare's writings. The story of the poet's emotional career were better left untold. It lies beneath crackling, sparkling ice, as the reader speeds across the surface of his work; and where a crevasse opens into the abyss, as in the epilogue to "The Tempest," we pull back in terror and avert our eyes. To all appearances, his work is extremely impersonal. A superman like Balzac produced it. It is the direct opposite of the work of Rembrandt, Goethe, or Byron. In thirty-six dramas he remade a world; on his narrow boards he completed a cycle of creation, and in the end he seems to have sunk back exhausted and completely emptied, the used-up vessel of manifold life, like an all-too-fertile mother.

What wonder that some have thought him the son of his Queen, while in the opinion of others he never lived at all, but was purely a creation of the fancy. For even his pictures, which are severe and reserved, seem to typify features which place us before new difficulties. We have evidence here that he suffered, perhaps even that he struggled, but hardly that he enjoyed. We catch

no glimpses down those secret passes to a great man's
heart where, as in the sulphur pits, magic grottoes un-
fold in twilight. What was the nature of his passions?
Did he, through choice or compulsion, actually duplicate some of those experiences which genius is able to
sense in advance? Did his narrow life as actor, proprietor, husband, and father in any way resemble that of
the powerful characters which he allowed to act, love,
betray, murder, or die in his name?

We know hardly anything definite about Shakespeare's tremendous inner life; and our imagination is
free to spin a network of conjecture about the dozen
definite facts we do have concerning him—much as with
the life of the prophet of Milan, who painted the smiling women.

Suddenly light flashes through the darkness. At the
end of his collected works, as an appendix—or even
omitted in many editions—there are two youthful epics
and a set of sonnets. These are usually considered as
much inferior to the dramas. Generally misunderstood
and frequently attacked, they are for the most part renounced by England's poets; and extrinsic issues make
them an object of controversy among scholars whose
solutions, even when they are adequate, throw no light
upon the soul of the poet. Wordsworth alone felt the
significance of this small book when he said: "With this
key Shakespeare unlocked his heart." Yes, here in these
graceful rhymes all the passions of the man are laid before us; here lie concealed the maddest love letters, written at the close of his youth.

The philologists see it all differently. Even though
these verses may glow to the point of scorching us, they
are looked upon as "exercises of the imagination with

which the poet entertained himself and his friends, especially since such themes were then the fashion." Another man brings evidence in several hundred pages that a lady, an untitled woman, and two young nobles, whom he describes, giving names and station, lived out a novel, and in the course of it one or another of them ordered sonnets from the well-known playwright of the Globe Theater, which he delivered singly or in groups as the occasion warranted. A third is disturbed by the question as to whether the rebellion of the Earl of Essex is involved, and whether the opponent in the competition was Marlowe or Chapman. A fourth cannot understand why the poet, instead of being satisfied with a hecatomb, wrote on to number 154. But all of them, who believe generally that some experience formed the basis of the poems, astutely avoid the question: Who is the boy, and who the woman, to whom they refer?

Thus the famous dedication which stands at the head of the first printing confuses rather than clarifies. These highly insignificant lines from a publisher to a Mr. W. H. have become a puzzle whose solution would produce nothing of value. Or do we know anything when we say that this young man was the Earl of Pembroke rather than the Earl of Southampton? Or did this dedication belong not to the begetter but to the collector of the sonnets, some dealer or other, perhaps the poet's brother-in-law? An Englishman has flatly demonstrated that the dark lady was the Catholic Church; another that the boy was not a boy, but Queen Elizabeth herself, to whom her poet writes as to a man in order to emphasize her strength and majesty. A German author proclaimed them the cries of a mortal to an immortal. But his colleague laid it all out in this wise: the sonnets are merely the creation of a free poetic fancy, for if they were the result of feelings experienced in actual life, then the greatest poet would have to appear before us as weak and unsteady, and deserving of scant respect.

And this is the point of issue which divides the generations. To us of today this glowing book, this collection of feverish pages from a diary, furnishes the most welcome testimony as to how passion once rushed into this superhuman soul, once broke on these rocky shores. But one should not be alienated by the formalisms and conventions of the work: he must think of the eternal notes beating beneath the wigs and ruffles which disguise the profound humanness of Mozart. A trim baroque park does not mean to us that everything beneath the soil is equally well ordered; we can imagine the unseen roots struggling as hungrily and avidly in their plot of earth as the roots of an untamed forest.

For beneath the patent uniformity of these fourteen-liners, beneath the smooth surface, there are the sighs and tremors, the groaning, quaking, and rejoicing of a man in love. If the literary fashion of his age led him to accept the somewhat jangling and unpliant form of the simplified sonnet, this is merely the expression of his trade and his period: Napoleon's love letters often read like military dispatches. This poet's fate had the same touch of ironic melancholy about it as underlies his own later comedies.

He loves and is deceived. This new Prometheus, who formed men out of the wax of history or legend and infused into them the fire of his breath until they came to life, pines and serves, pays court, grows angry, and bids successively for the favors of a boy and of a mature woman. We know nothing about them; and there is nothing of importance to be known, except that he was beautiful and blond, decadent and a noble; but she was dark, wild, pleasure-loving, and somewhat of a gypsy. He becomes wholly enamored of them both; they betray him, first individually and then together. Both, with native and impulsive cynicism, turn from him, and perhaps turn towards him, without ever a suspicion of his intellect. Distraught by love and jealousy, he runs a gamut of emotions, cajoling or threatening, hesitant or eager. And yet when he is betrayed and totally abandoned, he rises with the thirst of youth to so much beauty, so much refinement, that he threatens to exhaust himself in love-hate and to explode with madness.

The poet, who was always negligent in the publication of his works, could surely not have assembled even the least turbulent of these poems, to say nothing of publishing them. Further, all outward evidence would point to the contrary: such as the thoroughly disorganized text, the dedication from the publisher, his unliterary, masculinely stylized age—the book appeared seven years before his death—and above all the desire not to represent his love affair, the parties to which must have been known to certain circles in London, with the gesture of the confessor. Thus, we are more inclined to believe that in order to injure Shakespeare and the young earl an opponent published these poems, copies of which had been in the hands of friends for years. The mad years were over in which the poet dared frighten the bourgeois with the wild Ariosto-like songs of Venus and Adonis which did, it is true, pass the censorship of the Archbishop of Canterbury, although they were cited in a contemporary poem among the household utensils of his cocotte as a stimulant to seduction.

His contemporaries, although they were accustomed to sonnet sequences, and in particular to sequences involving men, admired the intensity of this collection. Then they were eclipsed, along with the dramas; but when the dramas returned to favor the sonnets were still neglected. Who reads them today? Who can find his way about in this trim park where all paths seem alike, and where any one who tries to walk here without a guide is wearied by their uniformity?

Since the arrangement of the sonnets was not made by the poet himself, later ages may, without encroaching on the rights of the individual pieces, attempt their rearrangement without fear of being more at fault than the original publisher. This task has long since been undertaken by English, French, and German scholars. Even on their republication thirty years after the first appearance, each sonnet was given a title.

The sonnets are by no means of equal value. Sometimes they express a mood, at other times they are hardly more than conceits—and a third of the poems must be omitted in order to convey the full force of this passionate story. Then one hears it reverberate. The first group, which is the most moral one, is also the least interesting. Perhaps it was ordered by a doting mother who was anxious for her pleasure-loving boy to behave well in early marriage. Then there are others which resemble monologues and are brought into an artificial relationship with the rest by a sudden twist at the end.

But the deeply-felt ones are also perfect as genuine occasional poetry. The poet cries out against the ignominy of his times; he runs against the wall of death which relentlessly encircles the garden of life; at one moment he suns himself in eternal fame, and in the next

he despises all striving; he complains of his plebeian
origin, and then points to his calling with professional
pride; ambition and envy, the pain of unrequited love,
and the delay of justice torture him like his own Danish
prince—and the reader feels that Shakespeare the man
is here. We listen to his heartbeat; we are enthralled by
this genuinely Shakespearean drama, while the poet
kneels before beauty, while genius humbles itself before
a corrupt dazzling youth, while the delights of a woman
skilled in love break upon his shore, and while at the
last the aging enchanter runs after his two laughing
betrayers, after these two simpletons—gasping, despised,
loving and hating, wholly the fool and wholly the poet.

Neither his marriage, nor his purchase of property,
nor even the burning of the theater, affected him as
profoundly as this experience. And while the universe
was mirrored in the palace within, and projected back
in images on the screen without, this adventure from
without seized him by the neck, shook him, and racked
him. This was the fate of Shakespeare.

REMBRANDT

REMBRANDT'S SELF-PORTRAIT

When I need relief from my work,
I seek not honor, but freedom.

IN all history, there is but one artist who combines all
the elements of self-portraiture: he alone depicts the
various stages of a man's evolution. His self-portraits
silently display a life: the yearning, despair, success, and
tragedy of Rembrandt van Rijn. Rembrandt's life is so
accurately disclosed in his series of self-portraits that one
can find here a record of all his suffering and his elation.

Eighty-four self-portraits are now considered genuine, and fifty-eight of these are paintings. He painted
the first when he was twenty-one, the last when he was
sixty-three. During the intervening twenty-four years
exactly twice as many copies of himself were produced.

In his first picture, a young man examines the world
with astute eyes—but the senses are sleeping. In the last,
when the senses are again asleep, his eyes are turned in-
wardly. At the same time he painted his last work: "The
Return of the Prodigal Son." There is more of a human
story in this series of pictures than will be found in
Rembrandt's actual biography.

In his early twenties he is somewhat uncertain, drop-
ping his head and eyes in confusion. His mouth is firmly
closed and secretive. But his eyes dart forth like the dove
from the closed ark, scouting to see what land may have
emerged. That earnestness of which youth alone is capable pervades him, such earnestness as old age is always

struggling to regain. Also, the vacillation and instability of youth are manifest.

Next he appears to himself as a beardless and passionate boy, with noble lips. And on another morning of the same year, he made himself a helmet of hair, raised his eyebrows, allowed a derisive smile to play about the corners of his mouth, and tried by dint of scanty beard and mustache to set before himself and the world the evidences of his sudden maturity. The next day he played the smirking, crafty peasant, obscuring his genius by his impudence. It was perhaps on the same afternoon that the etching needle examined in the mirror a young diplomat with a long, curly wig. And a few days later he discovered for the first time that gold chains laid about the neck over black velvet, and a barret with a delicate arabesque and a feather with a long baroque sweep, plus the gesture of the complete nobleman—that this can at least make a mask which not every one can don or doff at will. Thus his imagination riots at twenty-three, anticipating life, knowing the feel of events before their occurrence.

Soon thereafter Saskia came to him—the only person in the world by this name, just as no one else has ever been called Rembrandt. She glided down to him gently, a fulfilled dream, an inspiriting vision, a lovely image, each day astonishing, modest and passionate at night, intellectual without pedantry, changeable, but harmonious, endowed with every charm. When one thinks of how the artist looked at her, one thinks also of Othello. He was enchanted, exalted, and enriched, bound to her by all his senses—and the sight of her each day wrung from him these many pictures of her, which are the documents of a profound affection.

He saw the lovely creature in his company, and at the beginning he twice painted the two of them. Once, having appeared when she was putting on her jewels, he told her to put on twice as many, sat her down before the mirror and showed her how light and graceful her hands could be as she paused, in adjusting an earring, to admire it. Then, so that she might smile, he bade her watch herself in the mirror. He himself cocked over one ear a hat with a long feather, hung several chains about his neck, and stood waiting, ready to hand her a string of pearls. But imperceptibly he moves away in his thoughts; he no longer sees his charming Saskia, and still less he sees the observer: he sees the group, and paints. But in the other of these two pictures, which has been called "The Breakfast" and which could be called "The Midst of Life," she is sitting on his knee—and with rakish impudence, as lightly as the King of Life, he turns too obviously towards the observer, towards the world, and she too must turn her head. Sword and tankard are gleaming, the bright wine is shaking in the high goblet, the feathers are waving, the large hand of the artist is laid across Saskia's hip in firm possessiveness, and the lips speak laughingly: I see your head no longer, Gorgon!

During this period he painted himself twelve times in one year. The absorptive expression reappears in his eyes, yet he manifests a type of composure which comes with the knowledge of beauty and the sorrow of fulfillment. Again his mouth is closed—but this time only to the world. For her, the beautiful escutcheon of his fancy, these lips have surely spoken words which, if she could not hear them, she could feel like the pulse of her own child.

Now he basks in happiness, or what people call happiness. He has wealth and reputation, and is still in those years when it is a joy to give the world a spectacle. He holds himself like a prince. He was not born so. Chains, placed decoratively and sparingly and not with the indiscriminate enthusiasm of the Turk, give him a new claim on our admiration.

His hair is well trained; his beard is soft and fashionable. Embroidered jacket, furs, and collars are worn not as a mask, but to befit his station and his bearing. Now, he feels, I am a citizen of importance; I am a redoubtable warrior. He tilts his enormous plumed hats, then replaces them with helmets; he hangs golden chains across his breast; and once, noticing that the two sharp feathers of his barret cast shadows like ghosts upon the wall, he painted these shadows too. Whereby he painted his future.

Four years later, he turns from his observance of a profound and ardent world to rediscover himself; and again he is seized by the desire to depict himself. He did so four times. In the unusually beautiful picture of himself at thirty-two his finery is sparse and subdued. He is more composed, more representative, more melancholy. The man of genius always anticipates his destiny.

At the same time in England a self-portrait was produced which might have been the text to this picture. Hamlet.

Then Saskia died.

At once he laid aside his finery and his mundane mask. The time of defiance, of the waking dream, is over; again the man stands alone. Saskia is dead. In these years he sees himself as a burgher: prudent, substantial, retiring. Did we not know these features, we should mistake him for a merchant, or sometimes for a member of the city council. Lugubriously in his dark domino he attends the masked ball of life. But he paints Saskia once more after death. And this touching picture, this greeting which he himself exacts from the dead for the living, is like a self-portrait of his soul. Then, over a space of five years, the picture-diary is silent.

When he next paints himself, he has begun to develop the expression which we usually associate with Rembrandt, just as we generally turn with impatience to the last pictures of Goethe. He is again dressed with care, and in unusual garments. But as a lansquenet he has about him something of a sorrowing knight; and in the self-portrait in the possession of Lady Rothschild his bitterness is plainly in evidence. Then he is silent for five more years.

Lo, in the middle of his fifties, the youth with the large questing eyes appears again. Again he is beardless and wears his velvet cap, but two long folds flank the mouth like watchmen. In another picture of the same period he is even short-necked and sturdy, as though he ate and drank plentifully in order to sleep well. At the same time his charming son Titus rises before him—the heir to Saskia's beauty, the heir to early knowledge, melancholy and appealing.

Meanwhile he had taken a second wife, who was a good woman and said little. Deliberately, he took his stand before the world. In fact his expression was sometimes so resolute that it might better have suited a military commander. He still had a grip on himself, although his affairs were in confusion. He was self-contained, but one blow might destroy him. When the collapse of his finances occurred, his artificial swagger soon broke down, and over night he became an old man.

One year after he had looked at such a determined Rembrandt, he saw an impoverished, embittered old man who was sitting in his house-coat, since all his fine garments had been sold at auction. He saw that he was unshaven, that his shirt was worn, and that his face was haggard. He took a staff in his left hand and painted Rembrandt the solitary. This is Rembrandt at the beginning of his last stage, and the picture is the first of his final series: self-portraits of satanic melancholy. For now he paints himself again seven times in one year. Of these pictures, in the one at the Louvre he is the most terrifying; the Munich one shows him as indigent, the Aix one as frantic. The wrinkles of his forehead are increased; the collar is turned up high in order to conceal the fallen neck; some of his teeth are missing; and the large eye looks out helplessly.

Three years later he can hardly be recognized. There is something flaccid, almost weak, about his face. Yet as though attracted by the strains of long familiar music, he returns to his mirror, to the dance. He pulls himself together once more, resumes his old-time gestures of nobility. Nothing is left but a white night-cap and a fur; yet he transforms these into the purple of a king at once uncrowned and deposed, his bearing and his expression are such. And here for the first time, near the close of his life, after so many mirror pictures, so many different poses and moods, Rembrandt paints himself for the first and only time as a painter.

Once in his middle period he had etched himself in

the act of etching; yet the little sheet in no way shows the artist, neither as inspired, as studying, nor as working.

Rather, we are allowed to notice as little as possible. Not only his drawing, but also the paper on which he is drawing, are invisible—and only one little corner of the pencil indicates that he is not reading. But now, as an old man, on the other side of life, after having painted his own portrait eighty times, he finally seized the traditional symbols of his power—palette, brush, and paint-stick—in his left hand, while he rested his right hand on his hip, thereby demanding of the world what it once gave him freely without the asking.

Two more times he was lured into painting his head. Contrary to his earlier custom, he now omitted the decrepit body; he knew that now the face alone was his. In the Carstanjen picture, he laughs out from his frame at the spectator with diabolic coquetry and pokes with his stick against a mystically cold creature lost in shadow. Here he has dared to paint his demon.

Now, after the second wife, he had also buried his son, the one remaining symbol of his vanished dream. Yet instead of shattering him, this possibly gave him a kind of strength—as though he now understood his fate and knew that there were no more blows in store for him. He puts on his old cap attentively. He finds the pallor of his face more noticeable than his wrinkles. Mouth and eyes lie deep. The lips remain firmly closed, as they were in his earliest youth. Then they would not disclose what they expected of life; and now they kept silent as to what they had experienced.

But the hands, which created all this, are no longer visible.

The greatest self-portraitist known not only to painting but to all art, more profoundly lost in his ego than even Byron or other analytical tragedians, he concludes the record of his career and his work without a sign, without emblems, a man without a mask.

So at the end prototype and copy fall together as though in deep likeness, and whoever wrote the psychological history of the self-portrait would automatically write a history of the other self.

For the artist continually strives to meet himself again in his art, yet he never meets himself corporeally as in his own figure. Play and counterplay are familiar to him; he continually feels the other self; and he would be as unfruitful as it is, did not his God compel him to copy it.

In this one work alone the great inimical powers are united: the demon calls forth the genius, and the genius gives us his image.

VOLTAIRE IN EIGHTEEN TABLEAUX

*I am as slippery as an eel, as lively as a
lizard, and as tireless as a squirrel.*

IN an upholstered rococo room in Paris an elegant old
woman, shrunken but vivacious, is sitting by the window, blinking and smiling in the sun. It is noon, the
time for the daily visit of the Abbé, who composes
verses, understands women, and writes on music. As he
enters he is leading by the hand a boy with alert features, the same boy whose verses he had told her about
the day before. Recently, so the story went, an *Invalide*
who had served during the more brilliant years of the
now ailing Roi Soleil appeared in the school to ask the
teacher to write him a memorial poem to the Dauphin.
The teacher being absent, the boy promptly sat down
and wrote him a poem in twenty verses. This had been
handed about, and had been subsequently shown to the
old lady.

Now as he stands facing her, his aggressiveness
is subdued. He hesitates, and respectfully kisses the
wrinkled hand on which, as he perhaps already knows,
the lips of Molière had rested half a century ago, when
this hand still exhaled the fragrance of a Venus. Now
she smiles at the young man; and a year later, when her
will is opened, it will be found that she has left him a
legacy of two thousand francs with which he is to buy
books. Ninon de Lenclos, eighty-four years of age, and
the ten-year-old Voltaire.

The twenty-one-year-old littérateur is sitting in a café storming and raging against King and Court, and in particular deriding the dissolute Orléans. His auditor, an officer whom he has met by accident, imperceptibly draws him out more and more. The young political poet begins to exaggerate and in an excess of zeal he boasts of having composed certain French and Latin lampoons which were being circulated anonymously at that time and had in reality been written by some one else. The spy promptly reported all this, the Regent learned of it, and a few days later Voltaire is sitting in the Bastille, where he has brought from his parents' house two volumes of Homer, two lace handkerchiefs, a hood, two collars, a night-cap, and a bottle of carnation perfume.

He sits in the tower for eleven months; and since he is not allowed to have paper and ink, he writes his verses with a piece of lead, between the lines of a book.

The Comédie Française is overcrowded. Court and society are divided into two parties, each outdoing the other in pearls and stones and in expectancy and malice. The "Œdipus" of young Voltaire is about to be performed; and the duchess of Maine and her faction hope that the regent and his daughter, who as every one knows are living as man and wife, will feel the force of their poetic opponent's innuendoes, like the royal pair in Hamlet, and scandalously collapse. Perhaps they will be hissed. But Orléans is more suave than that, and the times are less tragic than in legendary Denmark. He smiles placidly beside his daughter; the duchess sits proudly under her canopy, surrounded by her thirty ladies. She makes no attempt to hide from her father the evidences of her pregnancy—and as the tragedy progresses they themselves give the signal for applause. Voltaire, behind the scenes, is in high spirits, for he feels that he has scored a victory. Finally he has himself made up as a page and helps carry the train of the high priest in order to observe the public from the stage.

When at the end the applause lets loose (for there are still more Œdipean pairs in the company) and the author shows himself in the *loge* of a marshal, the chorus calls up from below to the marshal's beautiful wife: "Kiss him!" And she does so, amid universal rejoicing.

In the *loge* of the great Adrienne Lecouvreur one winter evening Voltaire meets a young noble who is irritated to find the lady in the company of this bourgeois littérateur. "Just what is your real name," he asks sarcastically, since Voltaire had merely adopted this name, "Monsieur de Voltaire or simply Monsieur Arouet?"

"My name begins with me; yours ends with you!" the poet retorts. The chevalier raises his stick, Voltaire reaches for his sword, the actress feigns unconsciousness.

But some days later when he was stepping from the palace of a duke, where he had been an intimate guest for several years, he was beset by a pack of rowdies and beaten while the chevalier, a few steps away, looked on and laughed. As soon as the victim was able to make his escape, he returned to the dining room of the duke to call upon him for assistance, since such an outrage involved the duke as his host.

But the duke refused to help him. Though his intellectual attainments had made him a favorite with the high nobility and a protégé of the woman who was the real ruler of France, and though he had felt himself set for a great diplomatic career for which he was in so many ways fitted, Voltaire saw that he had not even scratched the surface of class prejudice. Now he practiced fencing, from morning till night; he repeatedly challenged the chevalier, and publicly insulted him, but the man's relatives, many of whom were cardinals and princes, contrived to prevent the duel, preferring to have the bourgeois first arrested and then banished.

Thus he came to England.

On one of the narrow side streets of Paris there stands an old house which belongs to a grain-dealer. Voltaire, towards the close of his thirties, has returned, and after a period of hiding he now makes no further attempt to conceal his presence. He moves about from place to place, and finally locates with this grain-dealer, whom he also gets to act as his broker in grain speculations. In his quarters here Voltaire receives every one. Today the Duchess of Saint-Pierre and her friend are visiting him; and they have brought with them a woman who, though not exactly beautiful, is very striking in appearance. She has a large nose and a lovely mouth; her chin is firm —and she has clear green eyes, and her high pure forehead is framed by black hair. She enters unpretentiously—yet she is highly educated and has had a world of experience. The poet is quick to recognize that, for all her knowledge and her intellectuality, the Marquise du Châtelet is profoundly passionate. As they sit down to an improvised meal, he proffers this little stanza:

> Ciel! que j'entendrais s'écrier,
> Marianne, ma cuisinière,
> Si la Duchesse de Saint-Pierre,
> Du Châtelet et Forcalquier,
> Venait souper dans ma tanière!

From this evening on, the "divine Emilie" remained his intimate for seventeen years, first as his mistress and later as friend and patroness. For whole years he lives in the family château on the border of Loraine so as to be able, during his periodic persecutions, to get out of the country at a moment's notice.

In a barren room of a castle at Cleves a frail man of twenty-eight, wrapped in a Prussian riding-cloak, is lying in a fever. He is waiting for the arrival of his idol, as he has been waiting for the last four years. He has been writing him letters both in verse and prose which contained the most passionate eulogies, comparing him with Apollo and Socrates, with Cicero, Pliny, and Agrippa. Yet the Frenchman has not come. He has been holding him off with the baldest flattery, until the title which this man was due to inherit should become a certainty. He has called up the names of Trajan and Virgil, Titus and Augustus, in order to tell him how highly he thinks of him. Now, when they finally meet, the German is down with intermittent fever.

But the younger man's emotions at the sight of the master are so intense that the fever abates, and for three days these two men, despite their fundamental differences, enjoy their first intellectual encounter: Frederick and Voltaire.

At the table of Richelieu, who was friendly to the poet and resembled him in intellect and cynicism, in chivalry and craftiness, they are discussing critically a new glorification of the Maid of Orléans; and it is suggested that Voltaire, who is present, could have handled this subject much more ably. The story of a barmaid, he

answers smilingly, who abandons her tavern to die at
the stake is purely a subject for satire! They prevail
upon him; he retires, he finds the first four cantos, and
shortly afterwards reads them to the same company.
Every one applauds and presses him to continue.

This is the beginning of "La Pucelle," one of his
boldest works, which he treats like a hidden vice, like
a talisman, for years making it the secret repository of
his free thinking and his cynicism, himself disguising
the copies of the poem so as not to pass as its author,
though it did none the less go the rounds of Paris society and became unmistakably allied with the name
of Voltaire.

Versailles. Voltaire is fifty. He promptly turns his
attention to those modes of the day in which he alone
became immortal. Today, on the little court stage in
the palace, in the presence of the King and Queen, the
Dauphin and the Infanta, chevaliers, princes, and cardinals, they are giving a performance, a fashionable
petit-rien, ballet and text by musicians, dancers, and
painters, the scoffer Voltaire having contributed nothing but the words. The commission to do this work for
the court had been procured for him through the influence of a woman of bourgeois birth who loved his
works and was now omnipotent: Pompadour. Voltaire
as national poet in the stalls of the royal palace.

"Versailles, April 1, 1743. In consideration . . . His
Majesty has found no one more deserving of being distinguished by an honorary title than Sieur Arouet de
Voltaire, who by the superiority of his talents and by
his enduring industry has made the most rapid progress
in all those sciences which he has studied."

Smiling to himself, he pockets his new annuity of 2000 pounds, and secretes the verses:

Mon Henri quatre, et ma Zaïre,
Et mon Américaine Alzire,
Ne m'ont valu jamais un seul regard du roi:
J'avais mille ennemis avec très peu de gloire.
Les honneurs et les biens pleuvent enfin sur moi
Pour une farce de la Foire.

Gambling table of the Queen at Fontainebleau. Voltaire's friend, the Marquise du Châtelet, loses 400 louis d'or. He helps her out with the 200 which he still has left and she loses them. A servant gets another 200 from the nearest money-lender at a high rate of interest; a friend scrapes together 180 more. The lady, warned in vain by Voltaire, loses it all; 84,000 francs are gone. Voltaire, an unwilling spectator, ventures to say to her in English that she has not observed that she was playing with cheats.

Which is the truth, but this is the table of the Queen. The same night they both are forced to flee, in order to avoid drastic consequences.

A duchess houses him in a castle not far off, but she is so uneasy that for three months he has to remain in a remote room with the door locked and the shutters bolted. Each night at two he is brought to the bedroom of the old duchess, where he finds a dinner waiting for him and reads to the lady what he has written during the day. In this way he turns out five short novels.

Castle Commerci. In an old park. They are the guests of the King of Poland, who has been holding court here for a time with his friend. The Marquise, who is now beginning her forties, had ceased to be the mistress of Voltaire ten years ago, for Voltaire aged rapidly so far as women were concerned. Though she has always remained his intimate friend, she has recently fallen head over heels in love, in an affair which was to be her last. The man is shallow and negligible, ten years her junior, a Monsieur de St. Lambert, who is also the lover of the King's mistress.

This evening Voltaire, who is now fifty-four years old, leaves his rooms just before dinner and enters his friend's apartments unannounced. He finds her in a very intimate position with the young man. Scene, accusations, bitterness, decision to leave this very night. His valet, in the interests of a reconciliation, sees to it that a coach is unavailable. In the night he finally hears a conversation between the two of them, who have been cronies now for over fifteen years. For the Marquise has hunted up her friend and is trying to placate him.

Voltaire: "Do you want me to believe you after what I have seen with my own eyes? I have sacrificed health, prosperity, every advantage for you, and you deceive me!"

Marquise: "I love you as much as ever, yet—for a long time you have complained that your strength was weakening. That is deplorable, still I must consider your health. Since you yourself say that you could do nothing for my comfort without injury to your own, how can you be angry with me when one of your friends assumes certain of your responsibilities?"

Voltaire: "You are right. But hereafter be careful that it doesn't happen under my very eyes!"

The next evening his rival appears before him, and begs him to excuse his impetuosity. Voltaire: "My son, I alone am in the wrong. You are in the happy age when one can love women and appeal to them. Take advantage of this brief period. I am an old man, and an invalid, and am no longer fitted for such pastimes!" The third evening they all sup as usual with the mistress of the King. Several months later when his friend is with child and they are all three trying to decide whether the married man shall be named as father, Voltaire says: "We will simply include the child among Madame's miscellaneous works."

She is brought to bed, and Voltaire is near by, having refused the most pressing invitations of the King of Prussia in order that he might be present to comfort his friend at the birth of his rival's child. Every one in the château is cheerful. Suddenly, after a week, she has an attack of fever and dies. Husband, lover, and friend stand at her deathbed: then Voltaire goes slowly down the château stairs. At the foot of the stairs he falls, knocking his head against the flagging. His rival hurries to him, and picks him up unconscious. When he awakes, he looks at the young man and says: "You have killed her!"

In Potsdam a Berlin *Schutzjude* lends the famous Frenchman a couple of diamonds which the poet intends to wear when acting the part of Cicero in a play of his to be given before the King. Frederick has had Voltaire with him for several months now, and has appointed him a Prussian chamberlain with an annuity of 20,000 francs. But Voltaire has always depended more on financial transactions for his living than on the uncertain income from his books, most of which appeared anonymously. There is some mention made of Saxony tax receipts, the purchase of which is strictly forbidden in Prussia, but on which one can, at the present rate of exchange, realize enormous profits. Voltaire fails to distinguish between Berlin and Paris; and thinking that here too a favorite of the king is immune from such rulings, he sends the Jew to Dresden to buy him Saxon papers for 40,000 francs. The King is secretly informed of this, and flies into a rage.

A long lawsuit is vigorously conducted by Voltaire, who offers a different explanation for the whole matter in order to defend his honor at court. The affair is finally settled by compromise, but in the eyes of the King it casts a lasting shadow upon the person of Voltaire.

When another incident, Voltaire's anonymous attack upon Maupertuis, his fellow-countryman and table companion at Sanssouci, arouses Frederick to still more violent anger and prompts him to burn the pamphlet in the public street, Voltaire returns his key as chamberlain, his *pour le mérite*, and his appointment as pensioner, with the verses:

> Je les reçus avec tendresse,
> Je vous les rends avec douleur;
> Comme un amant jaloux, dans sa mauvaise humeur,
> Rend le portrait de sa maîtresse.

On the same evening the King sends back these things to him, and will not let him depart. Some weeks later, after further quarrels, reconciliations, and caustic encounters, the poet serves notice on the King during parade.

"Well, Monsieur de Voltaire, you definitely desire to leave?"

"Sire, urgent matters, my health—"

"Then I wish you a pleasant journey, monsieur."

They never see each other again. But soon thereafter

the correspondence, with its mixture of admiration, malice, and tenderness, is resumed, to be maintained until the death of the poet twenty-four years later.

He is now past sixty, and lives near Geneva like a provincial noble, his little castle always filled with guests who come from all countries to see him and to hear him. Coach, lackeys, the cook from Paris, the secretary, a succession of dramas on his little private stage, where the nobility also perform, and which arouses the resentment of the burghers.

Here, on the boundary line of his native land, which persecutes and threatens him for free-thinking, he lives for more than twenty years. He goes about in gray shoes and stockings, a wide silk jacket, and a little velvet cap or a large wig. He works incessantly. He is always doing things and always learning things, with enough time and energy left to spend weeks entertaining the leading men and women of his day. As a matter of precaution, he has one estate on Swiss soil and another on French, so that if persecuted he could slip from one to the other.

Yet as he grows older he becomes less interested in satisfying the curiosity and the intellectual demands of guests, and turns his attention rather to the plight of the peasants and their cries for help. From the city council of Geneva he obtains permission to drain the swamps around his estate (half a century before Faust is finished) ; he reclaims stretches of heath, and protects his people from the despotism of the dominant class.

Now the aged man follows the plow, and sows a small field which is called Monsieur de Voltaire's field, and which is reserved exclusively for him until he is past seventy-nine and can no longer be active. He is generous with his funds, even too generous at times. To assist the destitute in his locality, he inaugurates the manufacture of clocks; and he is the first in this section to introduce silk weaving. The theater is converted into a house for silk-worms.

At the same time he works for months to free a family in Toulouse which was unjustly condemned by fanatical judges; he fights against the corruption of the French courts, against serfdom.

Justice is Voltaire's last and most passionate ideal.

One February afternoon a coach halts at the west gate of Paris; and when the customs officials ask whether there is any prohibited matter on board, the shrill voice of an old man answers: "I don't believe, gentlemen, that there is any contraband here except myself." One of the officials looks in, and then says to the other: "By heavens, that is Monsieur de Voltaire!"

After several decades, he is revisiting Paris for the first and last time. His ostensible purpose is to assist with the staging of a new tragedy, and to attend to various other matters—but in reality he wants one more opportunity to see Paris. And Paris wants an opportunity to see him. He has become quite a problem to both the court and the church, since the former is as eager to keep him at a distance as the latter is to attract him. But he receives the homage of the Academy, and of leaders in politics and the drama, as many as three hundred people coming to see him on a single day. He on his part visits before all others the woman who had been his first love, and whom he has not seen since this unsuccessful attachment of sixty years ago. He is horrified at the results of the visit; and she seems to have been so too, for the next day she laconically returns him a picture of himself as a young man.

For the first time in seventy years Voltaire, who is suffering from hemoptysis and increasing feebleness, has a religious conversation with a priest. Yes, he, Voltaire, confesses—though of course no one knows what. He also allows them to wheedle a statement from him wherein he asserts that he wishes to die in the Catholic religion, and "in case I have ever grieved the church, I beg God and the church for forgiveness." He was brought to this through a strange fear that his corpse might be cast into the boneyard. But when the Abbé was about to administer the sacrament to him, the old man stopped him with the words: "Remember that I am still spitting blood; we must be careful not to mix God's blood with my own."

He repulses all further advances on the part of the clergy, saying angrily that he would not even have made the concessions he did had he remained in Geneva. Then suddenly he becomes well again. His trip to the Academy is a triumphal march. In the theater he receives such homage as Paris never before paid to a poet. When he is led forward from the back of a *loge* by his friends, he bows so deeply that his forehead touches the railing. And when he lifts his head again his eyes, which had remained sharp and clear for eighty years, are full of tears. But at home he smiles again and says: "You don't know these Frenchmen! They welcomed Rousseau in exactly the same way, and the next day they had issued an order for his arrest!" Then he buys himself a house and decides to end his life in Paris.

But the end comes two weeks later; he declines rapidly, and dies in peace.

The church refuses him a grave. At the dissection the doctor takes his inordinately massive head, a friend takes his heart. At night the little corpse in dressing gown and night-cap, looking like some one asleep, is quietly packed up and shipped away. The omnipotent church will not allow the Academy to have a mass read for the miscreant; the papers are not permitted to print a word about him. A prior is dismissed for having failed to prevent the removal of the body. The dead man is secretly buried beside a relative in the provinces.

Twelve years later they are writing 1790. With the advent of the revolution, Voltaire's remains are brought back along a *via triumphalis* to Paris and placed in the Panthéon. The room where he was once confined in the tower of the Bastille is now a profusion of flowers, songs, and inscriptions. Amid torches and music, past hundreds of thousands of people, the twelve-span carriage drives on to Paris. The sarcophagus is inscribed with the words: "As poet, thinker, and historian he gave the human spirit a mighty inspiration. He prepared us for freedom."

A night in May, twenty-four years later: the lead coffin in the Panthéon is broken into, a band of young reactionaries stuff his bones into a sack, take the sack to a remote building plot, dig a hole, and allow his last remains to vanish on the edge of the metropolis.

No one knows where Voltaire's body fell into dust.

BYRON

LORD BYRON AND LASSALLE

The great object of life is sensation.

EXACTLY one year after the cannons of Missolunghi had fired thirty-seven shots over the corpse of Lord Byron, peer of England and poet of international fame, Ferdinand Lassalle first opened his eyes in the bed of a German Jewess.

These men were both adepts and victims of egocentricity. All their activities were aimed at the development of their own personalities; their primary purpose was themselves; they lived lives of passionate intensity, distorted by a certain fundamental skepticism; great play-actors of life, they carried their innate ideas to the extreme, the one playing the optimist, the other the melancholic.

We of a later day pass across the bridge of the impossible, from the grave of the one to the cradle of the other, hoping that their shades will forgive us should we be misled by profound similarities and pregnant antitheses. Yet the histories of these two men flow together, like a wave eternally renewed.

I

Lassalle's mythological forebears felt themselves chosen of the Lord among the peoples of the earth; Byron traced his lineage back to the gods of the north. But Byron's historic fathers sailed forth on adventurous galleys to plunder the merchandise with which Lassalle's

ancestors did business. The father of the one still took
his accustomed route to the exchange when half blind
with age; but the father of the other, while still a young
man, ended a career of folly by cutting his throat. At
ten Byron was a peer of England; Lassalle at fifteen secretly shut himself up to study for an examination as a
clerk.

But the differences between them seemed to increase
with the years, as the sides of an angle recede from
each other the further they are extended; for they were
nearest alike in their boyhood. Both of them were insolent, disdainful, domineering, ambitious, and cold-
blooded.

At twenty Lassalle was much more brilliant and more
stupendous than Byron. At that time Heine wrote of
him: "He is impatient of the gestures of resignation and
modesty with which we more or less hypocritically
dawdled through life. This new generation wants to
enjoy things, and to make its influence felt in tangible
objects. We, the older generation, bowed humbly before
the invisible, stole shadow-kisses, and sought the odor
of blue flowers, renounced and whimpered, and yet
were probably more happy."

In those years Byron was hardly more than an unusual bull in a china-shop. Lassalle hastily took up the
case of the Countess Hatzfeld as an outlet for his
genius; he was accused of inciting to robbery and political crime, and in a four-hour speech in his own defense
he both won his freedom and proved himself the ablest
speaker in Germany. And at the same age Byron was at
best an authority on neckties, who alternated drinking
bouts with dieting, and was followed about by a girl
in a page's uniform.

Vigorously and passionately Lassalle followed the standard guideposts to power. He studied three sciences; and for all his extravagance as a young man he was an adventurer with a very definite end in view. Byron does nothing, learns nothing, yet knows everything, writes little, plays Lucifer in the arm-chair. His first work is called "Hours of Idleness"; Lassalle's was the speech in his own defense.

Both were quick to recognize their potentialities, and soon began to stylize themselves, thus arriving early at a perfect development of their type.

But had Lassalle awakened in the cradle of Lord Byron, with this advantage, which he could never enjoy as a democrat, he would have met with unlimited success. Byron, rising from the cradle of Lassalle, could have given us at the best a Heinrich Heine turned genius.

Yet youth wears double masks.

II

Byron had planned to enter politics. He became a romantic politician, while Lassalle was a realistic politician with a romantic style. The most important trait they have in common immediately becomes obvious. It is centripetal monomania.

Their self-love and hero-worship contrasted so strongly with the insipid national politics of their times that they both developed into apparent revolutionaries.

Neither had revolutionary antecedents. The one was peer of England, the other was a descendant of middle-class Jews. Lassalle liked to call himself a revolutionary on principle; Byron was a revolutionary by temperament. But in reality both wanted the supreme power;

it was the ecstasy of tyranny, or at least of absolutism, which trembled before their eyes.

Byron saw, as he said, the first place usurped by Bonaparte, and so he turned to the second place as poet. Lassalle dreamed of his triumphal entry through the Brandenburg Gate. He was, Bismarck said, "ambitious in the grand manner, and not at all a republican. He had pronouncedly national and monarchistic leanings; the idea which he fought for was that of German emperorship—although it was of course doubtful whether the dynasty was to be Hohenzollern or Lassalle."

But Lassalle wanted to be dictator. Byron "Washington or the Aristides—the leader in talent and truth. . . . Franklin, Penn, and next to these, either Brutus or Cassius—even Mirabeau—or St. Just." They agreed on the name of Sulla. But Lord Byron's demon had always restrained him from playing the agitator, a rôle with which Lassalle had to be content.

However paradoxical it may seem to attribute to the poet a greater realism in his strivings than to the politician, Byron wanted all that Lassalle dreamed of. "Who would write," said Byron, "who had anything better to do? 'Action—action—action'—said Demosthenes." But after his writing and his speeches, Lassalle's capacity for action was exhausted.

Byron's position was of course an easy one, for he composed political dithyrambs. "Vide Napoleon's last twelvemonth. It has completely upset my system of fatalism. I thought, if crushed, he would have fallen, when fractus illabitur orbis, and not have been pared away to gradual insignificance; that all this was not a mere *jeu* of the gods, but a prelude to greater changes and mightier events. But men never advance beyond a certain point; and here we are retrograding, to the dull, stupid old system,—balance of Europe—poising straws upon kings' noses, instead of wringing them off!"

Lassalle hesitated for a long time before calling himself a socialist; and even in the year '48 he exhorted the workers not to proclaim a republic.

Both were men without a country, Lassalle in that he was a Jew, and Byron in that he scoffed at his fatherland until it banished him, although in spite of his thoroughgoing cosmopolitanism he could never succeed in forgetting England.

III

Their style gives us an insight into the deeper basis of their political views.

This is the heavy surf of Byron which beats against our ears: "The king-times are fast finishing! there will be blood shed like water, and tears like mist, but the peoples will conquer in the end."

And after this biblical rhapsody, hear the French accent in Lassalle's demagogy: "Well, now, gentlemen, I will not only overthrow the constitution, but probably I will have done so even before another year has passed! The games where the stakes are biggest, gentlemen, can be played with the cards on the table! And so I announce to you in this solemn place [in the courthouse]: perhaps not another year will pass before Herr von Bismarck has introduced universal suffrage!"

Is this the same demagogue who exclaims: "How? Some one in his Faustian ambition . . . has worked all the way from the philosophy of the Greeks to modern statistics, and you can believe in all seriousness that he

would desire to terminate this long discipline by pressing the incendiary's torch into the hand of the proletariat? Can one have so little insight into the moral
force of science?"

And is it the same rhapsodizing Lord who exclaims in
his first Parliamentary speech: "After months of inac-
tion and months of action worse than inactivity, at
length comes forth the grand specific, the never-failing
nostrum of all state physicians from the days of Draco
to the present time. After feeling the pulse and shaking
the head over the patient, prescribing the usual course
of warm water and bleeding,—the warm water of your
mawkish police, and the lancets of your military,—
these convulsions must terminate in death, the sure con-
summation of the prescriptions of all political San-
grados."

It is obvious how these two apparently irreconcilable
temperaments approach, or even attract, each other:
Skepticism is the coast towards which both are headed.

And are these Lassalle's words when we hear: "Give
me a republic, or a despotism of one, rather than the
mixed government of one, two, three. A republic!—
look in the history of the earth—Rome, Greece, Holland,
Venice, France, America, our too short Commonwealth
—and compare it with what they did under masters."
The fact that these are Byron's words throws further
light upon Lassalle.

But of course no one will think of the English aristocrat when he reads what the German upstart cries to his
judges: "Give thanks to the men who at the cost of
their own intellectual exertion have taken over a work
the results of which can eventually serve to benefit you
all! Banquet these men in the prytaneum, but do not
put them on trial!"

There is something strongly polemical in Byron's temperament, and he does not mind the awkwardness of adding notes to his poetical works in which he annihilates his literary enemies. One evening he dispatches four messengers to a friend in order to procure in Italy an English paper in which he had been attacked. Lassalle on the other hand has periods of peace, which he attributes to the study of Hegel.

Both love the superlative. In Byron it has a dithyrambic quality, in Lassalle it approaches the gasconade.

Their monomania looks steadily towards the mirror. Lassalle portrays himself in Hutten, his dramatic hero. Byron pictures himself as frequently as Rembrandt; for all his heroes, from Childe Harold to Lucifer, bear his features.

Their temperamental conflicts and their complex artistic development protected them both from improvisations. Byron never improvised, and it was only on rare occasions that he would recite a poem which he had just written. Lassalle, who wanted to become a dictator, would gladly have improvised with passion—yet he wrote out his speeches carefully—being actor enough, however, to make them appear like inspirations of the moment.

Yet there seem to be differences in the styles of these two authors which point to differences in character.

But style is one of the most impervious of masks.

IV

The face is seen more clearly beneath that frailer mask which we call style of living, or behavior.

Though Lassalle never loses sight of the common people, he is none the less an arrogant climber. Byron, while despising the nobility, is none the less a peer. His birth and caste allow him to soar as lightly as a feather in a world into which Lassalle bounded as though on springs.

Both had scant respect for the life from which they came, yet both cling to it, Lassalle through sentiment, Byron with the bitterness of the outcast.

However similarly the climber and the peer may dress, the two are always distinguishable by the one's obvious deliberateness. When Lassalle spoke before sooty laborers, he wore an elegant dress shirt, waistcoat, and patent leather boots. Byron, particularly as a young man, was an indolent dandy.

By the testimony of their contemporaries, they were both charming hosts: Byron in Piccadilly, Lassalle in the Bellevue-Strasse. And when Lassalle planned to build himself a house in the Tiergarten and embellish it with frescoes from the Edda, he was indulging in his favorite vision of himself as a leader of the fourth estate who moved among the best circles and gave the most exquisite dinners by the side of a countess. But Lassalle always gave the impression of a man trying to lift himself above his class by extravagance, and Byron was always a fantastic lord.

Furthermore, Byron had infinitely more leisure. "Today I have boxed an hour—written an ode to Napoleon Buonaparte—copied it—eaten six biscuits—drunk four bottles of soda water—redde away the rest of my time— besides giving poor —— a world of advice about this mistress of his." These are the pages from a diary which no climber can duplicate.

Byron's title was part of his character. And it was such a genuine asset to him that he could afford to despise it. When he was the lover of the Countess Guiccioli in

Ravenna and the Austrian authorities feared complications on account of his presence there, they banished the countess's family in order to compel the lord to follow her. When Lassalle was the friend of the Countess Hatzfeld, and her relatives feared that complications might result, they engineered Lassalle's expulsion from Berlin.

Since the lord could never meet with such experiences as these, many of his powers were left dormant which would otherwise have found expression in acts of rage.

Lassalle was also intellectually a usurper, as is made all the more evident by his theatrical manner. *Le grand oseur et le grand poseur.* In the mountains he happens upon his mistress: "By all the gods of Greece, it is she!" Such bombast comes only from the lips of dilettants. Byron on the other hand was amused by the disillusionment which he caused a young enthusiast by his unpoetic bearing. He was a born man of the world, and thus was thoroughly one; but Lassalle was never the perfect man of the world, having become one through deliberate effort.

Lassalle did not always succeed in mastering that native insolence which clung to Byron only as a boy. "You have the right to be insolent, we others but usurp this divine right, this heavenly privilege." The man who wrote him these clever sentences was, to be sure, no born man of the world himself. It was none other than Heine.

As a reaction, he sometimes lost his poise. "I am very, very unhappy, a thing which no one as yet has ever heard of me. Have pity!"

Have pity? Compare that with the ideal poise which Byron preserved in the parting letter to his wife, when he writes: "The ring is of no lapidary value, but it contains the hair of a King and of an ancestor, and I wish it to be preserved to Miss Byron."

Naturally Byron would never have associated with Lassalle, for he possessed the proper modicum of class prejudice. He could be on equal terms with every one but a petty climber. And Lassalle would have appeared to him as such, since he played the rôle of the enlightened aristocrat, and played it well.

But Lord Byron too was always prepared to meet the world on its own terms. A brilliant business man: he counts the stanzas of a song and frankly haggles with the publisher over a thousand guineas, offering, should he receive a large sum, to throw in various odds and ends, such as translations and lesser originals. Then he begins his capers again. One day he cuts down his stud, and the next he takes a large family under his roof and pays out a thousand pounds for a yacht. He dines alone for a couple of *paoli,* and lavishes money on dinners for his friends.

Lassalle too was often an adventurer in money matters, but he also knew very well where he stood.

While Lassalle revolved in steady motion, Byron— who seemed always to be resting—was usually moving in a way of his own. What would he have learned of life, he asks, had he been bent on a stodgy career in politics? A man must travel and fight—without which no life was genuine. And we cannot help but smile at the paradox of these sentences, for the truth is that Lassalle fought while Byron traveled.

Thus it was also infinitely more difficult for Byron to master the style of movement in repose. When he was very young, he addressed the upper house in accents which, some of the lords thought, were better fitted to the lower house. Nevertheless they left their seats and came closer to hear him, as though he were some exotically colored bird. And afterwards he himself spoke of the Don Juan element in his speech. But as he grew older and more famous, he learned better how to unite peer and poet in one style. In a certain sense, his own development in this respect was the opposite to that of Goethe.

Lassalle, it must not be forgotten, had only a slight European reputation when he died at the close of his thirties. But Byron was famous while still in his twenties. The fact that Byron was pampered, added to the beauty of his posture. The world had a strikingly different treatment for each of them. Lassalle was waylaid after he had refused to fight a duel, but fought his assailants so brilliantly that a historian made him a present of Robespierre's stick. Lord Byron—without the beating—received as a present a lock of Napoleon's hair.

Both are remarkably untrustworthy in self-criticism. We read "Cain" as a mystery. When the work appeared the poet was sitting in his Italian castle as though in an editorial sanctum. In one week he received a hundred opinions in the mail; he listened to the liberals, discussed in his correspondence the opinions which court and clergy had of the work; he held a barrister's speech over Lucifer's self-defense, and computed by how many verses Milton's Satan beat his own record.

He was extremely sensitive to criticism. In his youth, when his first work was rejected by a large paper, he became indignant, and composed a malicious satirical polemic. And a friend who observed him reading an adverse criticism when at the height of his fame, tells

of how he changed color, how his lips went white, and
how he threw the paper to the floor, half-minded to
return to England and demand satisfaction like a nobleman.

He sends recent poems to Thomas Moore and others,
asking for an opinion and giving instructions to burn
the poems if they are not considered beautiful. In Pisa
he shows a new poem of his to Shelley. Shelley does not
like it, and suggests that two verses of it are by his
enemy Southey. Byron grows pale, recognizes the two
verses, throws the poem "laughing" into the fire. (Epilogue: Two years later the poem appears in print, without the two verses; and it would seem that he had
written down the poem from memory immediately
after destroying it, or that he had had another copy of
it.)

Yes, he cites precedents; at every objection to his
work, he shows how Milton, Goethe, Dante, Æschylus,
Scott, would have sinned still more in this or that particular.

Lassalle too, who was much more deeply overshadowed by vanity, continually sought arguments for his
own worth, citing precedents, and even boasting before thousands of workmen that he had attacked an
opponent "amidst the thunderous applause of the greatest savants, who have congratulated me in writing and
in person."

The basic questioning of self and work which is betrayed by such appeals can only be accounted for, when
it is found in such proud and deliberate characters, as a
reaction from the overstressing of their own ego. It is
a kind of autosuggestion: if one circumscribe all circles
around himself as center, these circles run at uniform

distance and speed before his eyes until he finally believes that he himself is turning. That is revenge.

At times they were caught in the firm grip of sinister thoughts. Is it Lassalle or is it Lord Byron who writes to a friend: "I know the precise worth of popular applause, for few scribblers have had more of it; and if I chose to swerve into their paths, I could retain it, or resume it, or increase it. But I neither love ye, nor fear ye; and though I buy with ye and sell with ye, and talk with ye, I will neither eat with ye, drink with ye, nor pray with ye."

Did Byron or Lassalle say this? Do they disclose themselves? They played well, the one assuming the rôle of brilliancy, the other the rôle of gloom—but they were both perfectly aware that a person cannot be either of these types to the exclusion of the other, but must be a mixture of the two.

So that even their conduct becomes a mask.

V

Lassalle was like a mirror which became brighter as the light was increased. Byron was like a metal shield, its power of reflecting light being steadily diminished as it became more and more dinted by the invisible strokes of the demon.

Byron was ambitious in the beginning, but as he grew older and his fame increased he became more and more proud. Lassalle's vanity was increased by his successes.

As a youth Byron was elated when his name appeared with the names of great writers, and he admired his book in the shop windows. Then, at twenty-two: "I have done with authorship, and if, in my last production, I have convinced the critics or the world I was something more than they took me for, I am satisfied; nor will I hazard that reputation by a future effort. It is true I have some others in manuscript, but I leave them for those who come after me."

In these sentences a jewel is caught in a lava of glowing slag.

Lassalle on the other hand looked upon his life as a continual prophetic prelude. When he was almost forty, he apostrophized his bride: "Are you ambitious? What would my darling say if I were to lead her into Berlin in triumph, drawn by six dapple-grays through the Brandenburg Gate, the first lady of Germany, exalted above them all? . . . Do I look as though I would be content with second place in the state? Does a political martyr look so?"

In these sentences a stream of gleaming ore is poured forth which trickles away like magic.

No one can pronounce such proud vanities with impunity. Let him make good! And woe to the man who talks like this only a few weeks before his death!

A drama by Lassalle was a much bigger instance of dilettantism than a parliamentary speech by Lord Byron. But even an admirer cannot forgive him for printing and publishing this drama in later years. Yet the worst of it is that his verses are not bad enough to be defended as the work of a splendidly naïve genius. In his drama "Franz von Sickingen" there are passages which disclose many aspects of the author's character. Hutten exclaims:

> If I am so constructed that the pain
> Of mankind grieves me more than other men,

And human destitution hunts me out
For pity—that, O Lord, I cannot alter.

When men of action write bad tragedies, their personal destiny seems to suffer as a result, for the tragedy of their own life becomes second-rate. At least this was Lassalle's experience.

VI

Their portraits display their intense vanity and the annoyance which they feel at their own limitations.

When Byron, at twenty-two, was received by a Turkish pasha, the pasha told him that he was convinced of his guest's high lineage since he had small ears, curly hair, and small white teeth. And throughout his life the lord was proud of his thought-line, the middle one of three horizontal lines on his forehead.

"To be praised for one's intellect is good enough," exclaimed Lassalle; "but 'the handsomest man'—that is really important, some day that shall be placed on my tombstone!" Also, Lassalle displays here his excessive primitivism. Byron would have let such thoughts go unsaid.

Lassalle had the profile of a somewhat irritated Cæsar, Byron that of an Alexandrian lord. Lassalle's predominant traits were forehead and nose, Byron's his eyes and mouth. Both loved their beautiful hands.

But each of them was rankled by an imperfection. All his life Byron wept to himself with profound rage because he was lame in one foot. Lassalle had to take protracted rest cures; further, his voice was ordinarily high and squeaky, and he stuttered slightly. But when he appeared before the public, he overcame these handicaps and spoke with power and beauty.

Such men are always *hommes aux femmes*. Lassalle's pretentiousness is clearly in evidence when he says, "By recovery I mean nothing other than a circle of beautiful women." And Byron gives us a spectacle of his naïve effusiveness when he tells of his practicing at folding a shawl, and of how splendid his performance would be if only he didn't fold it wrong side out.

Lassalle was changeable and domineering in his treatment of women, and was vain rather than sensual. Byron found something "very softening in the presence of a woman." He willingly subjected himself to their whims, he said, for "I am sick of scenes, and have imbibed a taste for something like quiet." In a word, Lassalle was driven to women by his thirst for living, Byron by his genius. Thus it happened that the one made his bride a replica of himself, while the other's sinister passions made him the lover of his sister.

VII

Neither of these men was suited to marriage, yet both burdened themselves with marriage. Both found wives of inferior birth and both—looked at from without—were ruined as a result.

These lines of Lady Byron's to a friend show what sort of woman the poet's bride was before marriage: "I am engaged to marry Lord Byron. Convinced by intimate knowledge and deep investigation that he merits my highest esteem, whilst he possesses my strongest affection, I feel myself honored in the choice, and I expect of your candor and kindness, that you will rely more on the opinion which we have had reason to form, than on the vague prejudices of the world." That is not a mere formality; it is narrowness. How! Lord Byron's wife! She was not complex enough to resist her own tendencies, with the result that from the start things were headed towards their final outcome. It is well known how she and her relatives turned public opinion against him until he was practically an outcast. For the fact that he was the victim neither of political machinations, nor financial disaster, nor legal action, but that it was public opinion which pursued him, made his banishment permanent and complete, without the possibility of return.

This banishment, which was the culmination of his life since marriage, was of incalculable benefit to him. It is true that had Byron remained in England with his wife and child, and had his home life and his reputation remained intact, he would not have fallen so early into that whirling vortex which drives men so quickly to their doom. But by a special dispensation of the Muses, he was exiled—and this was his richest source of inspiration; for his poetic genius needed a real gallows on which to hang his melancholy.

However unfair it would be to Helene von Dönniges to couple her with Lady Byron, it is certain that she had nothing to give her husband except what he could supply from his own imagination, even her title and her social position necessarily standing in his way. But the more her wild temperament, her splendid figure, and her cultivation meant to him, the less we can forgive her for having failed in the two decisive moments of her life and his, and of having lost everything through the most miserable indiscretions. He wanted her to elope with him and to marry him in France in order to avoid useless complications with her titled parents, but she refused "to consent to such a romantic seduction." And later, when all arrangements had been made for an attack on the family, and she was sworn by him to complete silence, she pusillanimously allowed the celebration of her sister's engagement to play upon her sympathies: she "confessed" to her mother, thus breaking up all their plans and indirectly causing Lassalle's death.

Both of these men, Byron as well as Lassalle, were unsuited to marriage; or at least they took the wrong road to marriage. Lassalle fell in love in a few moments, carried the woman of his choice down exactly three flights of stairs—and then, as though his intellect had interfered to dampen his emotions, he let the whole matter drop; and had they not been brought together by accident a year and a half later in the Alps, the decision would have been put off for years. Finally he wrote to one woman, an old friend of his, the cool words: "In the first place I can no longer come back, and besides I see no reason why I should come back."

Down three flights? Why not an abduction, a seduction, which would have excited stronger pulses in him? And one asks: Why an aristocrat, which he treats as such?

Byron in his time sought a woman who was willing to swap her money for his escutcheon, and we are refreshed by the plain dealing of this tone. But he committed the mistake of taking a wife who was not rich enough, for whom he had too much respect, and whom he finally began to love.

Had Lord Byron married a millionairess with whom he had absolutely nothing in common, and Lassalle a girl who gave herself to him in simple delight, the results could hardly have been called marriages, yet as conjugal relationships they would have been much more decorous, more fruitful, and less disastrous.

Their blindnesses, which is to say their subconscious purposes, prevented this. For they would also have become fathers of numerous children, and this was not their vocation. Lassalle died before marriage; and had he had children he would not have felt them as a kind of vicarious immortality. Byron himself hardly knew his attitude towards his legitimate daughter and his natural one. Nature avenged herself: causing his natural daughter, Allegra, who did not live with him but for whom he provided generously, to die early, while Ada, who was born in wedlock, and for whom Byron in the growing loneliness of his banishment began to feel more and more affection, was permitted to grow up in hatred of her father, before whose picture a green curtain was hung and whom she was taught to consider as a renegade while all Europe was singing his praise.

Fertility is not the purpose of such characters. Only centrifugal forces can throw out circles from within.

VIII

The mule tracks lie side by side. On one the loaded animals are driven to the harbor; on the other they climb back up, freed, for new burdens. Similarly, many souls travel endlessly up and down the pathways of romanticism and skepticism.

"The great object of life is sensation—to feel that we exist, even though in pain," cried Byron, and Lassalle could have said the same. But it is only a very superficial aspect of romanticism to intoxicate one's guests with hasheesh as Lassalle did, or to drink out of a skull, like Byron.

In reality, Lassalle sought romanticism as a way of magnifying himself, of knowing; Byron as a way of forgetting. The genuine romantic is fated to grow bored whenever he cannot lose himself. Lassalle could never be bored; he was too active and too vain—and for this reason his romanticism was much more primitive: "Shall I give up everything, and shall we go off together and live just for our own happiness, our studies, and a few friends?" Or, in less elegiac mood, to his bride: "I will act and fight, but also enjoy the right of purchase, and will press the diadem of victory on your brow. Believe me, it is just as proud a feeling to be a president chosen of the people as a king by God's grace. Come to my side before the mirror!—Is not this a superb, a royal pair? Were not these two made by nature in her most joyous holiday mood? And do you not believe that the supreme power will well become us? Long live the republic and the golden-haired wife of its president!" In these painful sentences Lassalle's whole soul is exposed: simple romanticism, naïve theatricalism, a glittering dream of the future, a genuinely popular genius.

On the other hand, Byron's romantic gestures—beginning with those of the noble romantic: "My daughter, my wife, my half-sister, my mother, my mother's mother, my natural daughter and myself are or were all only children. The fiercest animals have the rarest number in their litters—as lions, tigers, and even elephants, which are mild in comparison." Then the flattering romantic who apostrophizes Goethe: "You have been fortunate, Sir, not only in the writings which have illustrated your name, but in the name itself, as being sufficiently musical for the articulation of posterity." Or the impulse of the meditative romantic which causes him to halt at Stromboli and to lose one day in his hurried voyage to Greece's war of freedom in order to watch the eruption of the volcano. Or the emotions of the gallant romantic when with forced merriment he plays the part of the adventurer at the Venetian carnival. Or the seriousness of the royal romantic, when the embittered exile from England, though he has no sons, expressly asks that he be sent his "summons as a peer to the Coronation," and asks to know "if we have any claims in our family to carry any part of the mummery, that they may not lapse, but, by being presented, be preserved to my successors." Finally the insolent irony of the romantic in the Colosseum at midnight invoking Nemesis to avenge him against Lady Byron and her mother.

Both these men were skeptics—and it is in their skepticism that they are most alike.

Lord Byron had the exact amount of skepticism proper to a melancholy romantic; Lassalle exactly as much as was necessary to balance an enthusiastic program. This skepticism may account for the arresting fact, as reported by a friend, that when Byron was reading "The Tempest" aloud, he laughed to himself, as he often did.

Lassalle on the other hand was occasionally overwhelmed by a profoundly skeptical dejection. "I am weary unto death, and however strong my system may be, I tremble to the very marrow. The mad exertions, the profound and painful disillusions, the corrosive chagrin which the apathy of the working class as a whole produces in me—this was in itself too much for me. I am engaged in a *métier de dupe* and I am angry to the point of death, the more so in that I cannot air this anger but must let it assert its sway within me."

The medallion on his grave (which a cunning fate keeps locked) shows the features of the man who spoke then. It represents him in his last years; and although he is still under forty, a deep furrow, such as might derive from misanthropy, curves about the mouth. Many masks have been removed.

IX

Lord Byron was temperamentally melancholy; Lassalle merely had attacks of despondency. Byron suffered because it was his nature to do so; Lassalle suffered from actual reversals. His soul was like a broad lake, Byron's a deep well.

Lassalle possessed an endless optimism and vitality which were enough in themselves to indicate his race. He had a strong desire to live long. "I well know that we are our own destiny, and thus I do not want to push our cause with haste. We are entitled to a long life, so patience," he writes his bride a few months before the end. He is always active, and almost always believes in the importance of his activities. Equally optimistic and Hegelian, he divides the world's history into three stages, the first two of which are contrasting, while the third combines the enduring elements of them both. Naturally the new era, the "synthesis," begins now, 1848, with Lassalle. This is not merely the overdoing of a theory; it also represents a temperamental aberration.

Lassalle understood the journalist's art of converting

life's accidents into necessities. Thus as the occasion demanded he became jurist, philologist, attorney, poet.

Lord Byron arrived at power (at fame) in a flash—and yet he exclaimed: "The most I can hope is, that some will say 'He might, perhaps, if he would.'" This is fate's ironic way of handling the careers of remarkable people.

With calm and discernment, Byron gives us the whole complexion of his temperament when he speaks of suffering from a kind of hereditary sadness which he naturally suppresses when in company but which breaks out against his will in his writings and when he is alone.

Lassalle was never alone, he was always surrounded by people or tangible ideas. Byron was surrounded by phantoms which never once originated in his own imagination. The eyes of the demagogue were turned towards the future; the bard, with a kind of spite, looked to the past. Thus when Lassalle came in contact with the traditional past, and Byron became inspired by an ideal future, both perished.

X

Commenting on the death of these men, it is usual to say that Byron fell for Greek freedom while Lassalle was the victim of his vanity. But this does not go deep enough.

The truth is they both had come to the breaking point. The bow, already taut, yearns to be drawn still tighter. At the close of their thirties—at that period when a well-grounded life begins to blossom and an adventurous one nears collapse—they both turned to en-

terprises which might give them one last new sensation;
but at the same time the thought slumbered in both of
them that things were rapidly coming to a close. Lassalle's haughty optimism obscured this thought; Byron
was far too much of a poet not to contain within himself some fore-knowledge of the future so that he could
talk of going to Greece to die there. The thought of
course did not take the same form in both men: Lassalle, who felt himself for ever mounting, pressed his
strong sense of life more tightly at the last so that it
shot up still higher; Byron, who felt himself for ever
sinking, lowered his body in a ship sailing for the islands
of Greece.

With Lassalle the symptoms announce themselves in
his last two years. His agitation turns into a nervous
trembling; he works like a man who desires life and fore-
sees death. An enormous productiveness, which fate now
granted him with a smile of malice, allowed him to
sink deeper into the veil of Maya.

Now he writes twenty different articles, makes speech
upon speech, confers with countless deputations, carries on a dozen political trials, founds the German
Workers' Union. A final triumphal march is permitted
him. As he goes down the Rhine on the first anniversary
of the Union, he is everywhere received by thousands
of workingmen, his coach and his home are crowned
with wreaths, honorary gifts are lavished upon him.
Garlands, banners, triumphal arches, serenades are in
order, while the coach of the president is deluged with
flowers. For a few moments he is allowed to feast upon
all this—for a few moments time stands still.

But immediately afterwards he writes: "I wish nothing more ardently than to be totally out of politics, so

that I could turn back to science, friendship, and nature. I am sick and tired of politics. Of course, I could become as passionately enflamed as ever if I had power or saw the means of getting power. . . . But for this child's play I am too old and too big." One feels that it won't go on, and it is only a wild trick of his Parcæ to let him fight the final duel in the well-known affair.

After all obstructions he now has the bride in his power. At last she is with him and is ready to flee with him. The angry mother of the bride appears, accuses him of having stolen her child. Then once more the lawyer and actor comes to the fore. "Smiling," he gets his bride to assure him that she will do whatever he asks of her. Then he leads her to her mother and bids her return. "And now, dear lady, I give you back your child! From your hands I will receive her; you will follow us to the altar. She goes with you because I so desire. Do not forget that, and now farewell!" Yes, he attained the brilliant exit of the demagogue, the actor. His short-breathed romanticism was sunning itself in its own glowing reflection. Three days later he was cold.

Immediately afterwards he saw what he had done. "I was an ass to play the comedy of magnanimity and decorum! I am so unhappy that I weep for the first time in fifteen years. . . . What tortures me most is the crime of my stupidity! What have I come to! I am consumed with remorse! But if I cannot undo this stupidity, I will shave my head and become a monk! If I cannot carry my cause through successfully, and I have grave doubts about it, then I am for ever broken, and through with everything!"

When a man of nearly forty, a person of active life who has learned how to dominate all sorts of situations, when an actor like Lassalle finds such touching tones, it is not because of a girl, not even because of a wish heightened to the point of mania by frustration, but it is the feeling: I have violated my own laws, the end is near.

Immediately before the ensuing duel with the bride's recognized fiancé, Lassalle presented the phenomenon of a man who was at once an unconscious *moriturus* and an incurable optimist. He, the challenger, did not bring about the duel with the intention of hurling himself upon his fate; but instead, with a kind of metaphysical blindness, he trusted in victory. When a friend advised him to practice pistol shooting, he called that nonsense; but his opponent, despite the fact he was an officer, fired one hundred and fifty trial shots the day before. His vitality, a few hours before his natural end, was enlarged to the point of monstrosity, so that Lassalle lost all sense of proportion. Despite all the illogical, and thus fatal circumstances, Lassalle might, it is true, have laid down his life with reason had he been combating the code of aristocracy. But this duel had none of the dignity of principles; the effect was quite different from the cause, the reward was not the motive, and his opponent was a dandy who was not at all concerned with politics.

Lassalle fell, but we must not leave him without adding that, though mortally wounded and in great pain, he ascended the hotel steps nobly erect, so as not to frighten the Countess Hatzfeld.

With Lord Byron it all occurred more resolutely and quietly. If Lassalle's activity within the last few years had increased to hastiness, Byron's stillness had become inertia. He hardly ever rode, he drank more than formerly—but at the same time his imagination was staggering towards death: he even thought of becoming a farmer in South America. (This is the identical stage at which Oscar Wilde faced the law court.)

The fact that Lord Byron saw in the Greek fight for independence one last opportunity for excitement leads many to suppose that he was not honestly aroused. This is the sort of judgment one might expect of people who rubricate the brightest-colored butterflies with abysmal seriousness.

This poet belonged to Greece. It was here that his poetic fancy first flourished; here that the past, the landscape, the people, and the customs spoke to him. But as a man of intelligence, he first considered very carefully of what advantage he could be there, he gathered information, and really tested himself out as a practical person. It was no crusader or fanatic that shipped at Genoa. "I am at last determined to go to Greece; it is the only place I was ever contented in. I am serious, and did not write before, as I might have given you a journey for nothing; they all say I can be of use in Greece. I do not know how, nor do they; but at all events let us go." Does one observe vacillation in these arresting lines? The poet is becoming a romantic hero. Lassalle, the "hero," became an infernal romantic.

The subsequent acts of the lord, after he had become a soldier, are lamentable. He had to be content with arming forty *stratiotai* and sending bandages and medicines after the battle. For weeks he lay undecided before Cephalonia, finally landing and retiring to a village. All this has its political causes, but the reader of history groans. Then Byron, while "observing operations" on the island, resumes his usual pursuits. He engages in repeated arguments with a Methodist doctor who has a library of reference-books on theology—and meanwhile the fate of Greece begins to be disclosed.

Finally when the hour arrives in which he could have left his tent, mounted his horse, and seized the colors, he catches cold during a ride and becomes deathly ill.

He might have recovered, but when the physicians prescribed blood-letting he resisted with the obstinacy of a man pledged to death, explaining misanthropically that they called his illness serious in order to have the credit of curing it. "Do with me," he told them, "whatever else you like, but bleed me you shall not."

When the dying poet is delirious, his daughter comes down to him out of the fog. He complains and sighs. The valet is expected to understand his confused words, but he falters, and Byron cries: "It is now too late, and all is over. . . . My wife! My child! My sister! You know all. . . . Now I shall go to sleep."

He dies. Athens asks for his ashes. They are delivered over to his enemies: they are brought back to England.

It seems to be the compensatory fate of tragic characters that their intense desire for a magnificent end is distorted into the absurd. Thus, Lassalle's duel was senseless. And Byron died of fever before the battle in which he was prepared to fall. And yet on his last birthday he had composed those ideal lines which a more kindly destiny might well have allowed him to fulfill:

> Awake! (not Greece—she is awake!)
> Awake, my spirit! Think through *whom*
> The life-blood tracks its parent lake,
> And then strike home! . . .

> If thou regret'st thy youth, *why live?*
> The land of honorable death
> Is here:—up to the field, and give
> Away thy breath!

Both Lord Byron and Lassalle were unmoral, self-seeking idealists, but Byron's idealism was tragic, Lassalle's hedonistic.

Lassalle's self-love grew enormously while Byron's dwindled, yet Lassalle went from enthusiasm to skepticism, and Byron from skepticism to poetic melancholy.

Of the tragic epigrams which posterity sees upon their brow, Byron's was branded upon him from the start, while Lassalle received his against his will at death.

Byron first emerged as a politician, Lassalle as a poet; and although there was a preponderance of emotion in the former and of intellect in the latter, there is just as much keenness in Byron's verse as there is romantic fervor in Lassalle's speeches.

Both were great play-actors at life, though Byron assumed a mask only in so far as he was driven to do so by his conflicts with the outside world, whereas Lassalle played so brilliantly that he himself sometimes forgot what he was doing. It was the will of an unseen stage-director to let this lord and poet play Thanatos, yet a simple empiricism forced upon him the rôle of Lucifer. The demagogue would have liked to play the part of Alcibiades, but a strenuous youth, an all-too-domineering intelligence, and an unharmonious century selected him to play the part of a Hutten who had no Luther to follow him.

As his style and the spelling of his name also indicate, Lassalle had French qualities and preferences, and yearned to be the great *écrivain*—but as a Jew he made efforts to be thoroughly German. In every way Byron resembles the city which he loved so much and upon whose bridges and canals he gazed with such feeling. And yet, had Lassalle been born in Paris and Byron in Venice, they might have been more perfect phenomena, but they would have been less interesting.

Anecdote and biography have carried their fame farther and maintained it longer than their works, which are read by only a few people today. The great successes of both came from one particular source: both possessed at times the temerity of the naïve mystic shipwrecked upon the shores of life.

Both were such thorough artists of living that they even profited by their romantic death. Their cult of the ego was as great as this.

But if Lassalle was in love with himself, Lord Byron loved his genius.

GOETHE AND SCHILLER

We recognize mankind by their weaknesses, the individual by his excellence; we all have our shortcomings and our destinies in common, but our virtues belong specifically to each one of us.

A FEW hundred young men are standing in line in a coldly lighted room—their heels together, heads and bodies erect, for their grim and severe old duke of Württemberg threatens to pass adverse criticism upon the students of his military school. Several court officials are standing behind him, in a subdued semicircle—and there are also some guests from Weimar present, notably the duke's young cousin, and next to him the poet and minister. The duke is now lauding the work of the industrious. Reading from a list which he has received from the instructor, he calls upon the best students to come forward, and with an expression less of congratulation than of warning he presses prizes into their right hands. The prize-winners silently express their thanks by a stiff salute, always keeping a close watch on their master's expression, for they fear him.

There is only one of them who is not looking at the master. However much he may have desired a prize for himself, he neither sees nor hears who is receiving prizes. His eyes are glued to the figure of that stranger over yonder in a dark suit, standing somewhat behind the others. How he tries in silence to fathom the depths of this silent man! So that is the way a poet looks who is adorned with fame and honors? No more brilliant, nor more beautiful than that? He looks pale and slender,

243

almost like his Werther. Soon he will turn his large penetrative eyes towards me too; now—if only I could hold him by staring, if I could fling myself upon him and cry out: Et in Arcadia ego! Yet you are proud; you do not see through me the way a poet should. You do not suspect what is going on within me. , . . How you smile and nod. You have become a prince's servant, merely a courtier. How I hate them! All! And you, too, who have betrayed your genius! Your pallor is from exhaustion, your frailness the result of excesses. No, you are no longer a poet. . . .

Friedrich Schiller! the duke calls loudly from the list. The youth awakens, steps forward in confusion, and dutifully kisses the hem of his master's coat. Hardly aware of the prize in his hand, he returns to the ranks somnambulistically.

A book, he thinks now. You pressed a book into my right hand? Duke! Soon I will press a book over your heart, until it turns to stone! Is this your prize? I am already twenty. When I am thirty, like that man, then I will feel a perennial prize upon my brow, and he shall look on while the whole nation presents it to me!

Eight years later, on a quiet August evening, Schiller is sitting over his Rhine wine in Goethe's summer-house. He has left the military academy; but through all his travels and wanderings, in periods of either destitution or glory, he has never lost this memory of Goethe, who had stood there in silence and totally failed to discern that here before his eyes a genius was receiving the prize. Schiller comes to Weimar and is well received there in intellectual circles; but the stranger does not find here the man on whom he could now finally test his mixed feelings of impatience and reverence, curiosity and skepticism. For Goethe is in Rome. There is nothing here to see but his house, and a little summer-house at that—for Goethe's friends have met there on his birthday, and the new poet is among the guests. And Schiller touches glasses with Knebel to toast the health of their host in this little house in which Goethe has lived for six years.—Schiller drinks to the health of Goethe, the absent, at the height of summer.

He has heard in Weimar remarkably conflicting reports of this strange man. Many persons have been unfriendly and have talked against him; a few have come passionately to his support—yet these few seem to be the best. Did not the Lengefelds at Rudolstadt, the wife of the Master of the Hunt and her two daughters, speak admiringly of Goethe's genius—and this was the most socially distinguished family to which Schiller had gained admittance. Yet the ill-humor of their friend, Frau von Stein, had already begun to affect his reputation unfavorably. Many an official twitched at the corners of his mouth when the stranger inquired after Goethe. How long would he remain, and what would he do? In any case his money was sent to him by the Chamber regularly, wherever he went. Again Schiller feels discontented.—How lucky this man is in everything, how regularly things drop in his favor—while we all have such hardship! Is he so much better? Only better housed and thus better educated; only happier; only ten years farther along! And in his conversation and letters he repeats all the malicious things he hears of Goethe.

When Goethe returns the following June, Schiller's curiosity reaches its height. "I am impatient to see him; few mortals have interested me so much," and he has friends who tell him "everything beautiful there is to

be told." Soon Frau von Stein comes to the country to
visit the Lengefelds, and from the lips of this woman,
who really ought to know, Schiller gets a cold and disillusioned version of Goethe since his return. "What a
turn I have for prophecy!" he thinks—but then
"Iphigenie" falls into his hands; he reads it again, and
it gives him "a very beautiful day, although the pleasure
it caused me was paid for by the depressive realization
that I could never produce anything like it."

Yet—will he not come to see me? And in total error
he writes to his friend: "Goethe would have visited me
had he known that his return route to Weimar brought
him so close to my own quarters. We were not more
than an hour from each other." He will be not more
than five minutes from you, Friedrich Schiller, and yet
will not come to see you!

A few weeks later, on a bright Sunday in September,
a day still warm enough to be spent out in the open air,
they finally meet in a society of nobles and gentry.
The Herders are there, also Frau von Stein.

"At last I can tell you of Goethe"—Schiller writes
to his friend, Körner. "The first sight of him consider-
ably lowered the high opinion which others had led me
to have of this attractive and beautiful figure. He is of
medium height, holds himself erect, also when he is
walking. He appears reserved, although his eyes are very
expressive and vivacious, and one follows them with
pleasure. He is very serious, yet he shows much benevo-
lence and goodness. . . . We became acquainted
quickly and without the least constraint. To be sure, the
company was so large, and every one was so eager to
engage him, that I could not have much time with him

alone, or talk with him on any but the most general
subjects. . . . I doubt whether we shall ever become
very intimate. He has already gone through many experiences which still interest me and are, with me, still
in the stage of desire and expectation. . . . He is so far
ahead of me that our paths can never cross again. . . .
His world is not my world, our ways of looking at things
seem essentially different. . . . Time will disclose the
rest."

Is that all? An account of what Goethe said of the
people of Naples, and other details of Italy? A chatty
Sunday among friendly and unfriendly ladies, and after
Schiller's proud expectations this had to be the historic
day on which Schiller and Goethe first met each other
face to face! How little he saw through Goethe's mask;
hardly even perceiving that he wore one. He was irritated by the fact that Goethe did not speak with him
alone, and never mentioned subjects in which they had
a mutual interest. Yet he rapidly recovers from his disappointment, and regains his self-reliance, placing himself on equal terms with Goethe. We are too different
ever to become intimate, he explains to a friend—but
he promptly adds: time will show.

Time passes, Schiller waits. That Sunday when he was
hoping in vain for an intimate word from Goethe, his
critique of Egmont—or better, his critique against Egmont—had already gone to press. It was good that it
had already been written and had not yet appeared: for
this enables us to see the two men shake hands for the
first time free of unrest and vanity. Afterwards Goethe
looks upon Schiller's critique as typical of the prevail-
ing attitude which he has encountered since his return.
Schiller is resentful because he sees in Goethe the favor-

ite of fortune, who conquers the world without battling with the world. Goethe is resentful because he sees in Schiller the usurper of the Muses, who believes that he can conquer them without battling with himself. It suddenly seems to Goethe that his twenty years of struggle from chaos to form, his genial methods of extracting gold from the mines of the demon, are being menaced from without, for this young man has again begun inspiring the Germans with chaos. Why should he meet Schiller amicably? Perhaps he need not positively hate him, but his ideas are at least repugnant.

Schiller however is beginning to develop a personal hatred for Goethe, whose ideas, besides being a guidance to him, are also an annoyance. From October on, he passes the entire winter in the same small town with him, just around the corner one might say, associating with his friends and often seeing Knebel and Moritz—yet Goethe never makes a single move, and even politely avoids him on the one or two occasions when they do meet. Meanwhile Schiller has to bear with Moritz's pæans to Goethe; he deliberately invites Moritz to talk about Goethe, and then suffers at what this colleague of his enemy says of him. Moritz returns to Goethe's stately house, in which he lives and to which Schiller alone is denied entry. And a few days later, when he appears again, Schiller waits eagerly to hear whether Goethe has mentioned "Don Carlos." For however strong his antipathy, what he wants most of all is to be judged by the poet as a poet, even though the verdict be adverse.

Goethe not only fails to criticize Schiller—he will not even speak of him. His only desire is to have Schiller established elsewhere. He is disturbed when people cautiously call his attention to Schiller. On his return home he finds his friends altered, listless, and evasive. But he refuses to have an opponent forced upon him. For Goethe, whose works and projects arouse Schiller to mixed feelings of enmity and admiration, is not at all interested in Schiller's art. In order to remove him from the city, he contrives to procure the poet a professorship in Jena. He proceeds rapidly with this sly plan; as early as December he sounds Schiller on the subject, and when Schiller assents he asks for the Duke of Gotha's approval the very next day. And simultaneously with the dispatch of this formal petition, Goethe notifies Schiller by letter that he may consider the matter as good as settled. Which is to say: as minister of education he appoints Schiller professor of history. Now Schiller must go and thank him. "Meanwhile I have paid one visit to Goethe. He has been very zealous in this matter, and shows a great deal of sympathy for what he believes will be to my best interests."

Does not this sophisticated judge of humankind discern the real motives of his opponent? Does he not notice that this man spoke to him only as a Weimar minister, without venturing one single step into that boundless realm which is the true home of them both? For the time being his desire to win this one man's favor was so great that it interfered with his judgment.

Goethe had also contrived to blunt his discernment in another way, for his treatment of Schiller was based upon his reading of Schiller's character. After ten dark years of roving and upheaval Schiller, who was now in his thirtieth year, wanted to conform. He wanted the certainty of a position and a home—and felt that calm and regularity were necessary for his work. True, when he is with the Lengefeld sisters, to whom he always

addresses his confessions jointly, he assumes the noble
pose of "heroic resignation." The offer is supposed to
have been "forced" upon him; he would like to reject it,
and speaks in praise of golden freedom. As a matter of
fact, he was not yet formally appointed, and could
have withdrawn at any moment. But he has no desire to
do so, and even admits to his intimate friend Körner that
he is very much pleased. He wants to anchor; and while
trying to extricate himself from a tumultuous love
affair with the gifted Frau von Kalb, he is on the lookout for a woman of wealth and good family, as he now
definitely desires both money and position.

He cannot choose between the two titled sisters. He
declares his love to them both, though at the same time
he writes to his friend of several other possibilities. Two
months before the engagement he again asks Körner to
help him make a good match, naming the minimum
sum which he needs.

Meanwhile the bride's friend, Frau von Stein, has
learned of Goethe's amour with Christiane. The atmosphere in which Schiller lives now becomes totally unfriendly to Goethe, although neither of the Lengefelds
will relinquish their admiration for Goethe's genius.

Schiller's patience is exhausted. "This man, this
Goethe, is simply in my way," he exclaims openly to his
friend. And with ill-concealed envy he complains at a
state of affairs which has made it so easy for Goethe to
attain his inimitable advantages. Yes, before going to
Jena, he openly avows the passionate love-hate which
Goethe has aroused in him:

"The idolatry with which Moritz follows Goethe, and
which he carries so far as to erect even his mediocre
works into canons and to praise them at the expense of

all other works of the human spirit, has kept me from
any close association with him. . . . It would make me
unhappy to be like Goethe. He never completely abandons himself, not even to his closest friends. He keeps
clear of every one. In fact I believe that he is unusually
egotistical. He has a way of attracting people and knows
how to win them over to him by trifling or important
favors, but he always manages to avoid entanglements.
He manifests his existence through his benefactions, but
in the manner of a god, without giving anything of
himself. This seems to me a consistent . . . policy calculated to produce the highest gratification of self-love.
People should not allow a person of such a nature to
come near them. For this reason I hate him, though at
the same time I admire him and am wholly attracted by
his mind. I consider him as I would a haughty prude
whom one must get with child so as to humble her in
the eyes of the world. It is a very strange mixture of
love and hate that he arouses in me, a feeling not unlike
that which Brutus and Cassius must have felt for Cæsar.
I could destroy him, and then love him again with all
my heart. . . . His mind is mature, and his opinion of
me is at least biased more against me than in my favor.
Since my only concern in this matter is to hear the truth
about myself, he is the one man I know who can do me
this service. I will surround him with informers, for I
myself will never ask him in person to discuss me."

Nowhere else has Schiller so well expressed his feelings
towards Goethe as in his tumultuous letter, which says
almost nothing of Goethe but tells everything of Schiller: he shows the poetic purity of his strivings, his professional honesty, his reverence for everything great and
beautiful; while there is also evidence of his ambition and

envy, and in the metaphor of the haughty prude he expresses his passionately virile longing to dominate the object of his love. In after years he never defended Goethe's character so ardently as he attacks it in this letter, where his antagonism impairs his judgment. Schiller never did definitely rectify this thoroughly erroneous concept of Goethe's character. Yet he has written friendly words to show that he now recognizes as devotion in Goethe what may appear from the outside like coldness. But at present Schiller sees in Goethe only what all the world sees, and what most Germans saw even a hundred years afterwards.

With this effusion he ends the Goethe matter. Three days later, when writing in the same vein, and often in the same words, to Caroline, he closes his letter as though he were summing up an issue. "Lay this judgment to one side. Perhaps the future will alter it, or still better, reverse it." And when Caroline undertakes to defend Goethe, Schiller declares that he would like to be alone with Goethe on a desert island to work out this problem of his character, but that he has other things to do. "If Goethe is such an amiable person, I will finally discover it in that world where we are all angels. In all seriousness, I have too much indolence and too much pride to wait until a man explains himself to me. . . . If a person works with all his might, he cannot remain hidden from another. That is my plan."

He has clearly decided upon renunciation, the abandonment of all further attempts. Yet at the same time he places himself on an equal footing with Goethe, and calls for competitive action. He is speaking now in the determined accents of a man who, after a protracted courtship, desires to punish his lady for her inflexibility by giving the world cause to wonder and herself cause to regret.

A year and a half later—Schiller, husband and professor, related by marriage to the nobility of Thuringia, honored by students, savants, and writers, is sitting in his tastefully furnished house at Jena. His wife has known Goethe since childhood; he himself meets him occasionally in the homes of mutual friends. Thus it is not surprising that Goethe—it is not certain whether this happened on more than one occasion—enters his house. The conversation—Schiller reports—soon came around to Kant. "Goethe is wholly incapable of attaching himself whole-heartedly to any doctrine. To him all philosophy is subjective. . . . His manner of thinking is positively too concrete, too insistent upon the tangible, for me. But his mind is active, reaching out critically in all directions and trying to construct for itself a unified whole—and to me that makes him a great man. Otherwise he is sufficiently involved in absurdities. He is beginning to age, and the interest in women which he so often carried to excess is about to wreak vengeance upon him. He will, as I fear, commit an indiscretion, and share the usual fate of the confirmed old bachelor. His maid is a Miss Vulpius who has a child by him. . . . He is supposed to be very fond of his child, and has probably convinced himself that if he marries a maid it is done through love of the child, and that this at least could keep the matter from being ridiculous."

A new tone. Schiller, who has been tortured for years with envy at Goethe's social position, while having nothing but admiration for his genius, for the first time feels himself socially superior to his opponent! Son-in-law, cousin, and brother-in-law of titled people,

introduced at court, professor, member of learned socie-
ties, highly cultured Kantian, sought after by German
producers and publishers, and now in reasonably good
health—and in contrast: this strangely recessive man,
who still tries to take hold of things which we philosophers have long since recognized as pure ideas, whose
plays are never produced, who has brought out nothing
new for years; aging in his forties, he lives with a maid
whom no one ever invites anywhere, he has an illegitimate child, and is about to tumble just like all the others.
Schiller is proud that he can pity Goethe, and only his
incorruptible genius hinders him from feeling superior.

Schiller's position improves. Two years later—it can
be avoided no longer—Goethe plays "Don Carlos" on the
court stage, yet their relations remain cold. For six years
Goethe has not written or spoken a single word concerning Schiller! "I resisted every effort of mutual
friends to bring us together," he recounts later. . . .
"Nor was his essay, 'Die Anmut und Würde,' very likely
to reconcile me. . . . I even saw how certain harsh
passages could be directly applied to myself; they showed
my creed in a false light."

Schiller's position improves still further. He is full of
worldly plans. He is soon tired of the professorship;
also his attraction as a teacher has fallen off. He thinks
of becoming instructor of the crown prince as a means
of assuring his future. He draws considerable revenues
from a count and a prince; he makes publishing arrangements and has financial dealings with four publishers at
once; his extensive correspondence keeps him *au courant*
with everything that is being written and talked about;
and a group gathers around him in Jena. He is entirely
the critic and philosopher, writing no dramas and little

verse of importance between the ages of twenty-eight
and thirty-seven. But about this time he has a tubercular attack, accompanied by convulsions—and this interferes with his many projects. It also hinders him from
accepting the offer of the ambitious Cotta'sche Verlag to
edit a new political paper.

For Cotta recognized in Schiller, along with his poetic
gifts, a great talent for political journalism. Now the
two of them found a literary monthly to which authors
are attracted both by the name of Schiller and by the
high rate of payment. Schiller has already made connections with the two Humboldt brothers, who are now
young men working at Jena, and with Fichte and several others. And he now tries to catch the three biggest
fishes, Herder, Kant, and Goethe, in the name of a "society whose admiration for you is unbounded."

When Goethe picks up Schiller's letter he realizes that
he would be doing more harm to himself than to the new
magazine if he were to avoid Schiller now. It is to his
own interests to associate himself with this paper. In re-
plying, he says that he would be delighted to collaborate
"with such sterling men"; and when returning proof
of the prospectus he suddenly drops into warmer tones.

A month after this letter, the two poets meet on truly
neutral ground in the Society of Natural History at
Jena. By accident—as people choose to designate such
dovetailing of events—they leave the hall together.
Schiller complains against the tendency to divide up the
study of nature into too many minor categories, saying
that this alienates the layman. Goethe, who feels like a
scientist in comparison with this philosopher, agrees
with him, and mentions another way of dealing with
nature. It is possible, he points out, to treat nature as

something which is alive and active, and to go from the whole to the parts. The philosopher pricks up his ears. From the whole to the parts? Inductively? How could such things be derived from experience?

Meanwhile they arrive at Schiller's house. "The conversation," Goethe reports later, "lured me in. Then I eagerly discussed the metamorphosis of plants, and made . . . a symbolic plant arise before his eyes. He listened to all this and watched me with great sympathy and with decided comprehensiveness. But when I had finished, he shook his head and said, 'That is not an empirical fact, that is an idea.' I stopped short, somewhat annoyed, for the point of issue between us was now clearly stated. . . . The old enmity was about to reassert itself, but I kept myself under control and said, 'That would be excellent—that I should have ideas without knowing it, and that I should see them with my very eyes!'

"Schiller, who was much shrewder and better mannered than I and who wanted . . . to placate me rather than repel me on account of 'Die Horen,' replied like a cultured Kantian. And as my stubborn realism frequently provoked vigorous opposition, we argued a great deal, finally declaring an armistice. Though neither of us could call himself the victor, each did consider his position unassailed. Sentences like the following made me thoroughly unhappy: 'How can there ever be empirical knowledge which would conform to an idea? For the particular quality of an idea lies precisely in the fact that an empirical fact can never be totally similar to it!" As Goethe leaves the house and strides back through the July night to his own quarters, he says to himself, "Schiller calls the same things ideas which I call empirical facts, so there must be some medium of communication between us!" And the next morning he travels back to Weimar.

In the arena where philosophers and scientists hold their unending contests, these two men met in this decisive conversation—and we almost forget that they are both poets. Yet there is no greater evidence of their artistic antagonism than this first flash of union between them. Here were two polaric currents which were to require the efforts of a decade before their adjustment to each other should be complete. "No one could deny," Goethe writes, "that the two intellectual antipodes are separated by a greater distance than the diameter of the earth, since each may serve as a pole to the other, but for this very reason they cannot fall together into unity."

As a thinker Schiller is incorruptible, and will not yield a single step. Socially, he contrives to match Goethe as courteously as possible. In Goethe's words, he held fast to everything that came near him, and his wife did all that she could to help him. But it was precisely this typically Schillerian mixture of purity in his desires and sophistication in his methods which now attracted Goethe! He always liked people who strove to attain their ends by subtle means, even if these people happened to be his opponents. In that scene too Schiller seems really to have been as much Antonio as Tasso. Since he admired Schiller's powerful intellect, and clearly recognized how things stood at the present time, after letting him wait for six years Goethe found every reason now to proffer his hand to this younger man who had made such great progress in power, intellect, and self-command. One day after this conversation, when sending material for "Die Horen," he wrote: "I hope that you will hold me in friendly remembrance.

And let me assure you that I look forward keenly to the prospect of a more frequent interchange of ideas with you."

Goethe knows exactly what effect every one of these words will have on the man who receives them—and Schiller handles the precious sentences like a statesman. Since Goethe is traveling, Schiller allows four weeks to pass before writing him. Should we call it a letter? It is a philosophic discourse on Goethe, suited for delivery at some public function such as a funeral or an address in commemoration of an aging man's anniversary, but not at all the sort of thing one would send privately to a man in middle age. And his only way of introducing this unexpected monograph on Goethe is by saying at the start that his conversation with Goethe had set his "own store of thoughts" in motion. Schiller writes:

"Everything which analysis patiently seeks, and more, lies within your unerring intuition; and only because it lies in you as a whole, your own wealth is concealed from you. . . . Thus such minds as yours seldom are aware of how far they have advanced, and how little cause they have to borrow from philosophy, which can only learn from them. . . . For a long while, although from a considerable distance, I have observed your intellectual development, and have watched with constant admiration the course which you have marked out for yourself. You are seeking for the basic facts of nature, but you seek them by the most difficult route. . . . You go step by step from the simple organism to the more complicated, in order finally to construct the most highly complex of them all, man, genetically from the materials of nature's entire scheme. A great and really heroic idea. . . . You could not have hoped that your life would suffice for such a plan, but it is worth more to set out on such a course than to finish any other. Like Achilles in the Iliad, you have chosen between Pythia and Immortality.

"Had you been born a Greek, or even an Italian . . . your problem would have been made much simpler, perhaps even wholly unnecessary. Then, even at the first sight of things, you would have perceived their form and their laws, and the grand manner would have developed in you concomitantly with your first experiences. But since you are born a German, since your Greek mind was cast in this northern mold, the only choice open to you was that of becoming a northern artist yourself or of employing intellectual effort to compensate the imagination for what is denied it in actual experience, thus creating, you might say, a Greece from within and by a process of reasoning. . . . Thus you had one more problem; for as you went from perception to abstraction, you had to transform concepts back into intuitions, and change thoughts into feelings, since intuitions and feelings are required before genius can produce.

"These roughly are my opinions as to your intellectual trend, and you yourself will know best whether I am right. But you can hardly be expected to know (since genius is always the greatest mystery to itself) of the perfect accord between your philosophic instinct and the purest results of speculative reason. . . . Of course the intuitive mind is concerned solely with the individual and the speculative solely with the type. But if the intuitive mind possesses genius, and seeks in the empirical the character of the absolute, it will it is true produce individuals, yet these individuals will manifest

typicality. And if the speculative mind possesses genius
and does not lose sight of experience when rising above
it, it will produce nothing but types, yet with the possibility of life and with a solid relationship to real objects.

"But I note that I am writing a treatise rather than a
letter . . . and even should you not recognize yourself
in this mirror, I earnestly beg of you not to avoid it for
this reason." There follows the question as to whether
"Wilhelm Meister" could appear in "Die Horen." "My
friends and my wife beg to be kindly remembered by
you, and I remain very respectfully your obedient servant Fr. Schiller."

This letter was written by a philosopher and a man
of the world. The poet remains invisible—and so the
purely poetic perception of the subject must remain in
the background. Surely this is the first time that Goethe's
development was seen through the eyes of genius; it is
only rarely that Goethe, either before or after, has been
able to read such profound comments on himself. But it
is the processes of the mind, not the movements of the
man, which Schiller depicts here—and for the next eight
years until his death, despite his intimate contact with
Goethe, he will never try to sketch Goethe's character:
which is astonishing in this psychologist and can only
be explained by the purely intellectual manner with
which Schiller handles their relationship. (Neither poet,
in his works, ever attempted to portray the other.)

But here too Goethe's mind is thought out rather
than felt. In this period of Kantian moroseness, Schiller
seems to deliberately put aside all psychological and empirical methods, and explains the idea of Goethe's mind
even where another inference was known to him.

Goethe's procedure was genetic it is true, but biogenetic; and furthermore, it did not go from the plant to man but from man to the plant. As a poet Goethe did lack the harmonic universal culture of the south, and he did look for Greece in Italy. Yet this was not because of his nationality, but was purely a method of solving his personal difficulties—and if he finally went from perception to abstraction, he had not felt it necessary to convert his thoughts back into feelings, but he arranged his system in such a way that it was separated by a glass partition from his perception: each part within view of the other, yet divided in space. It was Schiller's own influence which did at times favor a certain coalescence of the two spheres.

On the other hand the diplomatic art with which Schiller conceals his motives in this letter is thoroughly successful. With what delicacy he treats Goethe as the naïve genius ignorant of itself—and yet he is aware that Goethe knows everything about himself! And at the same time, how proudly he excludes Goethe from philosophy, his own special province! How bold, to tell him that his efforts cannot possibly succeed, and that the efforts themselves, had he been born in the south, would have been superfluous! How subtle, to offer himself even in the event that his mirror should be deceptive! For this letter is one grand offer of service, a bow to a superior, who is acknowledged, it is true, in a courtly manner, but with the important addendum that Schiller's reason accorded perfectly with Goethe's instinct, that Goethe was the intuitive genius and Schiller the speculative one—and that for this reason no one else was so innately fitted as Schiller to understand Goethe.

Goethe wrote a few such letters to his duke. And just

as he had always finished off such lists of claims and re-
quests with a tone of voluntary submissiveness, so Schiller finally closes the door of this secret and holy chamber with the sudden frigid expression, "very respectfully
your obedient servant."

But Goethe forthwith reopens it. Not for the last
twenty years, if at all, has he ever held such a letter
in his hands. He feels that he is being seen here in perspective, that he is being considered historically, and
even heroically! And out of gratitude he did something
which was not at all characteristic of him at any time in
his life, but was particularly unlike him at present:
Schiller's senior by ten years, he is the first to pronounce
the word friendship. He meets Schiller's advances much
after the manner of a beautiful and distinguished
woman, acquiescing without resorting to expressions of
equal warmth. It is the strangest letter of betrothal:

"For my birthday," it is his forty-fifth, "no more
pleasant gift could have come to me than your letter, in
which you generously present me with the sum and
substance of my existence and by your sympathy en-
courage me to a more vigorous and assiduous use of my
resources." He also considers their conversation as a
turning-point in his life; it now appears "as if we, after
this unexpected meeting, are henceforth to advance together. I have always highly prized the honesty and
high seriousness which appears in everything that you
have written and done, and now I dare hope that you
yourself will acquaint me with your intellectual devel-
lopment, especially in recent years. . . . Everything
within me and about me I will willingly disclose. For
as I feel very keenly that my ambition far outreaches
the measure of human possibilities, I should like to place

many things before you, not merely as a means of preserving them, but also as a way of increasing their vitality. You will soon see for yourself how great an advantage your sympathy can be to me when on closer acquaintanceship with me you will perceive in me a kind of darkness and vacillation which I cannot master however conscious I am of it. . . . I hope soon to spend some time with you, and then we can talk over many things together." The novel has already been given to a publisher. "Farewell, and think of me in your circle. Goethe."

He makes it clear that his suitor, in this intellectual union which they now contemplate, is cordially invited to join him in managing his riches, while Schiller on his part need provide nothing but the well-known honesty and earnestness for which he has always been esteemed. But as to what Schiller himself is, Goethe does not seem to have the least idea; for although his works are available and have become quite famous, he is here amicably invited to present his new friend with a résumé of himself. The question of equality does not enter.

Yet Schiller feels himself the victor; which he is, insofar as he has taken Goethe's confidence by storm. In time, he feels, he will awaken a deeper interest. He is already surer of himself. He seizes on the mention of their common career and expands it to the point of hoping "that we shall travel the rest of our course together, and with all the greater profit, since those travelers on a long journey who join each other last have the most to exchange." Thus he is inaugurating more than a life-long friendship—this attachment will be such that Goethe must find it to his best advantage even at the close of his career.

Schiller now writes with fire—and he is much less philosophical than in the cold glow of his first letter. He speaks of himself in very much the accents of a Marquis de Posa; and the more gallantly he tries to place himself in the background, the more nobly he speaks in his own behalf. "I am compelled to try and make a little go a long way, and when on closer acquaintance you have discovered how small a store I have of what is called acquired knowledge, perhaps you will find that I have sometimes been successful in this. . . . You have a kingdom to govern, I but a rather numerous family of ideas. . . . My understanding really works more symbolically, and thus, like a hybrid, I fall halfway between idea and perception. . . . Usually, when I should have been the philosopher, I was overtaken by the poet, and when I turned to poetry the philosopher in me became uppermost. . . . But unfortunately, just when I had begun to appraise and utilize my moral forces properly, I am threatened physically by disease. . . . But I will do what I can, and if the structure finally collapses, still I shall probably have rescued from the conflagration all that is worth saving. . . . I lay these confessions before you in all frankness, and I dare hope that you will receive them with affection."

How perfect, that he was overtaken by the poet where he had aimed to be a philosopher! How ardently and rhythmically all this was couched. We can detect in this letter the signs of a racing pen, while the first letter was carefully planned and worked over!

With affection—as the younger man has requested—Goethe receives these lines, and promptly invites him to Weimar. Schiller, in accepting, merely begs indulgence for his illness. Yet in order to mask the old pride once more, he stresses to Körner that he "could not very well refuse" Goethe's pressing invitation since their contact would have decisive consequences for both parties; and to his wife he writes that he has heard from all quarters "how pleased Goethe is over his acquaintanceship with me." Much more coolly, Goethe tells his friend Meyer that Schiller was putting fresh life into his stagnating ideas, and even three months later writes moderately, saying that he is "going on this occasion" with Schiller and the Humboldts, "and it seems as though we were to travel together for quite a while."

This fourteen-day visit of Schiller's with Goethe is like an inventory of all the property which each of the two contracting parties contributes to the menage. A program is now outlined, they decide on an esthetic correspondence for subsequent publication. "We now know, my worthy friend, from our fortnight's conference that we agree as to basic principles, and that the spheres of our feelings, thoughts, and activities partly coincide and partly touch. From this we shall both derive great advantage." And now the correspondence begins, their collaboration in "Die Horen" begins, a new party in Germany begins.

This alliance, with slight fluctuations but with no perceptible development beyond its first stage, is to endure for eleven years. At the time it begins, the two associates are forty-five and thirty-five years of age. Yet the younger man is pale and emaciated with disease, while the older is tanned and strong. Schiller is taller, lean and gaunt. Goethe is broader and stouter now; he is already beginning to grow fat. Schiller's mild, humid eyes are deep-set in an oval face; a pallid forehead, Gothic and commanding, looms to greater breadth than height; the pale and sensitive lips are like those of a priest; his short, prominent, aquiline nose is bold and aggressive—its lines seem to express most forcefully the sublimity of the head. Goethe's head is squarish; above the cheekbones his forehead is vaulted; it is higher than it is broad. Despite its bend, the nose is almost calmly classical in comparison with Schiller's. The lips are narrow and reserved, but the eyes gleam out upon the world darkly and absorbingly. Schiller's handwriting is agitated and inventive, and surges across the page in vast and rapid tides. Goethe artfully transforms his particular traits into the typical.

Schiller, the young councilor and courtier, dresses with utmost care, orders the most expensive material for his evening clothes, keeps up a large house; at thirty-eight he has his coach and horses, which Goethe does not procure until he is nearly fifty. In the first year of his marriage he cannot travel with his wife as far as Leipzig without valets and maids. He is brilliant in society, and in his court uniform with epaulettes he can be mistaken for a high officer by Madame de Staël. Goethe dresses very simply, has already dispensed with toupet and curls, seldom goes to court, rarely appears in society. As minister he lives like a private citizen, deliberately cultivates a stiff and formal manner, says little. Schiller, accustomed to learning more from books than from people, unused to life in the open, tubercular, and in constant fear of his attacks, passes much of his time indoors, never takes physical exercise, sits for whole weeks in summer in a closed room, smoking and taking snuff.

Usually sleepless at night, he can make no definite

arrangements for the next day, sometimes does not have his luncheon until eight, on bad days must bolster up his strength with alcohol, and writes best when the barometer is low. Goethe relies upon a high barometer, retires early and rises early, writes only in the morning, spends whole weeks in his summer-house, rides, skates, has his healthiest years between the ages of forty and fifty. The sort of air which is beneficial to Schiller Goethe calls poison; and one day when he detects the smell of rotten apples rising from his friend's writing desk, he feels himself growing faint and hurriedly throws open the window.

Schiller, who is often bewildered by the multitude of his enterprises, is completely prevented from working by sickness. Goethe discharges his offices and his duties promptly in order to devote himself to study and writing. Schiller's outward life is made more difficult by disorder, Goethe's is made easier by his punctiliousness. And yet it was more imperative for Schiller than for Goethe to distinguish between business and the Muses, because Schiller always had more projects on foot and thus was required to divide carefully his art from this life.

At the time when Schiller joined forces with Goethe —this is the time to which our antithesis applies—Schiller is in danger of journalism; he is excellently suited, as Goethe says, to become an editor. A man of genius, polished, interested in politics and esthetics, Schiller had several business men around him; and in his desire for power and money he would probably have taken this course had it not been for his illness and for Goethe. Comrades of his youth picked him out for a diplomat; Goethe calls him as great at the tea table as he would have been in a national parliament. He likes business. Expostulation, intrigue, everything of this sort which is found in his plays, suits him better than it does Goethe, is more characteristic of him and is given greater importance. He understands perfectly how to get good writers for his paper, and how to make propaganda— and he likes to do it. When "Die Horen" is about to expire after three years, he suggests that they get it suppressed by printing a few extreme articles, in order that the paper might seem to have been exploded rather than buried in silence. Yet his continued restlessness and hastiness soon causes him to alter his arrangements with publishers and papers, so that even Goethe does not rely upon him to carry anything through, since (he writes to Meyer) "one should not expect Schiller's assistance for any definite end." With so many rival schemes, Schiller's impetuosity finally prevented him from arriving at any practical results, however much he converted his intellectual idealism into its commercial counterpart.

Goethe's abilities lie in an entirely different quarter. "When observing nature, I am a thoroughgoing realist, so that whenever things present themselves to me I am incapable of desiring to apply them or to modify them, and my only distinction between objects is whether they interest me or not. On the other hand, in every form of activity I may call myself completely idealistic: I do not inquire at all into the objects, but demand that everything shall fit in with my ideas."

Schiller's enterprising spirit, however, is not driven solely by the external motive of gain; it is also nourished from within by his will to power. Goethe seems to be thinking of this in his old age when he says to Eckermann, "Schiller, who was much more of an aristocrat than I, but who weighed his words much more carefully than I, had the remarkable good fortune to pass as a special friend of the people." If Schiller shouted freedom in his youth, he meant first of all his own freedom; and in the announcement and foreword of his "Robbers," at the age of twenty-two, he was already insisting that his play was neither politically nor morally subversive. Fifteen years later, when he received the rights of citizenship in the French republic, he was interested in the matter only insofar as it might benefit his son.

Except for his servants, he had practically no subordinates. But when he had to do with actors, who were the mediators between his work and the people, he decided: "There is only one kind of relationship with them, the curt imperative, which I do not have to maintain." With this conclusion he seems to be admonishing Goethe to adopt more rigorous tactics, yet Goethe continues to act in an advisory capacity when dealing with his artists. Here too he is the antipode of Goethe, who desired to pervade all of his many activities with the same energy and order, yet had no wish to dominate. When he seems to be aristocratic, he is in reality punctilious. On the other hand, when Goethe in old age is trying to analyze Schiller, he says of him: "Whatever he thought of, had to be, whether it conformed to reality or not."

When Schiller writes, his thoughts are on the world and posterity. In the midst of criticism, vexation, competition, gossip, and factions he conducts an extensive correspondence. And though he is consistently successful as a dramatist, he is irritated by every journalistic setback. Then he speaks of how his blood boiled with anger when his "Musen-Almanach" receives mixed praise and censure. Goethe, who gave up trying to please the Germans twenty years ago, smilingly answers with the mature thought: "Unless one is willing to sow his seed at random like that unwise sower in the Gospel, without asking where or how it will take root, he had best not concern himself with the public."

Also in their erotic life Schiller's desire for domination stands in complete contrast to Goethe's more feminine devotion. Schiller has hardly broken with his mistress before he begins warning his new friend against her— and when she in turn becomes his bride he tries to make her in every way his disciple. There is no conflict in his relations to Frau von Kalb, his wife Charlotte, and his divorced sister-in-law, Caroline. At his marriage he takes Caroline into his house, and when she marries again he establishes her in Weimar because he himself has gone there. He lives on perfect terms with his wife—and in his letters always addresses her as "dear little mousey." Schiller is sensual and imperious in love, but Goethe gives himself with his whole soul; for which reason he loves but one woman at a time and has literally never possessed two mistresses at once. But to the one woman, it is true, he speaks in such tones that Schiller's widow, on reading Goethe's letters to Frau von Stein, is horrified at their intensity and confesses that Schiller had never loved in that way, "for he could not love out of pure passion."

Thus Schiller is the more passionate poet. During the three years just previous to their alliance he has been devoting nearly all his time to historical studies and the philosophy of Kant. From Kant he derives his esthetic, which in turn has a decisive influence on his work. But later when Goethe outlines his theory of colors for him in the categories of thought, Schiller only becomes confused: "In such a rigorous form this empirical subject must always appear an unmanageable mass—and in my very desire to grasp it in terms of philosophical concepts I must feel my empirical insufficiency." So impossible is it to force a Goethean idea into a Schillerian form! "I myself believe," Goethe answers with a polite shrug of his shoulders, "that the empirical mass of phenomena, which . . . cover such a wide territory, will not readily lend themselves to a rational unity."

For although Goethe has been induced by Schiller to read Kant, to whose work he had heretofore paid but slight attention despite the suggestions of Jacobi, he is still only partially won over. He does not, like Schiller, need philosophy to rescue himself from confusion, or to find himself, but "to get away from myself, which I can do all the more readily in that my nature, like separate drops of quicksilver, so quickly and easily unites again." And is it absurd or sublime to read in Goethe's hand that one should read Kant's anthropology only in the springtime when the flowers provide solace, and "I have read it while children were playing around me." When he is writing, Goethe avoids philosophy completely, asserting that it interferes with his poetry, "since I can never maintain a purely speculative attitude, but must seek a perception with every sentence, and thus fly off forthwith into nature." At such times, also, he avoids too frequent conversations with Schelling, who is closest to him as a thinker. When Goethe produces, he does not like to think, "since I can only think insofar as I produce."

Perception is always the big thing to him. He even decides that he could almost dispense with his other senses. In his study of Cellini, Goethe declares that we can get a better idea of Cellini's century when looking through the eyes of "this confused individual than in the dissertations of the most clear-headed historian." And he rebukes a physiologist, saying that his treatise, "The Organ of the Soul," should be entitled, "The Cerebral Termini of the Nerves," for an idea of the objects of experience is only an organ by which we may grasp them. Soon the whole Kantian furor in Jena and in Germany will become too much for him; he wants to get back to art and break clear of this environment where everything inclines to speculation. Even in his old age he regrets that Schiller chose to bother himself so much with philosophy. And Goethe epitomizes all the contrasts in attitude between himself and his friend in one genial sentence which seems to have been hurled suddenly like an erratic block across the steppes of his diary: "Experience is almost always a parody of the idea."

Such fundamental divergencies readily manifest themselves as differences in their work. The problem is merely broached in the concepts of the sentimental and the naïve by which Schiller has very beautifully distinguished their methods of writing. Goethe himself in his old age deduces the nature of Schiller's talent from his proud body and gentle eyes. Schiller, he said, would take hold of a large subject boldly, turning it over and over;

"he saw the subject, as it were, only from without; a silent development from within did not concern him."

These Goethean words accurately define Schiller's greatness and limitations and his departure from the method of Goethe. Schiller looks for material, Goethe finds it: Schiller selects material, Goethe lives it: if there is more allegory in Schiller, in Goethe everything tends towards the symbol. Thus Schiller's speculation, far from being inimical to his poetry, positively benefits it! He must always encompass both at once, and he explains that only by a parallel movement can he keep "both heterogeneous elements in a kind of solution." As he himself complains, Schiller must rely in his work upon this ambivalence of dream and thought for his inspiration. The third and most powerful ingredient of the poet—perception, life, contingency, nature—seems to have remained alien to him. And one is astounded to hear him, with his great variety of activities, complaining that he has no opportunity to study people.

The more profoundly he senses his own characteristics, the more profoundly he analyzes the opposite ones of his friend, whom he always observes inquisitively, like an object in nature. "While you are working, you are really in the dark, and the light is solely within you. And when you begin to reflect, the inner light emanates from you and illuminates objects for both yourself and others. With me both these methods are intermingled, not very much to the advantage of the matter at hand." Here he has defined that obscurity and innocence which Aurelie advises young Wilhelm Meister to guard as an artist and which even the aging Goethe was able to preserve. For with all his self-analysis Goethe can recognize nothing but his structure; but he can never, like Schil-

ler, say in advance what he will produce, since "this
regulated natural force" cannot be led. Thus an inner
voice compels him to keep silent as to his plans. In
silence he tests out by his new epic the results of the
theory which they have both worked out in common;
and even in very advanced years he regrets the one time
when he disclosed a plan to his friends and abandoned it
at their advice. Schiller, on the other hand, discussed his
later plays with Goethe scene by scene.

Of these two types of poet, we could expect that
Schiller would work more rapidly. His concentration
seems astounding, his method of writing is violent,
aggressive, and bold, much the way he rides or plays
omber, while Goethe waits for the occasion, and henceforth tends to employ the word "sport" in speaking of
his writing whereas he formerly spoke only of "work."
The contrasts in their writing also apply to their ways
of reading their works aloud. Schiller weakened his effect
by reciting stormily, rhetorically, and dialogically, while
Goethe—by unanimous testimony—recited masterfully.

Schiller's temperament and the nature of his literary
ability made the theater his natural medium of expression, whereas Goethe never felt at home here. Schiller
genuinely enriched the German stage with eight or nine
plays. Even the most important dramas of Goethe irri-
tate us; and while the internal dramatic values of these
works are slowly gaining recognition, Schiller's plays
have not lost any of their effectiveness after a century.
Schiller gets the last ounce out of his coolly chosen
material, heightening every figure to its most intense
expression, even trying to key up Goethe's characters
with his furor. When Goethe's play is being put on at
Weimar, he wants to have Alba appear in silence behind

the condemned Egmont, to gloat over his revenge, and
Orestes seems to him the most doubtful thing in "Iphigenie": "Without the Furies there is no Orestes, and
now, since the cause of his condition is not apparent to
the senses . . . this condition is an overly uniform and
overly protracted suffering without an object."

Goethe on the other hand avoids this sort of intensity.
He calls the more pronounced effects in Wilhelm Meister much inferior to the content of the novel, and in
this he seems to himself like a person who tampers with
large columns of figures with the deliberate intention
of "losing the sum total through caprice." Even for the
stage he rewrites the prose scenes of the "Urfaust" into
verse in order that the idea may be disclosed as though
through a gauze and the tremendous effect be
blunted. His humor increases, he hunts for diversions.
Schiller's methods remind us somewhat of Rubens,
Goethe's of Rembrandt.

But like those two masters, for all their polarity
Goethe and Schiller had certain traits in common; and
it would be too un-Goethelike to conceal their similarities in the interests of a clearer antithesis, since these
similarities were necessary to their continued union.

To both men birth and nationality are of secondary
importance as creative factors. The records of Goethe's
youth are evidence that his ambitions caused him to
forget father and mother. Schiller does love his mother,
but always remains aloof from his parents. We know
what Goethe thought of nationalism. He also writes
to Schiller: "Patriotism as a personally valorous endeavor
is as superannuated as government by aristocracy or the
church." Schiller, who took nearly all his themes from

abroad, says—almost verbatim—when he is in his thirties: "A patriotic interest is important only for superannuated nations and for the youth of the world. . . . It is an impoverished, petty ideal to write for but one nation." Or on the subject of his public, which he had no practical reasons for condemning: "The Germans want sentiments, and the more insipid these are, the more widespread their reception."

Even when they are farthest apart—when Schiller is the pure speculator and Goethe the pure observer—they occasionally signal across to each other. Wilhelm Meister, which is constitutionally alien to Schiller, overwhelms him because in contrast to his frigid philosophy it is so living, because "all nature is purely synthesis and all philosophy antithesis. . . . The poet is the only genuine human being, and the best philosopher is a mere caricature alongside him," he writes—and at the same time he begins to turn away from philosophy again. Yet Goethe meets him halfway! In preparing a "Physiology of Plants" he now distinguishes four classes of naturalists, and in so doing places the speculative class above the intuitive, on the grounds that, in beginning with an idea this class pronounces the unity of the whole at the start, even though they do to an extent ask that nature be made to fit a preconceived idea. In Goethe's mouth this sounds almost like a prologue to Hegel.

Goethe by no means sees in his philosophic friend a purely speculative nature; on the contrary, he finds in Schiller a strange mixture of intuition and abstraction. And on the subject of his work, Schiller himself once makes the strange confession that a certain musical mood, without a definite subject, precedes his writing. But above all, these two men resemble each other in the purity of their purposes. Indeed, with remarkable similarity, they both use the same figure, independently of each other, to symbolize their efforts. At thirty Goethe writes in his diary that he would like to point his life to a pyramid, and if this is impossible the attempt would serve as the evidence of his striving. "Every one builds himself a pyramid," Schiller writes at the same age and in almost the same words; "and even if he cannot bring it to a point, he could do nothing better than try."

At these points the curves of their nature approach. But normally they are in an antithetical position; and Goethe's analysis after their first conversation, when he said that neither was victor and neither felt himself vanquished, applied until the close of their friendship. For as soon as we fail to consider the relative strength of their genius and speak only of their characters and the manifestations of their characters in their life and works, they must stand facing each other as equally matched and fundamentally different opponents.

Schiller wants to dominate, Goethe to accomplish. Schiller never abandons himself wholly to a person, but always abandons himself wholly to his work; Goethe's devotion to affectionate people is complete, and at times he has a similar attitude towards his work. Schiller hammers at his poetry with cold passion: Goethe models with a loving hand. For Schiller life comes after art, which explains why his search for enjoyment was so unharmonious. Life for Goethe is the root of art, and thus art blossoms as though of its own accord. Schiller always thinks while he is feeling; Goethe always perceives, even when he is thinking. Schiller plants one tree after another, Goethe sows seed.

For Schiller can hate as strongly as he can love, and he is also the counterpart of his heroes like Goethe: except that Schiller's are repudiated by the poet as principles of evil, while those of Goethe are complex characters, exactly like the heroes of legend, "good and bad like nature." Schiller gives us the only complete depiction of himself in Wallenstein. Believing in the existence of evil, he stylizes in himself only the good. Goethe seeks to reconcile the conflict between the two equally powerful aspects of his character. Schiller wrestles loudly with the world, Goethe struggles in silence with his demon. Schiller battles, Goethe grows.

But there is one thing which gives the figure of Schiller the dully glowing patina of pure bronze, while that of Goethe seeks to emerge with the breath of life from the block of white marble: Schiller never forgets the presence of death—and even if we did not know this for a fact, we could assume from the sequence of his works that they would be terminated by an early, bitterly contested death. Once when Goethe's friend Meyer had met Schiller in the avenue, he wrote that Schiller's face resembled the picture of the Crucified—yet this is many years before the end. With an ever quickening pace he is driven forward by an inner fever; it is as though he were fleeing breathlessly on a speeding horse before the Black Horseman, looking back once each morning to see whether the rider had gained a few lengths on him the previous night—a process each day repeated through the years. Thus in the last and fullest ten years of his life, with so many circumstances in his favor, Schiller felt a steady and undeviating urge to pile one tragedy upon another.

Earnestly and helpfully, with sympathetic forebodings, Goethe observes this drama. His life is set for eight decades. Illnesses are for him brief, serious crises. He has faith in life and avoids tragedy; for death is not his enemy and from the beginning he lives in friendly communion with it. Goethe believes in transfiguration.

DEHMEL

If any should have sung his way through hell,
Ask him what you would learn of Paradise;
For he alone can know life's purposes
Who in despair has turned his eyes towards death.

No poet ever stretched forth his hands to mankind with a purer gesture; no poet ever tried so intensely to create happiness. But his stammered blessings, the purity of his strivings, derived their value from the gloom and violence of inner conflict. "To meet all, clamorously and open-armed"—this was his inborn mission, the special dispensation of fate by which he loved and wrote. But in the depths of this thoroughly masculine mind there dwelt a demon which sometimes turned unexpectedly to give battle to both its master and his fellows. He bore within him God and Lucifer alike: often his sympathy was canceled by self-sufficiency, and his ecstasy destroyed by analysis. These are the three aspects of his inner conflict—and his work is their reflection.

We, who did not come to know him until he was in his forties, found it easy to love him—for by that time, having become purer with the passage of each year, he was wholly lovable. In thinking over all the men whom I have met throughout my life, and some of whom I have known intimately, I can recall no other whose maturity was so graced by the rewards of a self-imposed discipline. Here was an equipoise of pride and kindness; a volcano, sleeping, but by no means extinguished. Yes, had he lived through the classic period of a second youth, I feel certain that in his sixties he would have set forth one day on new adventures, with the same youthful smile, the same naïve and steady eyes, as he had essayed in his thirties. For him, man-love was but a metaphor: his intense yearning, one time fulfilled, was to love mankind through woman.

It is easy to explain Dehmel's character and his works each in terms of the other, for they are really one, or nearly one. But if we wish to understand the sterling qualities of this man, if we wish to feel him as surviving death, we must avoid the immediate records of his life: his letters which, while they are painful enough in script, create in print the undeniable feeling that we are strangers here and are, however great our sense of kinship and sympathy, guilty of intrusion. The publication of these letters continues Dehmel's tradition in his weakest aspect. Here his darker side predominates; here are his shortcomings, which are shortcomings despite their identity with his high virtues, despite the fact that we may consider the crown of a tree and its darkly delving roots as one.

For Dehmel was a confessor. Exactly like young Goethe, he brought to the light the evidences of his personal distress. But Dehmel remained here; he never tired of confessing before the world; he spurned, and even scorned, the mask, donning only so much of a costume as the rules of art demanded—while Goethe's dignity and misanthropy soon drove him back into the torment from which he had previously escaped with the courage of a young lion. Dehmel always remained a youth, perhaps too long, for in the end he paid for this with his life. We meet with passages or statements which drop to a lower level and even repel us, and we are about to complain, when of a sudden we come upon one of those

confessional poems which radiate from his pages, and we
thank the powers of creation for having incited a temperament at once stormy and beautiful, majestic and
naïve, to mirror itself in verse. For also the heavy com-
bats between dignity and love of humankind which
were waged silently within him, were always decided to
his advantage, since he would never permit either factor
to triumph at the complete expense of the other.

Venus obsessed him. He has experienced and depicted
her in a series of transformations; yet unlike other poets,
he has not situated these different aspects in many
women, but in a few, by increasing the number of metaphysical facets to be found in each. This eroticist lived
monogamously, because he was essentially a moralist;
and it was precisely those transubstantiations which
lifted him from the gloomy world of the senses, where
he once brooded with impatience, into the brightness of
Dionysiac revels. His constant concern for the happiness
of his fellow-man served to release him from the bond-
age of his desires; and thus his lucid temperament could
become evangelistic without Protestantism. Impulsively,
as he liked to say, he settled the conflict of sense and
soul; and thus he was fundamentally, if not a Greek,
then not a Christian either. He would follow no voice
which did not come from within and he walked with
humble pride towards his fate.

In Eros he resolved all discord. Love for him was no
lyrical theme, no romantic adventure; it had become a
sacred service, a rite of procreation and birth, the joy of
fulfillment as the sexes grow and develop towards their
culmination in union. For him this was a blossoming
beneath the light of magic. And if this was the primary

content of his life, if his guiding purpose was to grow
ripe for fate in such a sense as this, then he did finally
triumph in his fifty years of struggle. Dehmel was a
typically untragic mind; perhaps no other mind of his
period is so brimming with life.

As poet, the confessor was inevitably a rhapsodist—
and from this too we may project his work, his fortune,
and his death. His deepest wish was to place his convic-
tions before the world. But was there a world around
him? Was there at least a people? Dehmel rose up, traveled through Germany, mounted with his young body
the podium of the concert halls, and recited his songs in
a remarkable tone of voice, to the accompaniment of
unusual and expository gestures. What did he find?
Merely a public, curiosity, literature. Out of a first lec-
ture, in which the two hundred young people charmed
him because he dared to charm them, there grew the dull
mind of a paying crowd who did not even lift their eyebrows, unless perhaps they did so through sophistication.

It was only when he faced an audience of laborers
that he could detect any sense of community, any folk
spirit. For all his ardor, for all his yearning to lose himself in the arms of woman and to see his image reflected
in a friend's moist eyes, he had to be content—reciting
to a few scant hundreds the protestations of emotion
which he would, with the wild cry of the rhapsodist,
willingly have expended upon the entire world. Thus his
folk-poems—superb as they are—are rare, whereas he
was fitted by both genius and desire to become one of the
greatest of social poets, with a formal power far sur-
passing that of his brothers in Flanders and America.

Yet also as a recluse he remained a rhapsodist. Are not

his strongest poems ballads, even if he does call them romances or work-songs? At thirty he found a form in which he could merge his intellect and his temperament; and in his principal work, "Zwei Menschen," there really are pieces of a wholly new finish. If these passages and a small collection of his poems were issued between the same covers, Germany would be astounded at the magnitude of this writer. He never wearied in his office of self-discipline; he struggled constantly in Faust-like oscillation between knowledge and ecstasy; and as he heralded in his works every slight change of direction in his life, he has left a great many inferior things—and of the twelve volumes which we now have by him, nine will collect dust in the libraries.

In the novel he failed completely. In his dream-plays and pantomimes he strings the butterflies of his phantasy on wires and puts fabulous creatures on creaking wheels. In the drama this ecstatic could not endure the cold restraint of dialogue. And his essays, despite their depth of thought, are all marred by that obstinacy which is the other side of German thoroughness.

But there are a dozen poems by Dehmel, or perhaps as many as twenty, which will outlast the work of any other poet who sang in Europe around 1900. Despite all his theorizings and his mannerisms, these poems are masterpieces, the genuine promptings of genius. And though he may have looked upon them afterwards in astonishment, and wondered how he could have done them, they enable us to rank him alongside Goethe—with whom he has nothing but this excellence in common—as the one lyric poet of his generation.

Music, the harbinger and concomitant of fame, has sensed this in advance—and even during his lifetime more of Dehmel's poems had been set to music than of any person now living or of most earlier writers. Thus we have also this indirect testimony as to his tonal and rhythmic perfection; and he, who had looked on with a mixture of bitterness and irony while youth stammered and grimaced and coquetted with chaos, really did become the father of all new verse forms in Germany.

There are some elements of his work which are overly theoretical, bringing him dangerously near to Max Klinger—and these are perishable. Other passages, where he is frank at the expense of tact and good taste, we might also desire to omit today, as well as practically all his attempts at humor. Also, his industry, his caution, and his program of writing led him into many fatal revisions, the noble original thus becoming entangled in these later additions, like Norman arches beneath Arabic cupolas in Sicily. Even certain passages of "Zwei Menschen" breathe with difficulty beneath the rigid meshes of the metal net which he has thrown over them. In this grim theorizing which sometimes caused his own talent to turn against itself, he occasionally reminds us remotely of Richard Wagner, whom he hated as his sultry antipode, although Wagner was superior to him in power.

Dehmel peered out in vain from the confinement of his century, to which he was so thoroughly pledged, for practical opportunities of becoming a rhapsodist. With the intimacy and remoteness of a dream, his verses display a process: a graded elevation above the strictures of the bourgeois, an exchange of heavenly love for earthly love, while this in turn he exalted to heavenly love, lavishing upon the two women of his choice both the gifts of feminine devotion and the ardor of masculine strength. What a drama, where so much modesty combines with so much license—what a scene in the delicate hands of this strong will! Dehmel was in reality the supersensual-sensual wooer.

His sense of responsibility, his thoroughness, and his kindness—all of them qualities which a writer can dispense with—prevented this born poet from setting out for those adventures to which he was by nature fitted. After spending ten uneventful years just beyond the city of Berlin, he spent ten more uneventful years just beyond the city of Hamburg—and though he had more leisure during this second period of quiet, and the immediate necessity of earning a living was removed, in all these years he created little or nothing that was decisively new. His original projects, his great rhapsodies, fall mostly in between these two periods of imprisonment which the singer graciously imposed upon himself. He endured his second environment, which was so alien to him, with remarkable patience, dreaming of palms or pines, loving, waiting, giving his life esthetic order. But occasionally, over his wine, he would flare up—and at such times one could sense his instinctive need of pilgrimage and travel.

Then the war brought him trumpeted release. He misunderstood the war completely; or rather, he was determined to misunderstand it, for here finally was the adventure—since he had never gone forth to find it, it now came to find him. And thus Richard Dehmel—friend to all the world, internationalist by reason of his strong love of mankind, connoisseur of foreign cultures, a singer of the classes but never of races, Dehmel, this Wendic German, who passed his life with two Jewesses, whose friends were Frenchmen and Poles, whose verses had been translated into eight languages—this social European became over night a nationalist. With a typically German seriousness and thoroughness, he voluntarily subjected himself at the age of fifty to the Prussian yoke and tried to overlook the discrepancies between his own martial adventurous mood and the icy business of modern warfare. Now at last, the rhapsodist felt, his moment had arrived. Now songs could be forged like swords, songs which would be sung by the armies at the front and by the millions of the population behind. Dehmel felt the people and crept into the trenches.

He failed pitiably. After a few weeks he saw his pure enthusiasm caught in the firm grip of a ruling class; he perceived the dull wretchedness of his suffering countrymen, he began to understand the reprehensible carelessness of those in command, he was horrified at the criminal actions of his superiors. But a sense of chivalry deterred him from withdrawing immediately. He persisted for years, depressed and skeptical. His war-poems themselves are evidence of his disillusionment, for not one of them has attained his high level or won popular favor.

Still true to his nature as a confessor, he wrote a long account of his struggles between his patriotism and his feeling for mankind as a whole. But he had recoiled upon the innate revolutionary aspects of himself so thoroughly that at the time of the collapse he advised holding out for a while longer, since in a few weeks the Red Flag would also be hoisted among the enemy.

Dehmel perished of a war illness, being denied the good fortune of an easier and, in the national sense at

least, more glorious death on the field of battle. In death
he looked like a workman.

Because he retained the perennial eagerness of youth,
because even when his hair was gray he still had a strong
sense of the adventurous, because his dithyrambic yearnings led him to mistake a petty era for a great age and a
bureaucrats' war for a popular uprising, because he
dared to be a rhapsodist as late as the 1900's, this beautiful poet's-madness caused his destruction earlier than
his simple lust of life had wished, and long before his
genius had lowered its wings in exhaustion.

For in the last few years before the war he had made
a new beginning. Mature, resonant tones were uttered,
at once sweet and pungent, like aging Burgundy; his
brilliance here was cautious, his clarity elegiac. Prepared
for an unknown destiny, vigilantly and patiently he
faces the future, who holds in her hands the scroll of his
own fate. Slowly he wrests from her the lines:

> until the moment comes
> when, before I shall have finished reading,
> the scroll
> slips from my exhausted fingers:
> and with fettered hands
> you leave it to the winds to say
> what I have done.

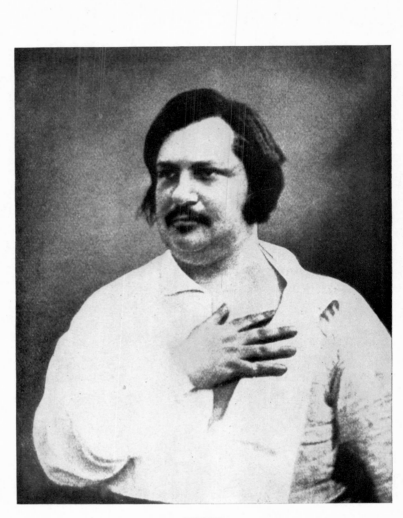

BALZAC

BALZAC

I

THE garret lies in the silence of night; the oil lamp is burning on the broad table; behind the green shade a man with an enormous head is bent over his papers. There is no other sound in the house; but up the steep walls from the depths below, through the window opened to the warmth of summer, comes the rustle of sleeping Paris. The last dancer has long since tossed his tuxedo down beside the bed, and the tradesmen who will be hurrying first to market are not yet awake. Even lovers merely interrupt their sleep for a time with soft whisperings which die away behind a thousand walls and doors.

But this lone man is sitting keenly awake at his table and adding one by one to the pile of white sheets which he has covered with the scratchings of a speeding, scintillant pen. This is the watchman of Paris, born to the task of peering at his century hour by hour, high above the metropolis, night after night, the warder of his age. But with this difference, that he does not strike a bell. Rather, he chronicles the histories of these yearning mortals who are sleeping now below; he records the legend of their most intimate experiences, describes the loves, struggles, and sufferings of their waking moments. Also, he tells the story of their brothers out in the French provinces—both the near and the remote— for he can see as far as that from his garret. For almost a generation he sits here, creating and assembling his characters, and adjusting their movements to one another. They are of all sorts; there are hundreds of them, two thousand in all, and they constitute a swarming world, a portrait of the period, a microcosm.

Now he rises to waken his comrade, for this typical Occidental has as his lone companion during these long nights an Oriental without which he cannot exist—his coffee, his stimulant. If he were to step before the mirror which hangs by his bed, he would meet the stocky figure of a monk in a white Capuchin cowl with the cords hanging loose, for he has already become quite fat from sitting so long over his work; also his bull-neck, which is always exposed at the throat, is too heavy for a man just entering his thirties, and his face has the flush of a person short of breath. A big nose protrudes from the gigantic skull, with sensually thick lips curving beneath it. Everything, including double chin and bushy black hair, seems to betray this monk's sybaritism, his delight in coarse pleasures.

"But there was nothing," says his friend, the poet Gautier, "like those eyes. They had life, brilliancy and magnetism. Despite his nightly vigils, the whites of his eyes were as clear and transparent and blue-veined as those of a child or a virgin, and contained two black diamonds momentarily pierced by flashes of gold: eyes to see through walls and hearts, to subdue animals, the eyes of a leader, of a conqueror."

And yet the cowl is no disguise. He does not look like a poet, or even a Frenchman. Short and thick-set, with the coarse features of a parvenu who is forcing his way up purely that he may glut when he arrives, this half monk, whose sweeping fiery eyes seem to lift him above the class of brutal energists without admitting him

to the sphere of intellect and meditation, in reality
spends three-fourths of every twenty-four hours (and
thus whole decades in all) in a self-imposed seclusion,
alone with his work.

For when morning comes now, and with it the noise
of the day, when the compositors return to their type,
still tired and ill-humored, they find bundles of manuscript in the splendid but unstable handwriting of
Balzac. And they sigh, for though it is hard to read, this
writer is always in a hurry and they must be quick.
The boy runs back and forth from the printer to the
author half a dozen times; the process of correction
begins, and it is endless. Passages which he dashed off
at top speed during the silence of the night, are now
hammered into shape in the cool light of the morning.
Whole pages are inserted and pinned on to others;
crosses and asterisks, arrows and signs of the Zodiac call
attention to new sentences and words. Everything is
pounded and tested. Six, eight, even ten times a sheet is
returned, and always with the speed of a journalist. For
the papers are usually waiting for the next chapter of
a novel, and his publishers for the end of a long promised
book. But besides, he wants to examine his work in the
perspective of print, and for days on end has corrections
made at his own expense until the grumbling compositors declare that they will not work longer than
one Balzac hour.

At noon a friend calls for him. He stands glowing
and steaming in the heat of victory, for every night is
a new battle. He has a huge appetite, eats a great deal
of simple food, smears his bread with butter and sar-
dines, tells stories and is mostly in good spirits, always
the life of the conversation, always active, always full

of plans and schemes and business projects; never at rest, and rarely in pursuit of pleasure.

Balzac was continually driven. What was it that drove him?

II

He was a proletarian like Rembrandt. His forbears were peasants and workers, day-laborers. The pastor had shown an interest in Balzac's father as a boy, and had taken him from the hemp fields and got him work in an office. With this as an opening wedge, his father had forced his entrance into the middle class. He procured some post or other through the Revolution, finally at the age of fifty marrying a young girl of the *petite bourgeoisie* and bringing her from Paris to Tours, in his native province, where he made money and served in the city government. There he wrote marvelous treatises against rabies and in defense of illegitimate children, and even had his portrait painted, pen in hand, but it did not suit him. As he sits there he might be taken for one of those peasants who went to war and became generals under Napoleon: hale, humorous, at peace with himself, Rabelaisian in his rustic cunning and love of pleasure, called by his mother a *chien de Gascoigne* and determined to live to be a hundred. All this health, heartiness, and boldness he bequeathed to his son.

Honoré, who derived this handsome name from the saint of his birthday, saw beside his father an anxious, parsimonious, and humorless mother who viewed the world with ill nature and discontent and who, as he confided later, hated her son. "I have never had a mother;

she hated me from my first day on earth. I was immediately entrusted to the care of a wet-nurse. . . . From my fourth to my sixth years I saw my mother only on Sundays. . . . Between seven and fourteen I saw her but twice. My father assured me that I would never have a worse enemy all my life."

Inspired by the remarkable changes in the social structure caused by the Revolution, the youth sought to escape from the narrow confines and the bleakness of his home. He found life at school in Vendôme very strict. He had to stay after class, was beaten, and was even put in confinement; but there happened to be an old priest here in charge of the library who gave him access to all the books. The boy, whose childhood had brought him nothing, now began reading, and he read steadily for the next three years. He read like a madman, greedily and haphazardly—and at the age of twelve he wrote a treatise on the human will. But this overstimulation of the brain proved too much for him. He was brought home suffering from fever and prostration, and lay for weeks in a state of semiconsciousness.

That was nature's first grave warning. Had Balzac heeded it, his life would have been much happier and quieter, and Europe would have been cheated of his works. But fate demanded that these works be written, and by him alone—so at the age of twenty, after a second school period at Paris, where he read omnivorously while studying law, he definitely decided to become an author. What brought him to this?

The two ideals which he confesses to his sister, *"Etre célèbre et être aimé,"* are often characteristic of talented youth in romantic eras. The unusual thing in

his case, however, was his ambition to write a successful play and quickly establish a name for himself, "in
order to enjoy the royal prerogatives of genius." He
did doubtless feel that he possessed a rich imagination—
but his choice of a career in letters rather than in politics
or business was determined principally by his preoc-
cupation with books. He was not moved primarily by
either a love of writing or a desire for immortality:
what he wanted to do was to arrive, and he turned to
art as a likely means of doing so. At the age of twenty
Balzac, of proletarian stock, began the steep ascent of
the pyramid, from poverty and insignificance up to the
narrower zone of money and position; and since he was
determined to press onwards to the very top, since there
was latent in the lines of this colossal neck an energy
without parallel in the history of art, he did cover this
intervening distance within the next thirty years—
though the effort was to cost him his life, and on reaching the apex he collapsed with exhaustion, a vanquished
conqueror.

These almost wholly realistic motives (the climber's
desire to improve his station and the petty bourgeois
wish for freer forms of living) drove Balzac from his
father's hearth into the garret. His parents had had
visions of their son as a model lawyer. Now they were
horrified, and by their embittered avarice converted his
two-year probation into a period of famine. "My breakfast," in the words which he later put into the mouth
of his *alter ego* in "Peau de Chagrin," "a stale roll
softened in milk, cost me two sous; at noon I ate only
every other day, so that my daily expenditure was but
nine sous. I used more oil than bread, the light of my
night lamp cost more than my room. This conflict with

destitution was long, intense, and comfortless." He spent
his days in a near-by library, for it was both his passion
and his program to read, and to learn, and to make his
own everything that gives this privileged class its self-reliance. And in times of need, he kept up his spirits by
a firm belief in his ultimate success: "Your brother is
already living like the great, which is to say he is starving. Coffee makes frightful spots, and much water is
needed to wash them away—but water does not come
up to my aerie (though on rainy days it comes down)
. . . I have eaten two melons—I must pay for that
with dry bread."

What then does he write, between the inkwell and
the coffeepot? In the sweat of his brow he scans Alex-
andrines, in an attempt to dramatize the life of Crom-
well. How hard it is to write verses. Something, either
a meter or a rhyme, is always out of place! And when
it is finally completed, and he goes home to read it to
the assembled family: utter defeat. A professor who
writes is consulted and gives as his expert opinion: "En-
courage the author to become anything he wants but
a writer." Will he now go back to law? Has he been
convinced? He shakes his head and answers cheerfully,
"Tragedy is not my forte. So perhaps it is to be the
novel." He returns home where, though he had to endure resentment and banter, he wrote two dozen novels
between the ages of twenty-three and twenty-six. These
books are wholly devoid of power and were merely
written to supply the market at the time and bring in
a little money to their author, who valued them so little
that he issued them under assumed names.

At the same time he took over a printing plant, his
parents gladly risking for this purpose a small holding

the income from which would have made him independent for life as a rhymester. His ideal was the then
famous Richardson who had made a fortune as the publisher and printer of his own novels. But since he saw
the goal so much more clearly than the obstacles, and
since his inborn peasant energy was victimized by an
overly rich and hasty imagination, within two years his
enterprise was in ruins. He next purchased a large type-
foundry, but when this in turn went bankrupt he gave
up the struggle. He was now more than a hundred thousand francs in debt. Henceforth these debts comprised
his negative nest-egg: around them all the calamities
of this life were to gather. The only other relic of this
venture is a work, "Balzac as Printer," which was issued
with all the appurtenant documents as a volume de luxe
on the occasion of the centennial of this same type-
foundry.

This failure at twenty-seven, and all the experiences
with promissory notes, money-lenders, usurious rates
of interest and court rulings that went with it, made
Balzac much more sensitive to the contemporary scene
in general while affording him deep insight into one set
of events in particular—thus, by providing him at once
with an equipment of facts and a corresponding attitude, it became magnified to the proportions of a
symbol. The gamut of emotions which he derived from
this *débâcle* as a business man made Balzac a poet. Hereafter he knew that this was no time for ranting in verse;
he now had the courage to use as the theme of a book
the ideas of life which he had developed out of his own
contact with actualities. Balzac had found that money
was the dominant motive of his age, and he wrote
accordingly.

Two years later he was famous. Now, under his own name, he wrote in the two years from twenty-eight to thirty the first two volumes of the "Scènes de la Vie Privée," the "Peau de Chagrin" and the first ten "Contes Drôlatiques." His first great original figure was Gobseck, the usurer.

III

He lived for another twenty years; and up to the very moment of death he nursed the mad hope that by reason of his talent he would cancel off his earlier failure and become a millionaire. While groaning under the necessity of earning six thousand francs a year to pay the interest on his debts and as much more for his current expenses, he was always on the lookout for a chance to make a fortune at one stroke. Neither Beaumarchais nor Voltaire had relied on the income from their works, but had on the contrary resorted to financial speculations; yet Balzac stuck to his theory and consoled himself with the lone example of Scott who was successful in doing what Balzac, with inadequate legal protection for his work, could not do.

Why? Did he have passions which cost him hundreds of thousands? Were there such items as extravagant mistresses, exacting minions, gambling halls, or jewels? Nothing of the sort. A good table wine, a beautiful vase, perhaps even a little celebration now and then, but neither women nor horses nor travels. His one driving force was the climber's hankering after some vague ideal of splendor; it was his ambition to be counted among the élite, to have his passport of genius viséed by the authorities. Also, he insisted that to get a good price in Paris one must have a prosperous appearance, and he assumed a sophisticated manner which was intended to dumbfound his publishers and editors.

Thus it happens that Balzac, who was not recognized when he stormed into the printer's in the morning wearing gray-and-black checked trousers, with heavy shoes, a red shawl around his neck, and a slouch hat on his head, in the afternoon drove his tilbury through the Bois in person while his groom behind was in readiness should the nag decide to bolt. He had a fashionable tailor fit a blue frock-coat tight across his stomach; he ordered of the leading jeweler of Paris a cane with a jeweled head; but he also appeared at tea with the duchess of Abrantès and was to be seen in the evening among the celebrities of the times in a *loge* of the Théâtre des Italiens. He was not disturbed when Gavarni, who mistook him in civilian clothes for a traveling salesman, caricatured him as a dandy. Nor did he suspect how these marquises and duchesses laughed at the title and the coat of arms which he bluntly bestowed upon himself, styling himself "Monsieur de Balzac d'Entraigues" although he had no trace of kinship with any such family and his father had been the first to write the peasant name of "Balsas" with a "*c.*" But the son insisted upon his nobility, and his pseudonyms were invariably titled names of his own invention!

This was Balzac, who as a man of letters was one of the first writers to portray the growing power and vitality of the fourth estate and who was past master at depicting the decadence of the flashy women of the aristocracy, but who as a man of fashion had no higher ambition than to be admitted into that very same society. This was Balzac, the most powerful critic of society, whose fondest hope was that he might become, not a popular leader in parliament, but a peer of France.

Rembrandt in his middle period also wanted to give the world a spectacle. But he only adorned house and wife, dreaming of chains, casques and mirrors, and feasting his painter's eye on effects of texture and light —and when all this was taken from him, he calmly withdrew into one little room and painted beggars like kings. Balzac, once he was gripped by this madness, never again got free of it and sacrificed his life to this illusory purpose. He furnished a house ornately and invited Rossini the epicure and his mistress as guests, borrowing the silver from his publisher since his own was in pawn. "I will provide the finest wines, the greatest delicacies, the rarest flowers, in short I will give my best." How? Is Balzac's best nothing but an imitation of Rothschild? "Rossini avowed he had never seen the equal at the home of any prince, that he had never eaten better or drunk better. He sparkled with enthusiasm."

His debts doubled under usurious rates of interest; the mountain which separated the poet from freedom became more and more impassable; court bailiffs followed him everywhere; in order to escape writs of execution he removed to a house with entrances on two streets, and he fled from Paris. Thus his rapidly growing reputation was dearly bought. He placed twelve volumes on contemporary society—not a word of which had yet been written—for an advance of 26,000 francs, and his letters show that he was much more gratified over this transaction than at the completion of many a novel. And now who would honor the publisher's drafts? An author was already asking himself this question a hundred years ago. Thus he paid his creditors with drafts, so as to get back now and then a few hundred francs in cash. Then he bought Chinese vases and took them to the pawnshop four days later.

He compared his publishers to the vulture of Prometheus, and on another occasion insisted that they "think of nothing but plunder." "Some day," he wrote to one of them while traveling, "and that day is not far off, you will have made your fortune out of me; our carriages will pass in the Bois; your enemies and mine will burst with envy. Your friend H. de B." Postscript in microscopic letters: "Apropos, dear friend, I have nothing left, so I have raised 1500 francs from Rothschild and drawn a draft for that amount on you, due ten days after sight."

The situation was chronic. As his reputation and earning power increased, his pretensions and phantasms increased proportionately. He lived like a hermit, requiring but a few hundred francs a month; but he doubled his debts by his absurd purchases and had to speed up the tempo of his work accordingly. "This frightful need of money, this demand, which has just driven me to write 'Honorine' in three days, will force me to finish 'The Last Love' in three days more. You do not know how this continued pressure humiliates me."

Thus in one year he wrote two totally different books, "La Recherche de l'Absolu" and "Père Goriot," the latter being turned out for a magazine in six weeks, during which time he had but eighty hours' sleep. He, a genuine poet, never once speaks of moods or other such ornaments of the soul. Figures, always figures. 200 hours a month, at y pages an hour, makes x volumes in half a year. "The 'Député d'Arcis' has four volumes, with one hundred characters in all, so you can well imagine how much headwork the book requires." Always like manual labor.

Since he considered writing as a routine to be learned, and since he claimed that he had written for so many years under pseudonyms "to limber up his arm," he was tireless in his attention to the details of his trade and looked upon his work with the practicality and self-confidence of a master. He instituted lawsuits to prevent the pirating of his works, and when he won his case he wrote a sensational preface within a few hours and set up two editions in two days. If he founded a magazine, it must forthwith "beat all the others," whereat he lost 40,000 francs. He organized an authors' league, proposing a vulgar farce to one of his comrades, and to another a drama for which he had nothing but the last sentence. In addition to his major works he was continually turning out sketches, editorials, feuilletons, and Paris letters for the newspapers, in which he chats about tobacco and wines, the new cabinet, the tariff policy, good food and gloves. "Everything must file past," he writes gayly to a friend; "the light penny literature as well as the society novels and the great thoughts which no one understands." As a way to get subscribers for an edition of his complete works, he thought of giving his readers annuity contracts in combination with the books.

He had such a reservoir of energy, and work came so natural with him, that he readily assumed new obligations. And under the pressure of these obligations he had to expend still more of his energies, so that his enormous innate capacity for work became even further developed during the course of his life. "If the artist does not plunge into his work like Curtius into the abyss, if he does not toil within this crater like a miner buried alive . . . then he is guilty of murdering his talent. For this reason the same reward, the same laurels, are held out to the poet as to the leader of an army."

Did he, through writing so much, write loosely?

He treated his galleys, he said, like a she-bear licking her cubs. He did not merely revise *ad nauseam*, he also consulted experts. He was never content, he knew how to profit by intelligent criticism; and often when getting out a new edition he would work over his old novels sentence by sentence, while writing at top speed on new ones. At times he even surpassed his own records: in a fever of work, he kept all the compositors in readiness until eleven o'clock at night, and in this same night, on two printer's sheets he accomplished the Ascension of "Séraphita," including all revisions. At the close of his life, twenty-two years after the beginning of his career proper, there were over a hundred completed novels to carry Balzac's name around the world.

IV

What was the source of this enormous output?

If one looks at his first portrait, one will observe a youth with wide open, eager eyes. The eyes have no expression of meditation or awakening; they are aggressively reaching out for things. He sees what he hears, he sees what he reads, converting everything into the present, into a picture, since only contemporary life can arouse his talent. He seldom dealt with the past, and the few books in which he did so can be discarded without loss. He despised authors who can only express themselves in terms of Rome or Hellas. The one thing in history that interested him was France, the France of the present and of the immediate past. At first this was a kind of instinctive economy; afterwards it became a deliberate program, but it was never mere nationalism. He needed a background for his novels, and he found it ready to hand in his own country.

Although he had read a jumble of everything, he had never studied, merely collecting whatever might serve his purposes. However, all this was stored away in a monstrous memory which retained everything—words, places, expressions—with the same fidelity. Since he possessed the power of creative imagination which marks the born writer, he did not need to parcel himself out autobiographically. He hardly ever borrowed situations from his own life, and even more rarely characters, never portraying himself, and only fragmentarily copying rooms, landscapes, or sensations. Like Shakespeare, he had no eye for individuals, but always saw beyond them to the type; he had observed every species of *homo sapiens* and for this very reason had never created a character *à clef*. Neither Vautrin nor Gobseck, Lucien nor Rastignac, Esther nor Delphine were drawn by him from nature, though the romantics regularly derived their characters in this way and even Goethe did so at times. Yet, while he produced types, his keen observation and his sound sense of reality spared him from the danger of empty abstractions.

It is hard to forget his characters because of certain subtle peculiarities of theirs which seem rooted in distant recollections. "Many little details which you have long since forgotten," he writes to his mistress, "will

keep me awake for half the night when I am hunting
without success for subjects. One time I see the foot-
path from Diodati or the gravel of the central avenue in
the Parc Monceau, another time it is a certain emphasis,
a certain almost childish pressure of the hand, while we
looked at pictures together."

To be sure, the types which annoyed him most in life
—brokers, lawyers, and usurers—are the ones with
which, through a natural thirst for vengeance, he was
most successful. But he also depicts with equal saliency
and color *petits bourgeois* and peasants, the class from
which he came; and marquises and duchesses, the class
towards which he was climbing; and soldiers and officers,
a class which he particularly envied. Yet he never went
out deliberately in search of facts. It was only at twenty,
while he was still scanning verses, that he purposely observed people—workmen in the suburbs, vagabonds,
and children—but at that time he had no thought of
copying them. Later, "observation became mechanical
with me. Without surveying the body, I could delve
into the mind: yes, through comprehending all the details of people's lives, I was able to go beyond them. I
could share another's experiences, by putting myself in
his place."

He did, however, study his backgrounds. No one has
ever had a more intimate and a more relentless understanding of the Paris of his times. He traveled through
certain departments purely in search of descriptive detail. The greatest landscape he ever studied, that vast,
unending Gobelin on which he never ceased weaving,
was the era of Napoleon. When Balzac was born, in
1799, Bonaparte was overthrowing the directorate.
When the emperor boarded his last vessel, Balzac was

sixteen. His father had already written an appeal for
a gigantic monument; the son saw in Napoleon quite
simply a kindred genius, and in reality the basic traits
of their two characters can be compared, since they
both owed their work to the same combination of imagination and energy.

Yet the statesman could only attract the epic poet
as a prototype, not as a theme. He collected in a notebook all the sayings of Napoleon he could find, and
later sold these 500 maxims for 4,000 francs to a hat-
maker who thought that they might help him to get
into the Legion of Honor. The poet would never have
undertaken to portray the emperor, who passes through
Balzac's great tragi-comedy solely like a god, intangibly
present, appearing only two or three times *ex machina*
in his own person. It was the environment or background of Napoleon that appealed to the novelist.
Thus, he absorbed the stories of an old duchess and of
an animal-tamer who had been with him in Egypt; he
drew out grenadiers and baggage carriers, priests and
provisioners; he learned of the battle of Wagram from
Schwarzenberg's son; and he devoured the anecdotes
of Metternich. Yet suddenly he goes beyond all
authentic detail, and in the "Country Doctor" an old
soldier who had become a rural letter-carrier tells the
peasants in a barn the story of the emperor as though
it were an ancient legend.

For what good would he—or any other poet—have
derived from keenness of observation if this observation
were not again and again lost in the diffuse light of the
common sun and were not the sharp outlines of reality
bathed in the golden glow of this delusion! Thus even
in his first novels he intuitively disclosed the empty ex-

istence of those titled women to whom he himself was later to fall victim; and if he expended much time, money, and brains solely that he might sit at a prince's tea table, he also portrayed the mistress of such salons, the beautiful Feodora, as she lies in bed at night and, before abandoning herself to sleep and paramour, studies the stock reports.

"My instability is the result of my imagination, which can receive one thing after another and yet remain virginal, as untouched as a mirror which is never tarnished by what it reflects. This mirror is in my brain. . . . To what do I owe this gift? I do not know. A second sight? I have never examined it; I possess it and use it. . . . With me nothing ages. Everything which ever moved me is as vivid as though it had occurred yesterday. A tree, a river, a mountain, a vista, a word, a glance, distress, happiness, danger, excitement, even the sand or the tiniest event, everything is reflected inside me, each day I feel it all anew and with greater force."

From this belief, perhaps, this feeling that his consciousness was mounting towards the universal, he arrived at a state of mind which might be called Balzac's unhappy love. For this falcon-eyed stalker of mankind, of all authors the most sensuous, had a remarkable hankering after the super-sensuous. Even in his youth he collected information about magnetism and mesmerism. Later he studied Swedenborg; he believed in mental telepathy, prophesying for Gall and Lavater the revival of interest which they are enjoying today. And in the last analysis he prized none other of his works so highly as his magnificent though imperfect "Séraphita," the only book on which he ever worked over a period of years. This and "Albert Savarus," his two mystical novels, are immersed in an overly brilliant light which is foreign to his realism. He believes in them, for "one can write a 'Père Goriot' any day, a 'Séraphita' but once in a lifetime."

And yet it seems as though despite his energy he recoiled from subjects which he felt to be beyond him— and in one letter he makes a confession whose full purport even he himself could hardly fathom: "If when I go to bed, I am not tired and sleepy, then I am lost, for the moment just before falling asleep, when one is delivered up to himself and the infinite, is a disastrous one for me."

Here are his natural limits. When he meets himself too much alone, without energy and movement, Balzac turns back obediently into the realism of his era.

V

"Today the writer has replaced the priest . . . he consoles, condemns, prophesies. His voice does not resound in the nave of a cathedral, it spreads thunderously from one end of the world to the other. Mankind, his flock, hearkens to his poetry, and many a word weighs more than many a victory. . . . He has become the choir-master of his century. That is a fact. It used to be Tacitus, Calvin, Voltaire, Rousseau, Chateaubriand, Constant, Staël. Now it is the newspaper. . . . If but fifteen men of talent in France were to be united under one leader as great as Voltaire, the farce of a so-called constitution, the enduring power of mediocrity, would be at an end."

This awareness of a social mission grew stronger in Balzac during his thirties; and however much of a con-

servative he was on the surface, at heart he was
thoroughly revolutionary. When he wrote against socialism—as when he asserted that the doctrine of
equality implies equality of brains and stomachs, that
capital was merely being frightened away to England,
and that the state should not meddle in the affairs of the
individual—he was prompted to this partly by the sense
of mastery proper to a man of genius, and partly by
the arguments of that class towards which his ambitions
were driving him. Yet the proletarian's resentment
against his superiors, the compensatory pride of the
frustrated, recurs continually; and social irony flashes
through his work in hundreds of places. He knows why
he jokingly calls himself *"docteur"*—*"docteur des
sciences sociales et des maux incurables."*

The incurable evil is money, for him who never has
it and is always trying to get it, and also for those who
do have it. Balzac, the first great unromantic author
after Goethe, dared in one of his first novels to trouble
a young man with two questions: was he loved in return, and would he be able to pay for the cab on the
trip home. During a period of sentimental fiction where
the hero joyously awoke in a neat, idyllic attic, he chose
to write of dusty, middle-class boarding-houses; and
while his contemporaries raved hellenistically, Gautier
tells of how Balzac stood before the Venus de Milo without much enthusiasm, "but there was an elegant
Parisian woman who was standing in front of the statue
admiring it, and he studied her eagerly down to the last
detail. He loved the fashions of his own day; he loved
Paris."

The more resolutely Balzac concerned himself with
the present and the farther his experiences as a climber

carried him into the criticism of contemporary society, the more definitely he came to face an architectonic task which he did not seem capable of solving. He was already well into his thirties and had just come to realize the full measure of his strength when, on looking back over a number of single, unrelated novels, he got the idea of bringing into one system all his past and future work, of writing the moral history of his period. Balzac fully realized the importance of this moment, wherein he ceased to be a writer of stories and became a writer of history. He immediately ran with this idea to his sister, swinging his Spanish cane, playing a drum-call, and crying: "I am breaking through all obstacles! Salute! I am now on the road to genius!"

His undertaking, even as a plan, is without parallel in French literature. For it is anything but French, and might at best be compared to the baroque projects of Michael Angelo, which nearly all were left as torsos. "In these studies of manners I will paint the play of the emotions and the turmoil of life. . . . Nothing shall be forgotten, not a single age or trade, neither politics, law, nor war. . . . Then in the philosophical studies I will establish the why of the emotions and the wherefore of life. . . . In this way I shall have imbued everything with life—by idealizing the type and making the individual typical." He decided that he would require twenty-four volumes of social studies, fifteen philosophical, and nine analytical. "Thus the individual, society, and the race will be described, judged, and analyzed without overlap, in one work which shall become you might say the 'Arabian Nights' of the West."

It was not until ten years after this epistolary sketch, and a few years before his death, that this project came

before the public with its present name and arrangement. The ambitious title, "Comédie Humaine," paro-
dying the title of a work which on its own score was
beyond ironic comparison, did not originate with the
author, but was suggested by a traveling Italian count,
perhaps as a witticism at table, to be afterwards parodied
by Balzac himself. But he soars magnificently in the
preface which he affixes to the first volumes in their new
framework.

Here Balzac associates himself with the new discovery
of Saint-Hilaire, "whose victory over Cuvier is welcomed in the last essay of the great Goethe." As the
animal kingdom, according to Saint-Hilaire, is developed from one primitive form into all its multiple
aspects through the influence of environment, so society creates different types: "Soldiers, workmen, savants, statesmen, merchants, seamen, poets, beggars,
priests are as distinct from one another as wolves, lions,
ravens, sharks, and vultures." What Buffon did for the
animal kingdom, Balzac wants to do for society—and
at the same time he is fully aware of all the difficulties.
"But how arrange the drama of the three or four thousand different people which go to make up a society?
At first I saw no way of writing a history of the human
heart in such a manner. . . . Then by taking an inventory of virtues and vices, selecting the most important events of human society, and constructing types
by the amalgamation of similar characters, I could perhaps succeed in writing the history of morals overlooked
by so many historians."

To plan a work of such architectural proportions, a
sense of unlimited energy was necessary; and only by a
clear knowledge of social criticism could it be arranged

into its various parts. But to put it successfully into
effect, one must have had long practice beforehand in
inventing and managing characters independently of
such a plan. The fact that so much of Balzac's work
preceded this superimposed outline saved it from the
danger of a schematization which even Goethe did not
always avoid in his revisions. In a list dating from the
period just before his death, the titles of 144 novels of
provincial, Parisian, political, military, and country life
are recorded under appropriate headings and sub-head-
ings as "Scenes of Private Life." Of these, forty-eight
were never written, while practically all the philosophical and analytical volumes are missing.

For the poet himself the plan, which he also called
his cathedral, his Madeleine, became a means of increasing his self-esteem, of indulging his sporting instinct,
and of dazzling his publishers.

The plan was thoroughly epic in its conception.
Nothing shows more clearly the difference between
Balzac and Shakespeare, writers who have as a trait
in common their unusual wealth of characters. Balzac
always invents, Shakespeare hardly ever invents. Balzac hunts for the type in the present, Shakespeare finds
it in history and literature. Balzac converts his contemporaries into myth, Shakespeare converts mythical
figures into contemporaries. Both succeed in the highest
task of which a portrayer of human beings is capable:
their characters escape from their own hands, break
away from their sponsors, and seek ways of their own,
and hundreds of years later we meet them in company,
on journeys, in love-affairs, in politics. Products of the
imagination have attained the reality of people who
once lived, people who will live tomorrow.

Wholly a prose-writer, in the double sense of an author who finds both verse and the stage unendurable and impossible, Balzac despised the drama and declared that it was superannuated. But he was continually trying his hand at plays, purely in the hopes that he might get rich suddenly by a theatrical success. He, who was in the habit of working out everything for himself, without documents or patterns, asked friends to turn out a few sonnets for his novels, and sought collaborators for what he alleged to be the lower art-form of the drama, farming out the acts among them and talking fantastically of the première in terms of hundreds of thousands of francs.

Gautier, whose essay on Balzac represents the finest tribute one poet ever paid to another, ascribes Balzac's limitations as a playwright to the fact that the chapters of a novel can be worked over indefinitely, whereas this is not possible with the scenes of a drama. This significant remark brings us back to the one set of conditions under which Balzac could produce. His continual restlessness, his writing under constant high pressure, the *tempo agitato* which was required for the development of his gifts, and a fiery temperament doubled in intensity by need, are all opposed to the calm of dramatic composition.

For in general dramatists and sculptors will prove to be more in repose than painters, epic poets, and musicians.

VI

Had he been calm, Balzac could never have become the Buffon of the human race. As his own tempo matched that of the era which he portrayed in his books, so he carried within him lamb and lion, poet, prince, and outlaw, giving them all free play within the confines of his mind. Even without definite documentary proof, every reader would inevitably conclude that Balzac was an author of pronounced emotional antinomies. But we have the documents to prove this.

The dark aspects of human character which he did not possess were envy, greed, cunning and intrigue. He was spared from all that by a pervasive good humor which rarely left him. "On the slightest provocation," Gautier recounts, "this hilarity broke out and shook his broad chest. The timid might be frightened, but every one had to join in. In this he had no thought of playing for the gallery. He was moved by a kind of inner drunkenness; in swift strokes, with intensely comical effects, and with no little skill, he would paint on the wall the mad phantasies which danced in the *camera obscura* of his brain." This joviality, inherited from his peasant ancestors, was the result of his enormous energy, which was always generating new plans for the future. "First finish the great comedy," he exclaimed to his friends at table, "then the monograph on virtue, then some fifty dramas, great wealth, marry, two children, no more, two are just right for the back seat in the carriage."

"Yes, by that time you will be eighty," said Gautier.

"What, eighty? Why, a man isn't really in his prime until then."

Here is the creator of the "Contes Drôlatiques," a giant plaything which he could always turn to after strenuous labor on the novels. That is the naïve legacy of his father, whose death in his eighties had been, we

might say, the result of a misunderstanding. Nothing
delighted Balzac more than the scurrilous notions
of lunatics and children. He would distribute pass-
words among his friends, who in order to gain admittance would have to say to the doorkeeper, "The
plums are ripe" or "I am bringing Brussels lace,"—and
then he would laugh like a fiend. And he formed a kind
of literary guild, "Le Cheval Rouge," with all manner
of queer rites and secret signs, for the purpose of mutual
public praise, with solemn banquets for which the
knights of the order finally lacked funds.

Further, his pursuit of wealth was nothing other than
a game with him. "What?" he exclaimed in the midst
of his plans; "30,000 francs—and is that all? That
would just pay for butter and radishes! Name me a
fairly decent house, if you please, where they don't pay
30,000 francs for butter and radishes. Incidentally, I
am prepared to live on nine sous a day." And he was
so modest and childlike about his work, making no show
of authority even when famous, pointing out new
talent, and admiring Victor Hugo despite their great
divergencies. He did not speak of his mistresses, not even
to his closest friends. When going on a journey, he never
disclosed whether a woman was involved. And even
after a hundred years no amount of prying has un-
covered the name of that middle-class woman by whom
he had a child. Yes, he was speaking the truth when he
once confessed to his friend, "My heart has always
dominated my life, that is my carefully guarded secret,"
and as though to illustrate this, in one of his first photographs he lays his great white hand broadly across his
heart.

And yet this is the same man who writes in an

anonymous prospectus: "I read somewhere that God put
Adam in the world and said to him: 'Thou art man.'
Could one not similarly say, that he put Balzac into the
world with the sentence: 'Thou art the novel'?" At
thirty he exclaimed that he would be counted among
the great men of his country; in the middle of his forties
he wrote confidently, "Four men will have exerted the
greatest influence in this first half of the century:
Napoleon, Cuvier, O'Connel, and I should like to be
the fourth. The first . . . inoculated whole armies
with his virus, the second chose the earth as his life companion, the third embodied a people. I will have carried
a whole society in my head."

Side by side with this vast self-confidence he possessed
such modesty that he refused to state his platform for
the national assembly, saying: "Whoever wants to vote
for me must decide from my work whether I deserve
this honor." His pride was even greater than his business sense, for whereas he took into his own hands the
sale of seats for his première, he excluded the claque and
thus prevented his piece from succeeding. At other
times the sums were beneath him, and after the suppression of one of his plays he refused the indemnity
of 5,000 francs on the grounds that he had been able to
earn 25,000 in the meantime.

A second aspect of his restiveness was his constant
battle between realism and an imaginativeness which,
through promising him much in the future, de-
spoiled him of the present. Only those who fail to
understand poet and madman can marvel that so great
a creator could judge the world so erroneously for himself when he explained it so accurately to others. These
phantasies were always concerned with money and

wealth. At midnight he came to his friend Laurens: "Get up, we must go away immediately."

"Are you insane?"

"Quick, we must go on a journey to the Grand Mogul. This ring which Hammer gave me in Vienna caused the Turkish ambassador the greatest astonishment last evening. 'Do you know you are wearing the ring of the Prophet? It was stolen a hundred years ago from the Grand Mogul, and whoever brings it back has been promised tons of gold and jewels.' " It was only with difficulty that he was dissuaded from taking the trip—this same man who knew all the shady practices of usurers and loan houses. Another time, when he was writing a story about a blind, penniless Venetian who is able to detect gold behind walls, he tried in all seriousness to persuade his friends to set out with him in search of the buried treasures hidden by Toussaint the Haitian. But unfortunately the money to charter the ship was lacking.

He bought a little house, Villa Les Jardies, near Paris, on hot treeless ground, and decided to plant pineapples there in long hothouses. These were to be sold for five francs each instead of twenty, and on the basis of 100,000 fruits this would yield him half a million, only a fifth of which would be needed to cover the costs. What did Balzac do first? He hunted a shop in the best quarter of Paris, deciding to have it strikingly decorated in black and gold, and to have painted on it: Les Jardies Pineapples. At times he recognized his fundamental error: when a woman in Venice laughingly said to him, "You always mistake your dreams for realities," he answered very earnestly, "In those few words you have hit upon the gravest secret of my life."

And yet, were not these hours, these weeks, of planning and hoping his times of happiness? What else did life offer him in the way of enjoyment?—and after all he did seek enjoyment.

"No one ever congratulated me on my birthday," he writes confidentially at forty-one, "except on one occasion Madame de C. And I am always sad on that day. My mother does not bother about me; and since I am always kept so much on the move, I proposed to my sister that we should no longer exchange greetings. So there was really no one to remember me. . . . And yet, I whisper this intimately in your ear, I much prefer happiness to fame, and I should give all my works just to be as happy as many a person I have seen." At such earnest moments we hear again the account of the man who might have lived for pleasure and who believed that he wrote merely to gain wealth by literature.

After thirty-five his growing fame brought him into the company of diplomats and artists, and to Rothschild's table. In Rome, Milan, and Vienna he was brilliantly received, and when he passed through Berlin the French ambassador immediately came to pay him the first visit, an honor which no German diplomat has ever shown to a German artist. In Paris, however, the leading romantics did not take him quite seriously; he was not pompous or exclusive or didactic enough; he was too close to life; and with their contemptuous praise of Balzac as "the most fertile of our authors," the *littérrateurs* tried—just as they do today—to dismiss a man who was their superior in power, industry, and devotion.

When entertaining his friends and showing them all his treasures in the two sumptuous rooms which he had fitted out with Oriental lavishness, with damask silks and rugs, and much red and gold; and when giving his stylish dinners in which there were all sorts of delicacies but no bread, where he could hold more wine than any of the others and consumed five enormous pears with the juice dripping down over his heavy chin, as his fathers would have done—yes, at such times Balzac in his naïve way was happy. And even more so when listening to music. At the time of Rossini it was not often that any one in Paris could appreciate Beethoven; yet Balzac was jealous of no one else, and he was continually expressing in letters and novels his admiration for the Fifth Symphony.

It also flattered him to entertain, not really as *causeur*, but with such *brio* that the conversation had soon become a monologue. "Then he would forget where he began," Gautier recounts, "leaping from an anecdote to an idea, from a custom to a scene. His eye caught fire, his voice changed with each impression; and at times came this magnificent laughter, when he was thinking over the absurdities to himself before describing them for others. In that way he announced, as though by a blare of trumpets, the beginning of his caricatures and sketches, and he soon carried his auditors away with him. His broad laughter, springing from these sensual lips, was that of a childlike man who is amused by the drama of human marionettes, and whom nothing can disturb, because he understands everything and always sees both sides of an issue. There was no situation or need, no weariness, no renunciation, not even a sickness, which could suppress this mighty joviality."

And yet Balzac, whose life was a continual quest for preference, splendor, and money, was only really happy when he forsook his salons and *loges,* his divans and Chinese vases, for the plain workroom which he had shut off from outside noise with mattresses and thus had artificially restored to the loftiness of his garret. Except that he now wore his tools over his cowl with the gesture of a prince: shears and a golden paper cutter hung from a Venetian chain! "My beautiful secret life consoles me for everything," he writes then. "You would tremble if you knew all my worries, but I forget them like Napoleon on the field of battle. When I sit down at my little table, then I laugh, I am so contented."

And once he encompasses mission and passion in the splendid sentences of a letter: "A vision, as brief as life and death, deep as an abyss, great as the sound of the sea; a woman, which even the devil would be made happy to possess; work calls, all the ovens are heated, the ecstasy of conception conceals the subsequent distress; such is the artist, the humble instrument of a will, apparently the freest, in reality a slave."

VII

"Artists must live wholly without women," Balzac demanded of his young friends, and when they tried to refute him by examples he exclaimed, "They would have accomplished entirely different things without women! You should see your mistresses not more than half an hour each year. Letters are permitted, since that develops style." But when his disciples entered the ornate divan room, they found that the only picture there was an engraving after Michael Angelo's "Leda." Or they had only to glance through the pages of the "Contes Drôlatiques," or to look into the master's face, and they would perceive a toper and a sensualist who contradicted his cowl in a truly Rabelaisian manner. Balzac saw women for longer periods than half an hour.

Yet he was much more economical in his relations with women than his portrait and his "Contes" and the *odeur de femme* in his novels would lead us to believe: both figuratively and literally, his nights were given to work. To see him in the morning on his battlefield, pleasantly wearied, sated, clear, and both contented and sobered by victory, was to recognize that the recipient of his masculine attention was his work. He never posed as a priest of art, and similarly in actual life he was no saint: he took what came his way, he had affairs with a duchess and a woman of the middle class; but these were never for long, and never passionate. This ceaselessly agitated man lacked one trifle—time. Love as well as the pleasures of the table were accessible only at odd moments. Thus he romanticized love, and love alone; it pleased him to treat his passion for work as a martyrdom of the senses and to picture this happiness as a sacrifice.

Once in his life, and only once, he experienced love simply, without romanticism or affectation, accepting it with a gratitude which kept him clear of either purposes or illusions. This was in his youth. For this once, Balzac was wholly in retreat, wholly the poet, abandoning himself to a woman of forty-five who was a grandmother or could have been, for her twenty-year-old daughter passed in the village as his fiancée. But from the class of the imposing women which he afterwards put into his books, none entered into his own life. This one alone was loved by him beyond her death: *"nunc et semper dilecta."*

Madame de Berny, whose father had been a German

musician and whose mother was a member of the lesser
French nobility, lived with an old partially blind husband and nine children on their charming estate where
Balzac came, at the age of twenty-three, to visit his
friend, her son. Her swimming eyes, her sensuously
heavy brows, and lips reluctantly resigned, betrayed a
whole world of yearning, devotion, and forgiveness,
such as unhappiness in love brings to women at
maturity. Her features aging unloved, with the searching expression of a virgin and the renunciation of a
mother, were certain to captivate the youth, especially
since he found here for the first time a woman of education, tact and breeding, who belonged to those circles
which vaguely troubled the little provincial.

First she refused him, then she acquiesced. And while
the yellowing leaves on this one stem tremble for the last
time, the buds on the other burst forth. Respect and desire were merged together, and the motherless youth
found two of his yearnings stilled at once. And he knew
well the purport of his words when he wrote later:
"Only a woman's last love can satisfy a young man's
first love."

This woman raised and educated Balzac, backing him
in business and in failure with money and sound advice.
From the nature of his devotion, she foresaw his talent,
and for twenty years she gave him the advantage of her
prudent and unindulgent criticisms. She never joined in
the applause of the rabble, but always marked out for
praise the elements of his work which were truly great.
Nevertheless, after a short period of jealousy, when the
vigorous young man turned towards his own kind, she
ceded her place to younger women. And his deep sense
of gratitude for what she had done never left him: "She

has created my heart. . . . Her criticism does its work; criticisms are so sweet when they come from the hands of a friend—one believes in them, yet they leave no wounds. . . . My friendship is of granite, nothing can outlast a feeling once it has taken root in me. She is sixty, her sufferings have so changed her that you wouldn't know her, and my love has doubled." And long after her death he called after her, "This creature was more than my mother, a woman friend such as only one human being could be to another. This can be explained only as the will of God. In times of great stress she supported me by her words, her deeds, and her devotion. If I am alive, it is thanks only to her. She was my moral sun."

And yet it was precisely this one friend of his life who could get the young man admittance into that titled set which he yearned to frequent. But because she was intelligent and knew what these people were like, she warned him not to overestimate them. No use. "It is too bad that you are so vain and do not know the dangers of this vanity. Not one of these people would give you 3000 francs if you needed it. These women are ungrateful on principle, self-seeking, sly, and designing, because they feel that they are weak; and they despise everyone who is not of their blood! How will you keep pure in the midst of such depravity!"

He was in Paris, and could no longer listen. The older, the more distinguished, and the more "refined" they were, the more quickly Balzac fell in love with them. There was the Duchess of Abrantès who might tell him endless anecdotes about Napoleon and also occasionally try out the famous plebeian *dans l'intimité*. There was the Marquise de Castries who, half paralyzed, always received reclining; "an elegant cadaver," she too wanted

to adorn her salon with the novelist, promised him
everything that an experienced woman can, lured him
to a watering place, though he had no end of trouble
raising the money. He came, fell out of the coach, went
limping among the dazzling *flâneurs,* was allowed to
burn with excitement, yet when his desires as a male
announced themselves, she laughed at him.

The same sort of thing took place with a Polish countess. And his refusal to leave her until he had conquered
her gave his remarkable career its decisive accent. On a
remote estate of the Ukraine, there sat the young wife of
a rich elderly burgher, whose money had won him the
impoverished descendant of a famous family. Despite
her little daughter and the Swiss governess, her ancestral
house and the serfs, she was bored. She read novels,
naturally from Paris. They had received some books by
a Mr. von Balzac, who knew how to write of love. If she
were to send him a letter, would he answer? Yet how
. . . by name? Impossible. Accordingly, he was com-
plimented anonymously, in the handwriting of the Swiss
governess: "Your genius seems exalted to me, but it
could be divine. Truth alone shall guide you. I see you
with the mind's eye, I see you in advance. That is my
only talent. It is pure and strong. Its source is divine,
its truth is holy. . . . I am all soul and have but one
virtue: love. My love is eternal. . . . For you I am the
Alien, and I will remain so all my life. We shall never
meet." Postscript: Kindly acknowledge the receipt of
this letter in a certain paper under letters which represent a play on your initials.

Was ever a man courted in such a mood? Here we
have the thorough stupidity of a bored landgravine, not
merely in Podolia. Yet what happens?

The author became excited, Balzac wrote the Alien a frightfully beautiful letter which contained many valuable confessions. She wrote back, still through the medium of the governess, still with caution, demanding that all letters be destroyed, and on her part hoarding every scrap (Eva Hanska's only service). She soon became his monitor, and began managing and reproving the poet from the frontiers of Asia: always astute, always dutifully appreciative of his genius, always a woman of the world, esthetic, aristocratic, romantic, pious, tender, coy, high-handed, jealous, a judge, a rescuer, an eternal mistress—a goose.

Balzac sent whole volumes in answer. He told everything that happened to him, all his plans, troubles, encouragements, and triumphs; his letters were diaries filled with the gossip of Paris, accounts of his debts and of quarrels with his publishers, descriptions of his most ambitious schemes—and meanwhile he was continually courting, always the admiring suitor of an unknown *grande dame* who had given him in tribute a portion of her heart. On this one point, as with the first of his mistresses, all his repressed romanticism poured forth. Because he did not know her, the woman seemed fantastic to him. Would not their first meeting destroy everything?

After a year and a day they arranged a rendezvous in Switzerland, with her husband as the third party. Prommenade in Neuchâtel, Eva's disillusionment with the short, stout, inelegant man. He on the other hand was a realist now, for the delusion was about to become a passionate reality. He neither expected nor sought intellectuality nor romance. What he did want was a dark, well-rounded, sensual woman, and this of course he could find: "The main thing is, that we are twenty-seven years old and are marvelously beautiful, that we have the most splendid black eyes in the world, the entrancing skin of the brunette, small amorous hands, and a twenty-seven-year old heart which is thoroughly innocent. . . . I say nothing to you of her colossal wealth. . . . In the shadow of a great oak we exchanged the first stolen kiss of love, then I made her swear to wait, and she swore to keep hand and heart for me [until her husband is dead]."

If one puts her portrait side by side with this letter to his sister, it becomes obvious why posterity's interest in Balzac's women has nearly always met with disappointment. Her nose was pointed and turned-up, the most pathetic excuse for a nose. Her mouth resembled his own description of her hands; and her eyes were cold, calculating, and malicious. Heavy, beautifully groomed hair fell across a neck which was almost as thick as his; and there was much white flesh on breast and shoulders. He himself was later to describe her mouth as "very sensuous, and at times even ominous." And when he talks about the childish tone of her voice and of her Slavic accent, we see the involuntary ascetic's idea of refinement, and we understand Balzac in whose imagination birth and wealth serve to complete the picture which his blissfully roving eye feasts upon.

It is clear, both from their portraits and from his "Droll Stories," that these two types were well adapted to each other. But Balzac was horrified when he learned that she had also read these stories, she who had so often reproved him for his "repulsive characters," a fact which gives us a very deep insight into the persistence of his self-imposed illusions. As rich and fresh and as thoroughly human as his letters to Eva are, when he speaks of his love they become sultry. "I saw you," he writes later; "our bodies and our souls have been united. . . . All the desires which an affectionate woman can inspire took hold of me. And if I did not tell you with what eagerness I yearned for you to visit me in the morning, it is my wretched living quarters that are to blame."

It went on for years. He followed her to Vienna, and here paid court to her while she was having her shoulders painted. He came to her estate, where they deceived her husband. She enjoyed his fame in public, and in silence delighted in the attentions of this powerful peasant who had previously lived almost devoid of women. And while she has no thought of giving up her safe berth for him, she held him with words which never left him: "Attach yourself to no one. I want your fidelity and your whole heart!"

He writes: "Before I can leave, I must get four volumes ready for the printer, get an extension on five notes, and pay out 8,000 francs; and the four volumes have 100 sheets, or 100 times 16 pages, each of which must be gone over from three to four times."

She writes: "Obviously other women are detaining you at Paris," or "You must earn yourself fourteen days of happiness in Geneva." Once when the rich woman offers a small sum to her hard-put friend, he replies with biting malice, "A thousand thanks for your drop of water, it is everything and nothing to me. You see what a thousand means when a person needs ten times that much a month."

His love gradually became more and more like a novel to him, and we can see how he distinguished his feelings as a poet from his epistolary sentiments by comparing

the same idea as it is written for her or for himself. To
her: "Twenty-three cities are consecrated. Geneva—a
glowing dream. . . . Cannstadt: all the sweetnesses of
dessert. . . . Baden was the summit, here was the fire
of Geneva. . . . All these riches were crowned by the
bliss of Naples." Could a bank clerk write more tritely?
On the contrary in his notebook: "Neuchâtel, a letter
in the hand. Geneva: a key. Dresden: bent over a violet.
Karlsruhe: an hourglass. Bourges: leaning against a
wheel. Brussels: holding six roses. Passy: a hand over
the eyes."

The notes of a poet, inimitable, pure air, music.

VIII

Nine years after the first letter her husband died.
Would she fly to him? She was now thirty-six, and was
already quite plump. He was entering his forties, and
had been complaining of his gray hair for years. At the
height of his fame he was again facing bankruptcy. At
thirty he had been 100,000 francs in debt, and by forty
this had increased to 170,000. His schemes and remedies
sounded like those of a stock speculator, and yet he almost never carried his projects beyond the stage of contemplation. At times he recognized the reason: "Napoleon could not be in Spain when he was in Essling. . . .
If you do not want to be outwitted in business or in society, you must refuse to think of anything else. I observe
that I am being duped, that so and so wants to trick me,
but even if I do notice this, I am forced to focus my attention elsewhere. Just when I discover it, I am in the
midst of work which would be ruined by interruption.
Often I am repairing the roof of a hut by the light of my

houses in flames." At times now he wanted to quit. He thought of Brazil, he wanted to give up writing, and he contemplated suicide. But his good nature would triumph, and following the failure of one of his plays his friends found him after midnight snoring in his box.

The death of Eva's husband gave him a new incentive: it was his last, but it was to be effective for years. Now all his struggles for money, rank, and position acquired a definite color, a purpose even. He wanted to enjoy a reputation in Paris, parading a countess as his wife. Now he began making the most ardent plans: he would lay his fame at her feet, he would become a member and salaried secretary of the academy, and a peer of France. He would open a cosmopolitan salon like Gérard, with Eva de Balzac as one of the queens of Paris. Her answers were cold. He is free, why doesn't he come. Besides her family is opposed to her marrying a writer. In order to get the money for his trip to Russia, he had to sit for weeks in a little printing establishment in the provinces, all for a few thousand francs.

New hopes, his fame mounts, David d'Angers makes a colossal bust which he wants to place with those of Goethe and Lamartine. Victor Hugo tries to get him a seat in the Academy, but the immortals prefer a little duke to the genius who might at any moment be cast into the debtors' prison. Another visit to Russia, with renewed courtship and renewed disappointments. "You are making the strangest mistake," he writes when she refers to his friends, "if you think that a man like me has friends. . . . I have wondered anxiously whether any one really understands me. . . . How could a woman like you forget how much work I do each day, how many pages I write! How could you always meet me with the same banalities!" In these fleeting moments of discernment he often thinks of the deceased Dilecta, and speaks in frank praise of her to the countess. Furthermore, his friends assure him that she merely wanted to flaunt his friendship and that she would never marry him.

He, a great judge of humankind, listened, pondered, and refused to believe them. He was enmeshed in this story like one of his own heroes. His weaknesses, passions and delusions bound him to this woman. He had decided to make his fortune with her, and he did not see that he was ruining himself! In a thoroughly romantic fashion his career was moving to a close. Everything became symbolic, just as though it were done by a Balzac. His house near Paris, which rested on a clay slope, showed signs of shifting, and had to be propped. His garden, where the experiment with the pineapples was to have been tried, dried up. Still he continued to believe in future opulence, writing in charcoal on the bare walls of his little house the names of the embellishments planned for each part: "Facing of Parian marble. A mural by Delacroix. Marble fireplace, inlaid floor of tropical woods."

His brain and heart were exhausted, and began to falter. His symptoms at thirteen recurred at forty-six: inflammation of the dura mater, fainting spells, intense headaches; also fatty degeneration of the heart, with dyspnoea at the slightest exertion. Finally, he could not take ten steps without discomfort. He grew thin. He felt all this, describing it much the way he might have done in one of his novels, and speaking of "these fifteen years of compulsory labor"; but he relied upon his peasant constitution: "My oxlike temperament is taking up the battle against death. I am a member of the opposition called life."

With this grandiloquent resolve he entered upon his final stage. At the marriage of her daughter, he arranged a formal engagement with Eva Hanska. Whereupon she let him wait for four more years. But he, with his world-wide reputation, his grave illnesses, and his debts, began like a youth in love to lay the foundations of his life's happiness. A long visit to the castle again brought the splendor of her rank before his eyes. The suite of rooms which he occupied, and the thousands of serfs dazzled him, although he knew of the financial difficulties of these large landowners and had fantastic schemes by which he hoped to remedy them. Lonely, wifeless, still a Bohemian, still thwarted in his social ambitions, he was determined to erect his house upon the foundation of this friendship. And once more he disclosed the madness of his entire life when he asserted that he hoped to advance as far through his marriage with this *grande dame* of noble blood as he had done through his books, and that if he could not have her as the crowning achievement of his life, he would elect to live in seclusion, as he had begun, on 100 francs a month.

He threw himself into his preparations ardently, almost furiously. While he felt his energies diminishing, he closed huge contracts with periodicals and publishers, and thought in terms of hundreds of thousands, yet he did not have a penny on the day of the fair. None the less, he bought *Henri quatre* chairs for their salon, their palace, their happiness. "I am devoting myself to our happiness. In 1848 we will own one of the most costly houses in Paris. I will not be a farthing in debt, and will have 500,000 francs in commissions, not counting the

returns from the 'Comédie Humaine,' which will at the
least amount to that much more. Thus, beautiful lady,
you will be marrying a million and more, if I do not
die."

If I do not die.

There sits Balzac in his little room. He has had the
one adjoining cleared out by the landlord, and here he
has piled up his chinaware, carpets and damasks, medal-
lions and clocks, pictures and chandeliers, which are intended to contribute to his happiness. Then on Eva's
behalf he purchases a little palace from a *Bankmann* and
slowly fills it with all his treasures—thoroughly the fool,
thoroughly the poet. His letters to her now are as care-
free as a boy's, but she answers nervously, fearing lest
everything be burned or stolen. Then he installs his aged
mother, the enemy, in his unoccupied house. He himself,
in his cell, writes two novels in five months, at times
with the thermometer at 104, while above him the laun-
dry under the roof is heating with coal.

And this situation went on for years. Towards the
close of this period of perpetual expectation Balzac, who
was always planning for the future, and though portraying the immediate present never lived in the present, rose to scenes of dramatic intensity. And while he
was buying paintings by Watteau and Palma Vecchio
for the walls of his married happiness, the woman already knew that he was soon to die. Yet he wrote her
that they still had twenty-five years before them.

Omens such as fill his own novels are allowed to pass
unnoticed. Eva's child by him is still-born. Her ring
slips from his emaciated finger. The coffer containing
their correspondence is broken into and the letters are
stolen. Finally he removes to the little palace, and dis-

plays his treasures to his friends; but he also shows them in the library, side by side with the "Contes Drôlatiques," a volume in black—"Comptes Mélancoliques," unpaid bills.

Gautier: "But you must be a millionaire!"

Balzac, humbly: "I am poorer than ever. None of all this belongs to me. I have furnished it for a friend whom I am expecting. I am merely the *concierge* of this house."

Finally, a few months before his death, on the occasion of her friend's last visit, the Polish woman realizes just how much she owes to the dying man, and she quickly closes the marriage. Balzac, finally successful after eighteen years of courtship, writes to his mother: "This union is assuredly a divine compensation for so much unhappiness, so many years of work, the enduring and overcoming of so many obstacles. My spring was not a happy one, but now I will enjoy a most splendid summer and the mildest of autumns. . . . I am almost beside myself with happiness." Are not these the accents of youth? Now follows a frightful wedding trip, a month through trackless Poland, with the groom dangerously ill. Eva writes bitter letters to her daughter, and the only time she grows warm is over his gift of a pearl necklace. Crises and scenes follow one another, for she is spoiled and nervous, he a bachelor in ill health.

Before their arrival in Paris, he tells his mother to have everything decorated with flowers, but to leave immediately afterwards, since Eva must pay her the first visit. Though he hates his mother, in making this superb demand of his countess the plebeian finally regains his self-confidence. They arrive in the evening, the windows are brilliantly lighted, the moment of happiness is at hand.

Yet why does no one open? Has the servant fallen asleep? They knock, they shake the door, finally they must get a locksmith and force an entrance. Inside they find the servant. He has gone mad from the excitement and Balzac has to take him to an insane asylum the same night. A scene such as Balzac might have written.

During the first days, he receives several letters addressed to "Monsieur le Comte de Balzac." It was neither his country nor his reputation which raised him to this coveted rank, but the zeal of his creditors, since he was now the husband of a countess. The envelopes contain bills, just as they did thirty years ago—only the address has become more elegant.

He is now fifty-one. He is suffering intensely from gangrened feet, and has barely three more months to live. Finally his eyesight fails: he creeps about in partial blindness; once as keen-eyed as Lynceus, once keeping vigil in his garret as the watchman of Paris, he now sits in his overladen palace sightless and inactive. At the close of a letter which he has dictated he adds in his royal handwriting: "*Je ne puis ni lire ni écrire.*" But when Victor Hugo comes, secretly to take leave of him, the invalid is cheerful, believes in his recovery, points to the chapel adjoining. He can no longer accompany the guest downstairs, but from above he calls to his wife: "First show Hugo all my pictures!"

Soon afterwards, on an August evening of the year 1850, the great master of eloquence comes to the death-bed of the great realist; he does not find the wife here, only the mother. The face of the dying man is black, as though his body were being corroded with suffering. So he lies there, exhausted by living, a victim to his passion for work. He is crumbling now beneath the hands of death, and before the close of another day there are no more masks to be removed.

Two days afterwards Victor Hugo, who is almost crushed during the solemnity, delivers before the people of Paris a truly Roman funeral oration in honor of the anti-rhetorical writer. A few weeks later, Eva seduces a younger admirer of her husband on his first visit. She lives for thirty more years.

IX

He was a plebeian like Rembrandt, and for this reason they both were prosaists, but Balzac was no mystic.

His worldly ambition headed him for calamity, yet in the absence of this passion he would have produced much less without improving in quality. For in the last analysis his genius lies in the extent of his works. No one of his novels in itself would be enough to earn him world fame; their significance derives from the fact that there are a hundred of them combined. In this respect he bears comparison with Shakespeare.

As his baroque manner of living oscillated between asceticism and luxury, so he has created both aggressive and renunciatory types. He has mastered all characters and all temperaments of both sexes. His herbarium is complete; no variety is missing.

There was really only one thing which he never portrayed: a person completely at rest. His only successful study in repose is his Dilecta, his *"lys dans la vallée."* For as God breathed into man the breath of life, so Balzac inspired his characters with his own *tempo*. And while they are not all so persistently harassed as Balzac himself, they are invariably in motion. Their birth is contemporary with the beginnings of the steam engine, which imposed its pace upon the century. They are all victims of money; yet not because their creator was such, but rather for the same reason as their creator: because the period, as he was the first to feel and to write, has forced this curse upon mankind and made repose impossible.

He is to be distinguished from the other writers of his century primarily by his combination of imagination and energy. These are the traits which permitted him to create and manage and dispose of so many characters with such skill. In this combination Balzac is reminiscent of Napoleon.

His life was sacrificed to his genius. When God saw a man who dared to create two thousand men and to supervise their destinies, He punished him with such blindness and calamities as the poet imposed upon his own creatures.

He made Balzac pay for his power as a creator.

AN OFFICER

PORTRAIT OF AN OFFICER

Gott erhalte Franz den Kaiser

HE was a cavalier of a vanishing sort, a cavalier who distinguished between *joie de vivre* and shiftlessness. A whole man, he loved life, was on good terms with death, and could match service and enjoyment so that each benefited by the other. The more brightly the flame of life flared up, the closer roared the dark and threatening sense of fate. No other life could have appealed to you— you who were adamant in meeting your duties and responsibilities, prompt in your decisions, courageous in your actions, while remaining an adventurer of the spirit, a servant of women, imaginative as a poet. . . .

Karl Gangolph von Sendler was the last of a Silesian family of Austrian officers, which had often distinguished itself in service, particularly at Aspern. A few bare facts, given in chronological order, cover the years of this full life prior to the war: born in Wiener-Neustadt, where his father taught in the Academy; military school; military academy; garrisons in Troppau, Galicia, Hungary; general staff; director of the commissary courses—the raw materials out of which a man of strong emotions may construct a life. And what an intense life!

Somewhere in Hungary half a century earlier, a woman, part Italian, was sitting beside her distinguished German husband, who had discovered her in Trieste and had won her in spite of her reserve. With Amazon-like beauty, she had preferred to shake her short locks on horseback rather than in the frenzy of love, and had refused every one until, past thirty, she finally followed the blond cavalry leader. Yet in accordance with her kind, she was determined that her child should be a boy, and during her period of expectancy she kept poison in readiness in the event that she should give birth to a girl. It was amid such remarkable passions as these that the boy came into the world—and for fifty years mother and son lived only for each other. This pact, sworn to by them both, was kept inviolate—and even in death one of them closely followed the other.

A difficult boyhood, for the father had to live on his wages, and the small holdings of the mother were soon gone. It was cold in the military school; often the water froze in the basin; and many years later the officer, although inured to all kinds of weather, could never get the room warm enough, as if he were trying to make up for the warmth he had lacked as a boy. But if one happens to be an unusually handsome lieutenant, proud of both physique and uniform, and if the beginning of one's career as an officer is also the beginning of one's career as a Don Juan, one may count on considerable success in both fields. There is no decline of charm here, no loss of art or zest; on the contrary, in the course of several years he gradually developed into a connoisseur who became more and more skilled at discerning in women the true image of life.

It is astonishing how well he preserved the same independence in both aspects of his life! Highly gifted, loyal and scrupulous in the performance of his duties, he was called early to the general staff. But this officer recognized the failings of his class. He avoided the casino, became more and more of a recluse from the society of his own set until he had no connections with any of them, and was looked upon by his irritated comrades as eccentric. Later, when his intelligence and energy landed him among the central military authorities, he still showed no pretentiousness; discerning that it was a mistake to underemphasize matters of provisioning, he promptly brought all the resources of his training and inventiveness to handling the problem of reconstruction. Again he was often spoken of slightingly as a queer chap who was more interested in boots, flour, and wood than in the high problems of strategy. Yet they let him alone; and for several years he was allowed to do almost as he wished, following his own plans for instructing the commissariat officers of the army in ways of providing food and clothing and of transplanting troops in war times. Finally his reports were recognized as fundamental documents on the question of reconstruction. But he always remains an outsider in his work, as in his private life.

For he felt that he could develop himself better, both intellectually and emotionally, in the company of women and artists. He sought humankind, knowledge and culture, quick to assimilate now all that a desultory education had failed to give him earlier. Thus for more than ten years he steered his strange course with perfect serenity and high seriousness through Vienna, avoiding the nobility and the court, preferring the society of the most modern minds, and determined that he should have only himself to thank for whatever of love or friendship was granted him. Though he was irresistibly charming, he always remained humble and compliant in his attitude towards women. And though he might be the best dancer at the *Volkstheater* ball, and parade in quite naïve vanity as a lieutenant-colonel with a lieutenant's *taille*, yet the next day he would impose upon himself eighteen hours of work if that were necessary. He always lived on his wages, and was paying off old debts at that; yet he was as generous as a prince. Such a life as his was a miniature work of art in which the opposing elements were never permitted to attain an audible conflict.

When he told a story, the literary men among his audience would be astounded. And if any one tried to write down these narratives, he would find it necessary to follow the original version in order to get the best effect. He would recount his experiences in a completely objective manner—very much like an official report by a member of the general staff. And although he dared not localize his anecdotes of love or the army by giving accurate names, a listener could easily imagine the light of forest or avenue, the room in the fourth floor or in the castle, such details being presented with the same singular plasticity as Flaubert demanded of young Maupassant in his first efforts.

The war developed his full productivity. At first the chief of Dankl's general staff of the First Army, he soon became Quartermaster-General. In this latter capacity until the spring of 1917, he had to take part in every advance and retreat, and to cope with the most trying conditions, in order to supervise the transport, provisioning, and quartering of 40,000 men and 20,000 horses in Eastern Galicia.

The happiest period of this rich life began. After a few months the "Quartermaster Division 14" was known to all the staffs in the monarchy. Here was an organizer of the first quality, operating in accordance with plans which he himself had been working on for years, and ruling in his realm tirelessly and in grand style, like a dictator.

He was the first to build factories for the production of leather, glass, wood, and other commodities. By sheer will-power he compelled his hesitant engineers to provide new roads and bridges. And when the number of the enemy was growing in Baden and Teschen, he was able, after continual threats of leaving for the front, to match this increasing power by wresting from his superiors the means for extending his own operations. An astounding knowledge of materials, down to buttons and glue, stovepipes and horseshoe-nails, gave him a comprehensive grasp of the reports submitted to him, and enabled him, since he would admit nothing as impossible, to fulfill his gigantic task by pressing the last bit of service from both men and things.

His subordinates and colleagues could hardly love such a leader; they feared him, and yet stuck by him, for even his enemies had to recognize the unselfishness behind his actions.

Thus it happened that after the fall of Budapest, when the life of the monarchy depended upon a prompt and plentiful supply of Roumanian grain, the young emperor could find no one better able to represent him than this friendless and patronless outsider, who had never breakfasted with the highest in command, had never concerned himself with official formalities, and once in his early years as an officer had even collided with the emperor. Now, when the emperor was appointing him plenipotentiary of the monarchy in Roumania, he told him: "You must do your utmost. Literally it is the fate of my people which now depends upon your energy!"

Sendler, exact and punctual, for long a critic of the typical failings of his comrades, had harbored from his youth a genuine reverence for the Prussian officer and had wished that the same type, despite its shortcomings, might be developed in his own country. But now he was brought into sharp competition with his ideal military type, as the result of that sinister war-within-war into which the allied belligerents of all the world, and particularly the hungering ones, were being forced. He had to turn diplomat, and work to reacquire for the monarchy, by measures not always gentle, the Roumanian territory which the Germans had long since covered with a network of systematic exploitation. They on their part were not accustomed to such energy; and with unconscious irony Mackensen angrily expressed his dissatisfaction with the new man from Vienna: "The fellow is going at it as though he were a Prussian!" Ludendorff tried to get him removed, but Czernin kept him; for it was observed with astonishment that within a few weeks the curve of the grain shipments into the monarchy had risen almost vertically.

Suddenly he found himself acclaimed everywhere. He became a general "out of turn," he was decorated with the insignia of the highest orders—and finally, at the beginning of 1918, he was called to Odessa on a similar mission. But after he had established the commissary service here, envious hands took it from him. At the same time the military situation began to affect unfavorably relations with the Ukrainian government. Personal differences with his superiors depressed him and stifled his old enthusiasm in his work. The hinterland disgusted him with his activities until—sick of the whole affair—in October 1918 he again asked to be given a brigade. This time he was to get it—in the first weeks of November.

The revolution, which occurred when he was on furlough in Vienna, suddenly left Sendler both materially and morally destitute. He had lost emperor and empire, power and money, influence and future. The man who had been exposed to the strongest temptations for two years, to whom Russians and Roumanians had offered all the treasures of the Orient as bribes for favors which would never have been detected, came home a beggar. At this time, when a career which had recently been so brilliant was in complete collapse, a new question arose. The revolutionary party was looking for a democratic and really capable general to organize a new central army. Sendler's name was the first to be mentioned, and old Dr. Adler said, "The imperialists always spoke ill of him; he is our man." On the seventh of November he was confidentially offered the new office. In every way this seemed to be the position for him, by reason of both his unprejudiced past and his present desire to raise himself from powerlessness and destitution to influence and security.

But the cavalier aspect of the man intervened. However skeptical he may have been of his recent master, his sense of loyalty to emperor prevailed; and the man whom the military authorities had, for the past twenty years, looked upon as too red, could not bring himself, despite his own and his nation's needs, "to break his oath." He refused, proposing another man instead; and in order to keep alive he acted for the cinema. An old attendant who had since become prosperous appeared on the scene and amidst much stammering offered his general his savings. When he saw that His Excellency would

not accept his assistance, he reached for the boots standing near by and begged that at least he be allowed to
black them.

A few weeks later he began working for an industrial-
ist who had learned to value his energy and honesty
during the war. For a while it seemed as though, with
his versatility, he would soon acquire a leading position
here as well. Yet the very rank and title which had previously been of advantage to him now acted to his detri-
ment. Both his fellow-workers and the officials resisted
him. His dealings with both superiors and underlings
disillusioned him, and he wrote: "The ascending curve
of my life is over." An attempt at the last to repeat
his great acts in miniature, in the country, as Stanley
did, was bound to fail. He lost his most vital incentive,
lost the very purpose and solace of his existence, when
his aged mother died. His own death occurred soon
after.

He was a nobleman, distinguished, keen and courageous, who carried the bounties of life in his heart,
while in his breast-pocket he kept a little poem to his
old emperor, torn from one corner of a newspaper; and
with it he had a Madonna, to which he turned only in
extreme moments. A worker and organizer of high rank
who ground his teeth at the vices of his class, a patriot
who recognized the shortcomings of his people, he
finally fell with the fall of Austria. A rare friend. A
cavalier, who loved life and who was followed until the
end by beautiful women, though he took none of them
in marriage.

Thus he remained the last of his race. His escutcheon
was broken over his grave.